HELICOPTERS IN COMBAT

HELICOPTERS IN COMBAT

The First Fifty Years

John Everett-Heath

ARMS AND
ARMOUR

Arms and Armour Press
A Cassell Imprint
Villiers House, 41-47 Strand, London WC2N 5JE.

Distributed in the USA by Sterling Publishing Co. Inc.,
387 Park Avenue South, New York, NY 10016-8810.

Distributed in Australia by Capricorn Link (Australia) Pty, Ltd,
P.O. Box 665, Lane Cove, New South Wales 2066.

British Library Cataloguing-in-Publication Data: a catalogue record
for this book is available from the British Library

ISBN 185409-066-8

Designed and edited by DAG Publications Ltd. Designed by David
Gibbons; edited by David Dorrell; typeset by Ronset Typesetters,
Darwen, Lancashire; printed and bound in Great Britain by
Hartnolls Ltd, Bodmin.

CONTENTS

LIST OF FIGURES

Preface

Many books about helicopters have been published in recent years but most of them have been concerned with general descriptions or their technical characteristics. Very few have examined how military helicopters have fared in combat. It is hoped that this book will help to fill the gap and redress the balance. It is directed at anybody interested in military affairs, not just professionals, and I hope that I have succeeded in eliminating all but the most essential technical terms; these are defined in a glossary.

During the preparation of this book I have been helped by many people who have given generously of their time, knowledge and experience. For information on the Algerian War, I owe thanks to General André Martini, Colonel Paul Gaujac, Colonel Christian de Saint Julien, Colonel Victor Croizat and Lieutenant-Colonel Bernard Blandin. American memories of the Vietnam War are still fresh in the minds of commanders and aircrew who participated. Indeed, it has not been easy to select from the wealth of information provided by Lieutenant General Harry Kinnard, Lieutenant General Bob Williams, Major General Carl McNair Jr, Major General Jim Smith, Lieutenant Colonel Wally Steward and Lieutenant Colonel Roger Wheaton. Their comments have also been most welcome. I must acknowledge, in particular, my gratitude to Nick Lappos, now Sikorsky's Chief Test Pilot for research and development, who never seemed to tire of the demands I made on him. Much of the material on Afghanistan was derived from Soviet military magazines, newspapers and TV film. It was enhanced by David Isby, who made a series of visits to that war-torn country and who has written widely on the war. Major Bob Wyman also made a useful contribution to this chapter. Major General Robin Grist read the manuscript of the last chapter, making many helpful suggestions and providing good advice.

Lieutenant Colonel Nick Parker responded quickly and comprehensively to a variety of enquiries and put me in touch with Regina Burns and Murray McGovern who kindly supplied photographs of helicopters in Korea and Vietnam from the US Army Aviation Museum. Similarly, I am grateful to Robert Senkowski for providing photographs of Soviet helicopters in Afghanistan. Finally, I must acknowledge my special thanks to Colonel Brooke Nihart, Deputy Director of the (US) Marine Corps Historical Center, who drew my attention to certain key events in the story of airmobility, besides assisting with the section on Korea and searching out photographs of that period. For any errors or misinterpretation I am responsible; the opinions expressed are mine alone.

The advice and help from my publishers has been indispensable and I am pleased to extend my thanks to David Gibbons, David Dorrell and Peter Burton.

Lastly, I must thank my wife who has not just tolerated the diversion of my attention but also given me strong encouragement throughout.

E.J.E-H.

Introduction

Any military operation today is almost unthinkable without the use of helicopters, even if only for the carriage of personnel and supplies and the evacuation of casualties. At the other end of the scale they can fight tanks and each other. As technology progresses their capabilities grow and the threat they pose to an enemy increases. This must be countered by all available means. In the 1980s helicopters fought each other for the first time and this type of combat is now being developed. A new era in helicopter warfare is dawning.

As soon as the helicopter had demonstrated that it was of practical use it was taken into military service. It proved its value in the evacuation of casualties, for observation and as a utility vehicle, and later, as its flying performance improved and capabilities expanded, for troop lift and logistic support. The need to provide the helicopter with some degree of self-protection became evident and so guns and rockets were fitted. Anti-tank missiles were soon added and the helicopter was further developed into an offensive machine. Other roles were not neglected: reconnaissance, command, control and communications(C3), electronic warfare, even mine-laying. Naval helicopter warfare is not considered in this book.

The helicopter did not really enter the battlefield arena until after the Second World War. Since then most conflicts have taken place in the Third World. In general, they can be divided into three types: colonial wars as the old European empires disintegrated; civil wars, some of which attracted intervention by an external power, for example, the Indians in Sri Lanka; and inter-state wars involving fighting between rival regular forces. In practically all of them, to a greater or lesser degree, helicopters have participated. Indeed, they are one of the few items of combat equipment that can play an important part across the whole range of conflict from internal security to general war. Not only do they have unique capabilities themselves, but there is no doubt that they contribute to the combat effectiveness of other weapon systems.

The first chapter attempts to set the scene and to show how helicopters came to be accepted as weapons of war. Brief references are made to various conflicts and military campaigns where they played a conspicuous part. In simplified terms, airmobility was born during the Korean War, received its baptism of fire in Algeria and came of age in Vietnam. Thereafter it was developed to become combat aviation. More recently the

Gulf War amply demonstrated the versatility of helicopters. Indeed, it is ironic that the Western nations involved had trained for decades for a defensive war against the Warsaw Pact and yet, in the Gulf, were forced to undertake a short offensive campaign. The possession of helicopter gunships and multi-purpose types is spreading as more Third World countries appreciate their capabilities. Not a day goes by when they are not in action somewhere in the world.

Three long guerrilla wars in which the course of the fighting was strongly influenced by the use of helicopters are examined in more detail. To provide a framework in which to place the part they played, a brief description of the general course of each one has been included. Unfortunately, lack of space has not permitted even a brief review of one vital aspect of helicopter operations: that of an efficient maintenance support system and logistic backing. Each of these three wars lasted for more than seven years, although US helicopters were sent to South Vietnam more than three years before the first American ground combat troops arrived. Algeria was a colonial war, a desert and mountain war, ending in virtual military victory for the French but political defeat. Vietnam was a civil war, a jungle war, with external intervention, ending in honours roughly even militarily but a political and propaganda defeat for the Americans. Afghanistan was also a civil war, fought in mountains and desert, with Soviet intervention; it ended in military and political defeat for the Russians although the Afghan regime survived. The American and Soviet withdrawals from South Vietnam and Afghanistan respectively constituted an acknowledgment that their interventions had been ineffective, and were economically and politically damaging both to Super Power relations and to their prestige and influence in the Third World.

All three major powers underestimated the strength of their opponents who were courageous, adaptable, resourceful, resilient and determined. The Russians entered Afghanistan not intending or expecting to fight a guerrilla war. Unlike the French and Americans, they did not deploy enough troops to attempt a widespread territorial pacification programme, and thus it would seem that they resorted simply to trying to kill as many Mujaheddin rebels as possible. All three countries started with their troops ill-equipped and trained for the type of guerrilla war with which they were faced. Immense efforts had to be made to realign their troops from being able to fight a conventional/nuclear war in Europe to a low-intensity struggle in a completely different climatic and topographical environment. Fortunately, air power was available and helicopters could help to provide a degree of mobility and bring intimate fire support to bear on the transient enemy. All three campaigns demonstrated that fixed-wing aircraft are not really suitable for the support of heliborne operations; thus armed helicopters were needed to provide an independent capability for close air support. The lesson was learnt, however, that air power alone, of whatever sort, does not defeat the guerrilla.

Not surprisingly in the 1950s, the French did not have the resources to build up a large helicopter fleet. At the height of the war in Algeria some 425,000 troops were supported by 380 helicopters, a ratio of one helicopter to about 1,120 troops. In Vietnam the ratio was one to approximately 125 troops and in Afghanistan one to 250. The Russians could have deployed more helicopters. That they did not may have been because of a problem of their protection on the ground and their technical support, as well as commitments on the Chinese border and in Eastern Europe. Both the South Vietnamese and Afghans also operated their own helicopters, but their contribution to the fighting, compared with that of the Americans and Russians, was small and has therefore been disregarded.

These three wars, and indeed most other recent conflicts, have served to emphasize the versatility and capabilities of helicopters, and consequently the importance of anti-helicopter weapons. This, in turn, has underlined the need for good helicopter survivability, both by tactical and technical means, despite the conclusion drawn from combat experience that the helicopter is much less vulnerable to fire than is generally imagined.

The world has been fortunate in not having to experience general war, conventional or nuclear, in Europe. Had even a conventional one occurred, it would have been a savage struggle and probably the most intense war in history, given the amount of sophisticated weaponry possessed by NATO and the Warsaw Pact and, ominously, the ever-present possibility of resort to nuclear weapons. There have, however, been general and limited wars elsewhere, where the fighting has been without pause, the full panoply of conventional weapons has been used and all available troops committed to action. Thus the final chapter of this book addresses the contribution that helicopters can make to this type of warfare, now and in the future. Most countries operate American, European or Soviet-designed helicopters but, despite references to them and those countries' forces, this chapter is not specific to Europe.

The 1990 Conventional Armed Forces in Europe Treaty recognized the importance of missile-armed helicopters as one of the five types of equipment to be limited; the others were tanks, artillery, armoured combat vehicles and combat aircraft. It was not a stringent limit but it may inhibit plans to equip some types of helicopter with anti-tank or air defence missiles and future unit organizations will have to take account of this. No restrictions were placed on helicopters carrying other weapons.

Since the Second World War guerrilla wars have far outnumbered conventional wars between opposing states. Yet probably more effort has been put into preparing for the latter (thereby to deter the outbreak of war) than for lower intensity, unconventional conflict. The years 1989–92 did not encourage predictions as to the course that international relations might follow or the way in which combat might change as a result of emerging technologies. The demise of the Cold War may have ushered in a new world order, but challenges to it there will be in plenty. From now on perhaps the major powers should pay as much attention to countering insurgency and terrorism, and to conducting low intensity guerrilla wars, as they do to general war. A balance of capabilities must be kept to cater for any level of violence: in 1991 British forces were involved simultaneously in a general war in the Gulf and anti-terrorist action in Northern Ireland. Such has been the concentration on war in Europe for the major powers that the lessons of the past in numerous colonial and guerrilla wars are in danger of being forgotten. Equipment and training have to be tailored to meet any eventuality. This could mean a lesser need for anti-tank helicopters and a greater one for assault/transport and reconnaissance/surveillance helicopters, and also those equipped for deep penetration special operations by day and night.

An Army's effectiveness can be judged by the quality of its C3, firepower, mobility and logistic support. Helicopters contribute to the first and last and can also be a source of very mobile firepower; they have not yet made a real impact on infantry mobility, however. Although they are the means to increase this five-fold or more, no country possesses enough assault and transport helicopters to lift more than a few, usually specially trained, units. The potential is recognized but its realization is still far off, partly because of the costs involved and partly because of the view that the infantry still need armoured fighting vehicles (AFVs) to help them hold ground and co-operate with tanks. Indeed, the helicopter's potential overall has yet to be fully exploited, not only in terms of its physical characteristics and capabilities but also with regard to unit organizations and its place in the structure of an Army, tactics and as an instrument of war when grouped at corps and army level. The helicopter has not yet been put to the test of general war and operated in the face of co-ordinated fire from tanks, artillery, air defence and other helicopters. So far only the Americans and Russians have had the resources and the vision to put faith in large numbers of battlefield helicopters. Those countries with fewer resources have been understandably reluctant to reorganize their Armies around a piece of equipment that has yet to prove itself in general war. The *rotor revolution* is still awaited.

The Soviet Union ceased to exist on 21 December 1991, being superseded by the Commonwealth of Independent States (CIS) which may itself prove to be a transient body. The Baltic Republics and Georgia did not join the CIS. Of the remaining eleven former Soviet Republics only eight agreed to having unified armed forces for a two-year period, Ukraine being the principal dissenter. Nevertheless, for the sake of simplicity, I have referred to all inhabitants of the former Soviet Union and CIS as Russians and equipment in service before the start of 1992 as Soviet. NATO has a system of code-naming all former Soviet aircraft, giving helicopters a name beginning with the letter 'H'. Subsequent versions are identified by a further letter in sequence, e.g., Hind 'A', 'B', 'C', etc.

The Helicopter as a Combat Vehicle

It could be claimed that the battlefield helicopter has its origins in a proposal made in February 1916 by Lieutenant Stevan Petroczy, chief balloon instructor in the Austro-Hungarian Army. He suggested that a tethered helicopter would be less vulnerable to enemy fire than the hydrogen-filled balloons then in service for observation of the battlefield. He envisaged a cable with a maximum length of 800m (2,625ft) and the single pilot/observer being equipped with a machine-gun, camera and telephone. Petroczy received such help from two engineers, Dr Theodore von Karman and Ensign Wilhelm Zurovec, that the first machine, completed in March 1918, was designated the PKZ-1. It did not become operational because the engine burned out during the fourth flight and could not be repaired. Zurovec simultaneously applied himself to the PKZ-2, a more sophisticated three-engined version, which could be dismantled and transported to any part of the battlefield where it was needed. This machine flew for the first time on 2 April 1918. More than 30 successful flights were carried out but it, too, crashed and was not rebuilt. The impending collapse of the Austro-Hungarian Empire conspired to prevent a third version being constructed before the Armistice was signed by Austria-Hungary on 3 November 1918.

The Autogiro

More widespread interest in the potential of rotary-wing aircraft for military service began in the 1930s. But it was not, to start with, the helicopter that was the subject of interest but the autogiro. Having an unpowered rotor which rotates only as a result of air, generated by forward flight, flowing through the rotor disc, the autogiro could not hover and, at least initially, was unable to take off vertically. Nevertheless, after the Spanish inventor, Juan de la Cierva, had made the first successful flight in an autogiro near Madrid on 9 January 1923, development of this type of aircraft was pursued in France, Germany, Great Britain, Japan, the Soviet Union and the USA. In October 1925 Cierva took his newest model to Britain, where he remained until his untimely death in 1936. In the intervening years he was responsible for the design of a range of increasingly capable autogiros.

Because of its ability to fly low and slow, to take off and land almost anywhere, and because it was small and inconspicuous both in the air and on the ground, a military autogiro could be based much closer to the enemy than conventional fixed-wing aircraft. It was thought that it might be suitable for observation and reconnaissance. The British conducted trials in 1935 whereby artillery officers, flying as passengers, directed the fire of their guns by means of two-way radio communications. This was a vast improvement on the existing antiquated system developed in 1917 which involved fire directions being tapped in Morse code over a one-way wireless link. Often, however, the aircraft was facing the wrong way at the moment of the shell's impact and so it was suggested that the artillery officer should not only control the shoot but also fly the aircraft himself. After further trials this proposal was adopted – but not with autogiros; light fixed-wing aircraft were deemed to be more effective in this role.

American experience was similar. The United States Marine Corps (USMC) conducted trials with autogiros in Nicaragua from 1932, and additional trials of the type as a vehicle for casualty evacuation were undertaken in 1936. The results were not sufficiently promising to attract the necessary funds. In both countries it was concluded that, with its severe performance and payload limitations, there was no role that was suitable for the autogiro in support of the ground forces.

The First Practical Helicopter

In retrospect it can be seen that two events in the space of seven months in 1936 and 1937 heralded the demise of the autogiro, at least as a serious weapon of war. On 9 December 1936 Cierva was killed in an air crash, a tragedy that the autogiro industry could not sustain; and on 25 and 26 June 1937 the German pilot Ewald Rohlfs proved that the helicopter was the rotorcraft of the future. In a Focke-Achgelis Fa 61, which had made its maiden flight on 26 June 1936, he set five world records. The most extraordinary of these was to raise the altitude record from 158m (518ft), which had only been set in September 1936, to 2,439m (8,002ft); but the increase in speed from 44.69km/hr (27.77mph) to 122.55km/hr (76.15mph) was also significant. Just six weeks earlier, on 10 May 1937, the Fa 61 had carried out the first auto-rotative landing in the history of the helicopter, thus demonstrating an important aspect of safety. It proved that, in the event of an engine failure, the pilot could still land his helicopter safely provided he reduced the pitch on all the main rotor blades immediately. In this state, the helicopter became rather like an autogiro, the main rotor continuing to rotate at the same speed as a result of the air flowing upwards through the rotor disc.

The Second World War (1939–45)

Despite these successes more autogiros than helicopters were used during the Second World War, although it was only the Japanese and Russians who employed them in support of their ground forces – and then only in a very limited way. In 1939 a single American Kellett KD-1A had been imported by the Japanese Army for trials in the artillery fire direction role. It was severely damaged in a crash and rebuilt, with some modifications, by the Kayaba Industrial Company as the Ka-1. About 240 were built during the war but evidence is scant about how and where they were used by both the Army and Navy; it is known that more were in service with the Navy for anti-submarine warfare (ASW) and liaison work than with the Army.

The British deployed a couple of Cierva C.40 autogiros to France before the end of 1939 for Army observation and communications duties but the fall of that country in June 1940 put an end to their activities. Only a handful of Soviet TsAGI A-7 autogiros participated in operations against the Germans. In the summer of 1941, after the German invasion, they were rushed to the area of Smolensk where they were used for reconnaissance at night and for leaflet-dropping. They did nothing to stem the onslaught and were quickly withdrawn. But the A-7 does have a significant claim to fame: it was the first rotary-wing aircraft to be armed, having forward- and rearward-firing 7.62mm ShKAS or PV-1 machine-guns.

Helicopters made no impact on the course of the Second World War either, only the Germans being able to put a very small number into operational service. A few of these were engaged in the land battle in Europe, carrying out reconnaissance, supply, transport and casualty evacuation missions. The two-seat Flettner Fl 282 Kolibri, arguably the first fully developed helicopter, was the first in the world to enter operational service, in 1942: it was employed by the German Navy for shipboard reconnaissance and anti-submarine patrol. By 1943 twenty had been built and in 1944 an order for 1,000 was placed, but Allied bombing frustrated this ambitious programme. Allied air attacks also prevented full-scale production of the Focke-Achgelis Fa 223 Drache, a transport helicopter which could carry four troops or a load of 1,280kg (2,822lb). Less than ten entered Luftwaffe service from 1942, being used for supply, casualty evacuation and occasionally reconnaissance. Some of them were equipped with a machine-gun in the nose for self-protection.

Four American Sikorsky R-4s were sent to India in 1944 for trials. On 23 April, while these were in progress, Lieutenant Carter Harman of the 1st Air Commando, US Army Air Force, flew from India into Burma to rescue four men, one by one, whose aircraft had crashed behind Japanese lines. This was the first recorded rescue by helicopter of men behind enemy lines.

By the end of the war the helicopter had taken its first, tentative, steps in military service and had had the briefest taste of combat. Given that its first flight in November 1907 (by Paul Cornu in France) was only four years after the Wright brothers had first flown, the technical and tactical progress of the helicopter had been painfully slow compared with that of fixed-wing aircraft. It was thought that the helicopter was too fragile for the battlefield, vulnerable to all types of weapon and excessively difficult to maintain. Even the far-sighted and perceptive needed a faith and optimism beyond the ordinary, and the men who could appreciate the helicopter as a future war machine were few indeed.

The First Post-War Atomic Bomb Test (1946)

On 1 July 1946 the first atomic bomb test since the end of the war took place over Bikini Atoll. It made an immediate impression on one of the watchers, Lieutenant General Roy S. Geiger of the USMC, who felt that a few atomic bombs could annihilate an amphibious landing force. To lessen the risk dispersion would be essential, but this would lead to a much slower build-up of forces ashore. Various ways of achieving dispersion yet, at the same time, rapid concentration, were studied. Although the capabilities of helicopters were rudimentary, it was concluded that the helicopter was the most appropriate vehicle to introduce a new method of marine assault.

In early December 1946 the Commandant of the Marine Corps directed that two parallel programmes should be initiated to develop a transport seaplane and a transport helicopter; an experimental Marine helicopter squadron should be formed to train pilots and mechanics and to develop tactics and techniques for ship-to-shore operations.

This was the first time that helicopters had been proposed officially as the tactical means to convey combat troops from one place to another. As well as a helicopter for the carriage of assault troops, the USMC also wanted a larger helicopter capable of lifting all loads in a Marine division.

On 1 December 1947 Marine Helicopter Squadron One (HMX-1) was commissioned. Its principal mission was to develop tactics and techniques for the movement of assault troops in amphibious operations. The following year it began to receive its helicopters: the four-seat HO3S-1 (a slightly modified commercial Sikorsky S-51) for training and utility use and the tandem-rotor Piasecki HRP-1 with seating for eight troops; its payload was well below the desired 2,268kg (5,000lb) and it was regarded as an interim helicopter purely for experimental and trials purposes. Unfortunately for the USMC, it was not until March 1955 that it received its first Sikorsky HR2S (CH-37C Mojave in the US Army) with a stated payload of 3,027kg (6,674lb). A secondary mission for the squadron was to evaluate a small helicopter for observation and the direction of gunfire. For this purpose HMX-1 was given a two-seat HTL-2, a militarized version of the Bell 47D. The USMC grasped this opportunity with enthusiasm and quickly established a reputation for innovation in the use of combat helicopters. It is one that it has maintained ever since; in recent years it has been the pioneer for helicopter air-to-air combat.

The National Security Act of 1947 provided for the division of the US Army Air Force and the establishment of the US Air Force (USAF) in its own right. This reorganization was followed by two years of discussion on the form the Army's own aviation should take. Almost inevitably limits were imposed on both fixed-wing aircraft and helicopters: the latter were not to exceed 1,814kg (4,000lb) maximum take-off weight and their roles were to be restricted to observation, route reconnaissance, liaison, aerial photography and limited resupply within the combat zone. Nevertheless, the Army appreciated the need for larger helicopters to move artillery and bridging equipment and to undertake the tactical movement of troops. By 1951 the weight limitation had been abolished. The USAF, on the other hand, was merely interested in helicopters for search and rescue (SAR).

The Malayan Emergency (1948–60)

In 1946 the British War Office stated a requirement for three types of helicopter, ranging from a two-seater for observation to a heavy load-lifter. It was not envisaged that any of these helicopters would fly within the range of enemy small arms fire. But a higher priority was accorded to the Royal Navy for the procurement of helicopters for ASW and SAR, and this absorbed the limited funds available and the capacity of the fledgling British helicopter industry. It was the campaign against the Malayan Communist Party and its military arm, the Malayan Races Liberation Army, that proved to be the catalyst for the Army and RAF, with an urgent demand for three helicopters to be in Malaya by the autumn of 1949 to form a casualty evacuation flight operated by the RAF.

By the end of April 1950 three Westland WS-51 Dragonflies (licence-built Sikorsky S-51s) were ready for operational trials. These helicopters were the forerunners of a gradually growing number of Royal Navy and RAF helicopters which were deployed to Malaya in support of Army operations. Ultimately one Royal Navy and two RAF squadrons were deployed with some 40 Bristol Sycamores, Westland Whirlwinds (licence-built Sikorsky S-55s) and S-55s; none was armed. With so few helicopters, they had to be controlled and tasked at a high level. This meant that they were normally used only for pre-planned operations and few helicopters, if any, were available to react immediately to events or take advantage of opportunities. Thus one of the great attributes of the helicopter, its flexibility, was not put to best use.

Unlike in the later war in Vietnam, no independent role was given to air power. Offensive air power proved to be largely ineffective against terrorists in the jungle, so air power in all its forms was directed towards the intimate support of the ground forces in their attempts to separate the terrorists from the population at large and to eradicate their units.

In addition to the evacuation of casualties from the jungle – so important for the maintenance of morale – troops in very small numbers and supplies were inserted by helicopter into the jungle, thus saving much time and effort. As a light communications vehicle the helicopter was invaluable for the rapid movement of commanders. From time to time it was used for reconnaissance and observation, including searching for crashed aircraft and possible survivors, and crop destruction by spraying, all tasks more often undertaken by fixed-wing aircraft. An unwelcome discovery, however, had been made soon after the arrival of the first helicopters. The heat, humidity and high altitudes conspired to produce high-density altitudes: the air was thinner and thus less lift could be generated than in temperate climates. This, in turn, adversely affected the payload of troops or freight that could be carried. The Whirlwind and S-55 could lift ten passengers in Europe but at times in Malaya only two.

The helicopter did not have a decisive impact on the twelve-year campaign in Malaya because too few of them were present; but when they were used, their effect was striking and much appreciated by those who benefited.

The Korean War (1950–53)

On 25 June 1950 North Korean forces crossed the 38th parallel into South Korea and the Korean War began. Its place in aviation history was to be won not solely by the first-ever jet-versus-jet confrontations – between the MiG-15 'Fagot' and the North American F-86 Sabre – but also by the demonstration of the military potential of the helicopter, as yet untested in conventional warfare. As realization of its capabilities slowly dawned, new roles and techniques were investigated. Almost unnoticed by the tradition-alists, a new weapon of war was gradually forged, the first since the tank had made its dramatic appearance on the battlefield some 35 years earlier. Yet the very success of the helicopter in the casualty evacuation role tended to obscure its merits as an armed fighting vehicle, and these were appreciated by only a few far-sighted enthusiasts. The helicopter was quick and quite unconstrained by snowbound or muddy roads, often clogged with troops, equipment and refugees; minefields could be ignored; it had good communications; and although potentially vulnerable to all weapons and shrapnel, it showed that it could survive in the battle area much better than had been anticipated.

From 2 August 1950 the concepts of the USMC's HMX-1 were put to the test of war. The four HO3S-1s in Marine squadron VMO-6 were heavily involved in the fighting to maintain and later break out of the foothold around Pusan in the extreme south-east of the country. As well as tactical reconnaissance and direction of gunfire along the perimeter, they were also used frequently to take commanders about the battlefield, a heartening return to a more personal system of command. Although nominally a four-seater, the HO3S-1 could only carry two combat-equipped troops, in addition to the pilot, over a range of 260km (161 miles) at a cruising speed of 120km/hr (75mph). By the end of 1950 helicopters of the four American Services, acting as part of the United Nations forces, had all been in action, undertaking such varied roles as casualty evacuation, reconnaissance and battlefield surveillance, the direction of artillery fire, resupply, the laying of telephone wires, and the carriage of commanders and staff officers. Principal types were the HO3S-1 (H-5 in USAF service) and the three-seat H-13 Sioux (Bell 47; HTL-4 in USMC service), although in January 1951 a few Hiller H-23 Ravens were delivered to the US Army. The USMC also flew some four-seat HO5S-1s (Sikorsky S-52s) in the observation and reconnaissance role from 1952, although this type was overshadowed by the other better known helicopters. The H-13's casualty evacuation role has been 'immortalized' by the 'MASH' (Mobile Army Surgical Hospital) TV series.

During the three years of the Korean War, with more than 600 helicopters deployed, some 23,000 United Nations casualties were evacuated to field hospitals. Of these, about 18,000 were transported by US Army H-13s, which could have a stretcher pannier mounted on both sides of the fuselage. This service not only resulted in the lowest percentage of wounded to die in any war in recorded history to that date, but also did wonders for the morale of the fighting troops.

Within a month of the start of the war it had been realized that the rugged terrain, poor road system and the ubiquitous presence of the enemy made evacuation of casualties extremely hazardous and very likely to exacerbate their condition. USAF helicopters from the 3rd Air Rescue Squadron were thus requested to help, and the first helicopter rescue took place on 27 July 1950. At the same time it was decided to carry out trials with an H-5 using a Stokes litter – little more than a rigid wire basket – and the standard Army stretcher which had to have its handles sawn off if it was to fit inside the cabin. These trials were successful and on 10 August 1950 USAF helicopters were authorized for the evacuation of casualties from the front line. By the spring of 1951 the US Army had sent the 2nd, 3rd and 4th Helicopter Detachments to South Korea, each attached to a separate MASH; the fourth MASH was supported by the USAF. Even at the height of the war, only eleven Army H-13s specifically for casualty evacuation were operational but, by the time of the Armistice in July 1953, they, together with other US Army, USAF and USMC helicopters, had evacuated 17,700 American casualties alone.

So effectively had these three Helicopter Detachments contributed to American and United Nations morale, and therefore combat capability, that in August 1952 the US Army formally established helicopter ambulance detachments as part of the Army Medical Service; the three detachments in Korea were transferred to the US 8th Army Surgeon.

As the use of helicopters for evacuation accelerated it became clear that certain ground rules, procedures and techniques were needed. Only the seriously wounded, those in locations inaccessible to ground vehicles, or those who would suffer if using such vehicles, were to be evacuated by air. Medical helicopters were not to be used for any other tactical or logistic tasks, although when flying forward to collect casualties mail, cigarettes, beer and other 'comforts' were often delivered to the front line. Landing zones (LZs) were to be marked with panels and some indication of wind velocity given, but those susceptible to hostile fire were not to be used. To start with, because the H-13 had no radio, the ground tasking system was much too slow to be effective. To reduce reaction times a single H-13 was sometimes located at a casualty clearing station just behind a tactical HQ. But requests to give each division its own medical helicopter were never approved on the grounds that there were simply too few helicopters available to decentralize the service.

What received considerable attention and publicity was the rescue of aircrew shot down, often behind enemy lines. This dangerous task was undertaken by the 3rd Air Rescue Squadron which retrieved 996 aircrew. The first such rescue was made as early as 4 September 1950 when an H-5 crossed into North Korea. With fire support provided by ground artillery and fixed-wing aircraft, many dramatic rescues were undertaken in the mountains, in coastal waters and in rice paddies, sometimes under the astonished gaze of the enemy. The rescue helicopters were shot down themselves from time to time but, as experience grew, their success rate improved.

Conspicuously successful though casualty evacuation was, helicopters were also put to good tactical use despite their limitations. The payload/range of the helicopters in service precluded large simultaneous lifts of troops or supplies. The US Army and USMC, however, lifted both in emergencies and, on a more regular basis, they were delivered to remote and otherwise inaccessible locations, usually in the mountains. The H-19 Chickasaw (Sikorsky S-55; HRS-1 in USMC service) first arrived in Korea in March 1951 and was ultimately operated by all the US Services there except the Navy. It had a much greater payload than the older helicopters. At sea-level up to 700kg (1,543lb) of freight or ten troops could be accommodated in the cabin and large sliding doors facilitated rapid entry and exit. On 19 March a USAF H-19 was given an unusual task: the recovery of a MiG-15 shot down 56km (35 miles) behind enemy lines just west of 'MiG Alley'. The aircraft was at the bottom of a narrow and steep-sided ravine. Having landed, a small crew removed the parts of most interest – the engine and the tail section – and loaded them into the helicopter. Although 454kg (1,000lb) over weight, the H-19 managed to get out of the ravine and, though hit, safely deliver its precious cargo.

HMR-161, the USMC's first transport helicopter squadron, arrived in Korea on 31 August 1951 equipped with fifteen HRS-1s. Thirteen days later it undertook Operation 'Windmill', the first-ever tactical resupply operation by helicopter; ammunition was carried in, dead and wounded out. The first tactical troop lift in history took place on 21 September. In 65 flights and over a period of four hours during Operation 'Summit', 224 combat-equipped troops and 8,060kg (17,770lb) of freight were lifted, under enemy observation and exposed to hostile fire – although in fact unopposed – on to Hill 884, subsequently dubbed 'Mount Helicopter'. Six days later Operation 'Blackbird' took place. The 1st Marine Division had a frontage of 20km (12.5 miles) which made it difficult to maintain an adequate reserve. Consequently a company, with supporting mortar, machine-gun and anti-tank sub-units and a battalion command group, was earmarked to reinforce the most vulnerable, left, flank. Any emergency was most likely to arise at night and so a trial tactical lift in darkness was carried out. Useful lessons were learnt but no other lift of this magnitude was undertaken during the rest of the war.

Operation 'Bumblebee' built on the experience gained. On 11 October a dozen USMC HRS-1 helicopters carried forward the 3rd Battalion, 7th Marines, in successive waves to the top of a 915m (3,000ft) mountain to relieve another unit in the front line. The battalion of 958 men was put in place in just under six hours, each helicopter carrying a single pilot and six troops each time. Although not an assault landing under fire, this move demonstrated the potential of the movement of large numbers of troops by helicopter. Many other similar moves were undertaken subsequently, some over water. The biggest involved 45 Marine and Army helicopters. As it happened, no troop-lift operation during the war came under fire.

A few H-19s were equipped with multi-tube rocket-launchers mounted on the fuselage sides to provide suppressive fire. Other H-19/HRS-1s occasionally lifted 24-round 114mm (4.5in) rocket-launcher systems from one site to another, the purpose being to fire and then leave before the site was located and counter-fire started coming down. Three helicopters were required: one for the launcher, one for the crew and one for up to 22 rockets and fuses. These and other low-key attempts to use weapons from helicopters did not result, however, in a formal decision to arm them.

The USMC pioneered the tactical movement of troops and supplies by helicopter within the battle area, but the HRS-1/H-19's major roles were casualty evacuation, when it had the capacity to take six stretchers, and resupply, even to troops cut off by the enemy. These two roles, particularly the first which caught the imagination of all associated with the war, ensured the future of the helicopter as a battlefield vehicle.

The Korean experience was sufficient to convince the US Army and USMC, in particular, that more resources should be devoted to the research and development of helicopters and more thought given to their employment on the battlefield. It had not taken long for the US Army to learn that the difficult terrain, harsh climate and numerical superiority of the North Koreans and Chinese combined to give the Communist forces an advantage that was hard to match, despite the qualitative edge of the UN troops and their weapons and equipment. But the balance could be partially redressed by the use of helicopters – if they could be kept serviceable. What were needed were not only more capable helicopters but also ones that were more reliable and easier to maintain on the battlefield; such attributes would offer better serviceability and thus, most importantly, availability.

In 1952 a study into the concept of airmobility, the tactical movement of a unit by helicopter, was undertaken by the US Army. It was recognized that improvements in firepower had far surpassed those in mobility and the intention was to see how the balance could be redressed. Subsequently, in a typically bold move, a decision was taken on 21 August 1952 to form twelve helicopter battalions as soon as practical troop-carrying helicopters became available. The intention was to commit the US Army to the concept of airmobility even though the means were not yet in existence.

The Korean experience also led to a recommendation by the Surgeon General that '. . . all aircraft designed, developed or accepted by the Army (regardless of their intended primary use) be chosen with a view toward potential use as air ambulances to accommodate a maximum number of standard litters'.

Indo-China (1950–54)

The war in Indo-China in some ways paralleled the conflict in Korea. Flying American-built Hiller 360s and H-23 Ravens, S-55s and British-built WS-51s, the French Air Force used them mainly for casualty evacuation, the rescue of aircrew down in Viet Minh territory and the recapture of escaped prisoners. No helicopters were actually engaged in combat. The first two Hiller 360s arrived in April 1950 to form the nucleus of the first aerial liaison flight. The three pilots included a woman, Captain Valérie André, who was an Army surgeon. She later commanded a casualty evacuation flight and completed 120 missions, recovering 165 casualties.

On 16 May the first evacuation mission was flown by Lieutenant Santini who boasted only 28 flying hours in helicopters. Nevertheless, in a flight lasting nearly two hours, one hour of which was in darkness, he flew two wounded men to Saigon. A second helicopter unit was established in April 1952 after four of the more powerful H-23s had arrived. It was put under the control of the Tactical Air Command which had been brought into operation in June 1950. Between June and December 1952 eight WS-51s were welcomed as they were able to lift three casualties simultaneously. The arrival of these helicopters did not relieve the pressure on the two helicopter flights; if anything, the reverse was true as word of their capabilities spread. A major improvement in capability was achieved in September 1953 with the introduction of the first S-55, which could take six wounded and a medical attendant.

In November 1953 alone 400 French wounded were evacuated by helicopter from the battlefield, some flights taking place in darkness. The siege of Dien Bien Phu, however, saw the end of such evacuation when, in the space of four days in March 1954, four S-55s were shot down by Viet Minh 105mm artillery despite the red crosses painted boldly on the fuselage sides.

Although the 42 French helicopters played no part in actual combat, eleven were lost to enemy action. Their value was quickly appreciated however. On 22 November 1954, to man and operate its own aircraft and helicopters, the Army formed its own light aviation branch – Aviation Légère de l'Armée de Terre (ALAT) – from the existing Aviation d'Observa-tion d'Artillerie. Furthermore, experiences in Indo-China were invaluable for the war that had just broken out in Algeria. The veterans of Indo-China were to form the nucleus of the greatly expanded helicopter force that was to operate in that country during the next eight years.

The Mid-1950s

A significant event took place in June 1955 when Bell Helicopters were awarded a contract by the US Army for the construction and testing of three

XH-40 prototypes. The specification called for the ability to lift a 363kg (800lb) payload over a radius of 185km (115 miles); the helicopter was to be able to carry troops, equipment and supplies, and evacuate wounded. Powered by a turbine engine, the XH-40 in its production version was designated the Helicopter Utility No. 1 – the HU-1, immortalized later as the 'Huey'. The first HU-1A (reversed to UH-1A in 1962) entered service in June 1959 and so successful has this helicopter been that later variants are still in service today in considerable numbers in many parts of the world.

The mid-1950s were to see a concerted American effort to get to grips with employment doctrine and tactics in theory and practice. It was Major General James M. Gavin, a dynamic commander of the famous 82nd Airborne Division during the Second World War, who coined the title 'Air Cavalry' to denote the sort of attributes airmobile forces should have: speed, shock action and the indefinable quality of dash or élan. For the April 1954 issue of *Harper's* magazine he wrote an article entitled 'Cavalry, and I Don't Mean Horses!' in which he analyzed some aspects of the Korean War. Included was the following passage: 'Where was the cavalry? . . . and I don't mean horses. I mean helicopters and light aircraft, to lift soldiers armed with automatic weapons and hand-carried light anti-tank weapons, and also lightweight reconnaissance vehicles, mounting anti-tank weapons the equal or better than the Russian T-34s . . . If ever in the history of our armed forces there was a need for the cavalry arm – airlifted in light planes, helicopters and assault-type aircraft – this was it.' Later he wrote: 'Only by exploiting to the utmost the great potential of flight can we combine complete dispersion in the defence with the facility of rapidly massing for the counter-attack which today's and tomorrow's army must possess.'

In 1955 General Gavin started a programme to bring into Army Aviation officers in the combat arms of the rank of colonel and above. They were taught to fly and then given key command and staff appointments within the organization. They were thus able to combine their previous experience with their newly acquired aviation skills to further the evolving concept of airmobility. Equally important was the fact that they had the credibility within the US Army at large to *sell* Army Aviation, to enhance its image and thereby attract into it the best junior officers. Having senior officers with direction experience of Army Aviation, both in combat in Vietnam and in the NATO environment, was invaluable when the focus shifted to the European air/land battle in the 1970/80s, to the future shape and size of the US Army and to the new generation of helicopters and associated equipment.

Further studies generated the first serious, but often hair-raising, experiments and trials with armed helicopters. In June 1956 Colonel Jay D. Vanderpool was ordered to undertake an experimental programme into helicopter armaments by Brigadier General Carl I. Hutton, the Commandant of the US Army Aviation School at Fort Rucker. Hutton saw the need for the helicopter to have the capability to suppress enemy ground fire during heliborne assaults; he believed that, if the enemy had to keep his head down, his fire would not be as accurate and heavy as when the approaching helicopter could not fire. Vanderpool's unit was given every encouragement but told not to invite publicity for fear of having the project cancelled by Hutton's superiors. Although without any formal funding or charter, Vanderpool somehow managed to scrounge six H-13s, one H-19, two H-21s and one H-25, the latter two types being tandem-rotor transport helicopters. He had armed them with a wide variety of guns and rockets and taken them on field tests. Since these weapons had not been designed for aerial use, it was often difficult to predict the results of firing them. For example, by not initially providing for expansion for some 70mm (2.75in) rockets, they took their tubes with them when they were fired.

Nevertheless, these tests indicated that helicopters, thought by many to be rather fragile vehicles, could function effectively as weapons platforms. The imagination, initiative and sheer hard work of Vanderpool's unit, given the title 7292nd Aerial Combat Reconnaissance Company (Experimental) in March 1958, were to pay significant dividends when the first of many US helicopter units arrived in Vietnam in December 1961.

The Joint Experimental Helicopter Unit (JEHU)

Despite the evident success of helicopters in Malaya and in other campaigns during the first half of the 1950s, the RAF was reluctant to devote much in the way of money or manpower to helicopters for the support of the British Army. However strongly the Army felt, helicopters were simply too low a priority to compete with the RAF's need to build up its fleet of jet aircraft. The RAF's misgivings centred on the limited payload/range, perceived vulnerability and mechanical complexity of the helicopter, but eventually it agreed to the formation of an Army/RAF Joint Experimental Helicopter Unit (JEHU). Established on 1 April 1955, JEHU was to conduct trials into the uses of utility helicopters in the field. Until 31 December 1959 when it was disbanded, JEHU experimented with different tactical and technical procedures which were put to good use in later years by Royal Navy Commando and RAF Support Helicopter squadrons.

During its years of steady but unspectacular work, JEHU did enjoy a brief moment of glory. Dropping its 'E', it participated in Operation 'Musketeer', the assault on Port Said, Egypt, on 6 November 1956. All six Sycamores and six Whirlwinds of JEHU, together with nine Royal Navy Whirlwinds, ferried ashore the men of 45 Commando, Royal Marines, in the first helicopter-borne assault in history actually to be opposed by regular troops. Within 2½ hours 415 troops and 25,400kg (56,000lb) of equipment and stores, much of it underslung, had been transferred from two aircraft-carriers to Gamil Airfield. Casualties were taken back on each return trip. No helicopters were lost to enemy fire.

Some of the more important lessons learnt were:
● Troops in the first wave of helicopters must secure the LZs against an enemy counter-attack.

- Second and successive waves must be brought in as quickly as possible.
- Unarmed troop-carrying helicopters must have some kind of fire support.
- Once the troops have been landed, the ground commander must be able to call on some helicopters to exploit success.
- Rehearsals are necessary if the assault troops and helicopter crews have not worked together before.

The success of the helicopters during 'Musketeer' confirmed the belief, particularly within the Royal Navy and Royal Marines, that they could provide a highly desirable additional element of mobility. Beliefs were translated into action and the Commando carrier concept was born, the first fixed-wing aircraft-carrier being converted to the Commando role in 1959, the second in 1961.

The fact that the RAF had to buy and operate helicopters to support Army operations was a source of general dissatisfaction in both Services. It came as something of a relief when the Minister of Defence directed that the Army was to man and operate its own light aircraft; they were not to weigh more than 1,814kg (4,000lb) and they were to be unarmed. A new corps, the Army Air Corps (AAC), was formed on 1 September 1957 and it was not many years before both constraints were being quietly ignored. The RAF retained the manning and operation of the large transport helicopters. Thus the responsibility within the British Armed Forces for operating battlefield helicopters was split between the Army and RAF, an arrangement which still exists today despite its évident shortcomings. It is also an arrangement that is unique among the major armed forces of the world.

The First Soviet Military Helicopters

Possibly because she had no wars to spur her on, the Soviet Union lagged behind the Americans, British and French in the technical and tactical development of helicopters after the Second World War. It was not until September 1948 that Mil's Mi-1 'Hare' flew for the first time. The American use of helicopters during the Korean War had, however, quickened Soviet interest and in October 1951, fifteen months after the Korean invasion, Stalin ordered two new helicopters to be designed, built and flown within twelve months: a single-engined, twelve-passenger version, the Mi-4 'Hound', and a twin-engined 24-passenger version, the Yak-24 'Horse'. Both had clamshell rear doors and a loading ramp for vehicles. In the event only the 'Hound' proved to be a success and a few are still in service in parts of the world today.

An opportunity for Soviet helicopters to become involved in conflict arose with the suppression of the Hungarian uprising in November 1956. Although not thought to have participated directly in the fighting, 'Hares' and 'Hounds' were used for liaison and logistic support tasks.

In the meantime, the application of the helicopter to the battlefield was studied carefully. One particular role was seen to be the airlifting of troops forward, ahead of the main body, to capture key objectives such as bridges, road junctions, choke points and even airfields. A requirement for a bigger helicopter quickly emerged and in June 1957 Mil's mighty Mi-6 'Hook' flew for the first time. Able to accommodate 65 troops or carry a payload of 12,000kg (26,455lb), the 'Hook' allowed the Russians to lift large numbers of troops, together with a variety of guns, equipment and supplies, close or even on to tactical objectives, provided that they were not too heavily defended.

In August 1968 the 'Hook', together with the Mi-2 'Hoplite', 'Hound' and Mi-8 'Hip', played an important supporting role in the Warsaw Pact invasion of Czechoslovakia. A year later they were in action during the Sino-Soviet clashes on the Ussuri River, on occasion using the guns, rockets and anti-tank missiles that had been installed on some 'Hounds' and 'Hips'. No purpose-designed armed helicopter was yet available – but note had been taken of American experience in Vietnam and the Mi-24 'Hind' was to appear shortly.

Counter-Insurgency

In the years following the Second World War, conflict, rebellion and dissension broke out in many parts of the world. Some required just police action to contain them but others demanded the commitment of military forces. The helicopter did not begin to figure prominently until the late 1950s, but when it did it quickly proved its effectiveness in the various struggles to counter insurgency. Hard-won experience showed that the secret of success in such campaigns lay in winning the battle for the hearts and minds of the local populace. The insurgents could then be isolated and denied access to refuge, sustenance and information. Nearly always able to land close to where it was needed, the helicopter thus had a major role to play in winning hearts and minds, besides its more obvious military tasks.

If they are to prevail, guerrilla forces must seize and keep the initiative, select targets that are not too big for them and which they can attack when ready, and avoid confrontation with the security forces when the odds are against them. The security forces, on the other hand, must also try to gain the initiative by making contact with the guerrillas as often as possible, to keep them off balance and force them onto the defensive. Cordon, search and destroy operations have been much favoured in counter-insurgency. But the results, when good, are usually short-term and when bad, that is when the innocent suffer, long-term. Whenever possible, clear and hold operations – and thus the continuous domination of territory and pacification of the population – are much to be preferred. Whatever methods are used mobility, flexibility and speed are critical attributes for the security forces, and clearly helicopters have a major part to play in enhancing them and, with good intelligence, achieving all-important surprise.

While rotary and fixed-wing fire support can make a significant contribution, its indiscriminate use can backfire. Any target must be precisely delineated and there must be no danger of hitting innocent civilians. If such guarantees cannot be given and innocents, particularly women and children, are killed and wounded – as they were in large numbers in Vietnam, Algeria, Afghanistan and elsewhere – then more harm is done by alienating the survivors than any good achieved by killing a few enemy. At a lower level the same applies to the destruction of villagers' houses and property. Thus ill-planned and poorly executed air attacks can be, and often have been, counter-productive.

Apart from the French the British were probably busier than any other country during the 1950s and 1960s in confronting colonial insurgencies. In two campaigns, in Borneo and in Aden, helicopters played notable roles.

Borneo (1963–66)

In 1961 a plan was put forward to create a Federation of Malaysia to include Malaya, Singapore and the three territories of British Borneo (Brunei, Sabah and Sarawak). In September 1963 the Federation was established without Brunei. Its existence, however, conflicted with Indonesian ambitions and President Sukarno declared a policy of 'confrontation'. Shortly afterwards acts of terrorism and sabotage took place in Sabah and Sarawak and it was not long before regular Indonesian troops were making raids across the 1,600km (1,000-mile) border into these territories.

Such was the nature of the terrain, the vast distances and the shortage of combat troops that the successful prosecution of the fighting would have been impossible without the use of aircraft, particularly helicopters. The fewer the helicopters, the greater the number of infantry required. As the Director of Operations, Major General Walter Walker, said: 'Give a hundred men some helicopters and they will do the job of a thousand.' But the best the three Services could provide for him was about 80 helicopters.

Traditional roles absorbed much of the flying effort but the airborne command post role assumed ever greater importance. Reconnaissance was a common task and, although it rarely resulted in a positive contact because there were no permanent enemy camps or caches to be found, it certainly inhibited enemy movement, as testified by captured enemy documents. Care was taken, however, not to jeopardize surprise when trying to intercept Indonesian raiding groups; security forces were landed covertly some way away and they then moved forward to pinpoint the Indonesians, trap them and attack them.

Infantry battalions and artillery regiments usually had three Army Sioux helicopters for command and control and the direction of artillery fire. Having pilots on the spot, who were tactically up-to-date and at immediate readiness to fly, was of enormous value to the hard-pressed unit commander. Five-seat AAC Westland Scout helicopters were also in direct support of the Army, being employed for much the same tasks as the Sioux but normally at brigade level. The larger Royal Navy and RAF Whirlwind and Westland Wessex (licence-built turbine-engined Sikorsky S-58) heli-copters were initially controlled centrally. Experience soon revealed, however, that these helicopters should also be decentralized, so they were operationally subordinated to brigade commanders. This allowed a quicker reaction to events and a better chance of following up fleeting contacts. Only the few RAF Bristol Belvederes remained under central control at the main airport at Kuching.

Aden (1964–68)

In 1964 violent opposition to the Federation of South Arabia broke out, fuelled principally by the National Liberation Front and the Front for the Liberation of South Yemen. These groups, supported by Egypt and the Yemen Arab Republic, probably encouraged the tribal dissension and attacks upon Federal troops which took place in the Radfan Mountains in the Western Aden Protectorate. A British brigade group was sent to Thumeir, some 100km (62 miles) from the British base at Aden, in an attempt to restore peace.

The tribesmen, inherently warlike and helped by their remarkably long eyesight, were keen to open fire whenever they saw a target. Aircraft were a favourite, even if out of range. Nevertheless, they did achieve many hits on helicopters of all three Services as they carried troops to picquet positions on the mountain tops, delivered ammunition, water, food and other supplies and evacuated casualties. The Belvedere, the only British twin-engined, tandem-rotor helicopter ever to enter operational service, was particularly useful for carrying heavy loads, notably howitzers, their crews and ammunition, to mountain peaks that were inaccessible to other helicopters. It could lift 2,720kg (6,000lb) of freight or accommodate some eighteen armed troops over a range of about 150km (93 miles). But, as well as demanding excessive maintenance, it proved to be vulnerable to small arms fire and unreliable.

Tactical flexibility and mobility depended to a large extent on the immediate availability of helicopters. Their use to deploy infantry platoons to mountain tops and keep them resupplied helped to raise the tempo of the campaign and keep the guerrillas off balance. Some were armed: a few Scouts were equipped, for example, with two fixed forward-firing 7.62mm general purpose machine-guns fitted to the landing skid booms, one on each side of the fuselage. For many minor operations the most viable grouping was three Scouts and one Wessex. One of the Scouts was armed and carried the ground commander, the flight commander and a gunner in the back; the other two Scouts had four armed soldiers each and the Wessex fourteen. This force was well able to deal with opportunity targets or those spotted by hidden observers.

While the Army and the Royal Navy were in general agreement that commanders on the ground should have control of the available heli-copters, the RAF believed that centralized control was more effective.

Ground commanders believed that their helicopters should be based forward with them, but the RAF pointed to the maintenance complications of such a deployment.

The guerrillas also waged an urban campaign in the town of Aden itself. Even here helicopters had a role in monitoring the sudden formation of threatening crowds and watching for the surreptitious deployment of terrorist mortar or bazooka squads. Suspicious vehicles were followed and troops guided to intercept them.

The two most significant lessons to be learnt in Borneo and Aden concerned command and control. There was no doubt that helicopters were most effective when they were deployed as far forward as possible and their control was decentralized. The work of individual pilots and crews was of greater value when they were included in the planning and briefing process and understood the concept of operations; when they flew regularly in support of specific units and got to know the individuals in them; and when they were prepared to share the risks and discomfort experienced by 'their' units.

Panama (1989)

Operation 'Just Cause', to remove General Manuel Noriega from power, install the already elected Government and ensure the safe operation of the Panama Canal, began before dawn on 20 December 1989. The vast majority of the 171 US military helicopters involved had already been deployed to Panama before the assault. The Army's share was 162: 116 in Task Force Aviation and 46 in Task Force 160, an element of the 160th Special Operations Aviation Group. The wide variety of helicopter types in Task Force Aviation included Bell AH-1 Cobras, UH-1 Hueys and OH-58 Kiowas, Boeing Vertol CH-47 Chinooks, Sikorsky UH-60 Black Hawks and eleven McDonnell Douglas AH-64 Apaches. Task Force 160 had Black Hawks, MH-47D special operations Chinooks and two variants of the Hughes OH-6 Cayuse: the AH-6 'Little Bird' gunship and MH-6 troop carrier. Three MH-47Ds flew direct from Fort Bragg, North Carolina, to Panama with two in-flight refuellings, one by night with the crews using night vision goggles. By means of image-intensifying tubes, these enhance the existing light level and, in doing so, they also make it possible to fly comparatively safely at low level in the dark. These Chinooks were ready for operations on arrival, thus demonstrating the advantages of self-deployment. At least 30 hours are required to prepare a Chinook for carriage in a transport aircraft and to reassemble it ready for operations at its destination. The USAF used five Sikorsky MH-53J Pave Low and four MH-60 Pave Hawk helicopters for special operations.

Task Force 160 is structured and equipped for short-duration decisive operations, and that was what Operation 'Just Cause' turned out to be. The major military objectives were secured within 24 hours, by which time Panamian Defence Force resistance was largely over. Much of the actual fighting was carried out in darkness, most helicopter crews using night vision goggles and the Apache crews their integrated night systems; of the 246 hours flown by the Apaches 138 were at night.

The Apache made its combat debut in Panama. None was shot down although three were hit, one by 23 bullets. All were rapidly returned to flying duty. Four other helicopters were shot down: two AH-6s, one MH-6 and one Kiowa. Most of the damage to helicopters was suffered during daylight hours. Losses would probably have been higher had not about a third of the total flying hours been completed at night. The value of effective night vision equipment and good training was evident in greater survivability; and also in the attainment of tactical surprise.

War

It would be impossible to describe the helicopter contribution to all the various major and minor inter-state wars, civil wars and interventions that have taken place since the end of the Second World War (see Fig. 2). This contribution has been dramatic in some cases and a few brief examples are cited below.

The Ogaden War (1977-78)

In the middle of 1977 guerrilla operations by the Western Somalia Liberation Front in the Ogaden Desert spilled over into war when the Somali Army was committed to the struggle to unify the ethnic Somali population in this part of Ethiopia with Somalia itself. By November the Ethiopian Army had been driven out of the desert and had even lost the key stronghold of Jijiga. On 12 November the Somali leader expelled from his country the thousands of Russians who had been providing help and advice. Smarting from this treatment, Moscow immediately switched sides and started to pour aid into Ethiopia, together with advisers and aircrew, while simultaneously arranging for Cuban troops to be brought in to spearhead a counter-attack. The capture of Jijiga would unhinge the Somali defence and it was therefore decided to try to trap the Somalis there, having first cut off their supply and escape routes. Situated at the north-eastern end of the Kara Mardah Pass, Jijiga was dominated by the Ahmar Mountains to the west. In the view of the Somalis, these mountains were impassable to armour and prevented any outflanking move to the north. A conventional advance along the Pass and subsequent attack on Jijiga would invite heavy casualties and offer no guarantee of success.

If it were possible, a flanking movement to the north could bring Cubans and Ethiopians to the rear of Jijiga and permit a surprise pincer attack on the town. The only way such a move could be achieved in time would be to make use of the twenty Soviet 'Hip C' and ten 'Hook' transport helicopters available. An advance along the Pass to keep Somali attention firmly fixed in that direction was also included in the plan. During the first days of

March 1978 these helicopters lifted Cubans and Ethiopians in a series of waves into a staging area some 30km (18 miles) north of Jijiga. A further 100 'Hook' sorties were then flown to bring in ASU-57 airborne assault guns, airmobile and other light armoured vehicles, ammunition and heavy equipment. A logistic support base was set up and restocked by means of helicopter lift.

As the frontal assault went in from the west, so the outflanking troops attacked from the north. Within two days it was all over: Jijiga had fallen, the Somali Army had been roundly defeated and the Ogaden was soon to be free of a Somali presence. The astonishingly rapid collapse of the Somalis was brought about by the surprise attack from the north; this, in turn, was only possible because of the use of helicopters which proved that natural obstacles, in this case mountains, could no longer be relied upon to protect an open flank.

Iran–Iraq (1980–88)

The Iran–Iraq War broke new ground in being the first to see serious, though infrequent, clashes between helicopters. Within two months of the war starting, on 8 November 1980, a couple of Iranian AH-1J Cobras met two Iraqi 'Hinds' near Dezful in Iran. Chasing them back into Iraq, the Cobras shot down one of them and so damaged the other that it crashed a little further on. This engagement is believed to be the first-ever helicopter kill by another helicopter. Further Iranian successes were recorded but the Iraqis got partial revenge in February 1984 when 'Hinds' shot down three Cobras. Other engagements followed during the course of the war. Despite Iran's acute shortage of spare parts, she generally used her combat helicopters with more verve and skill than the Iraqis. The attack of

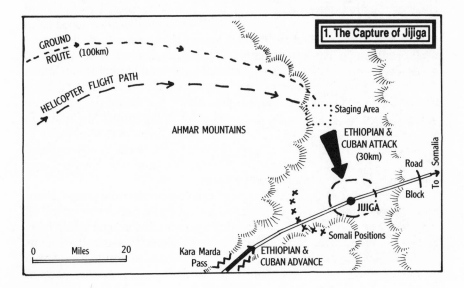

2. Helicopter Participation in Major Conflicts

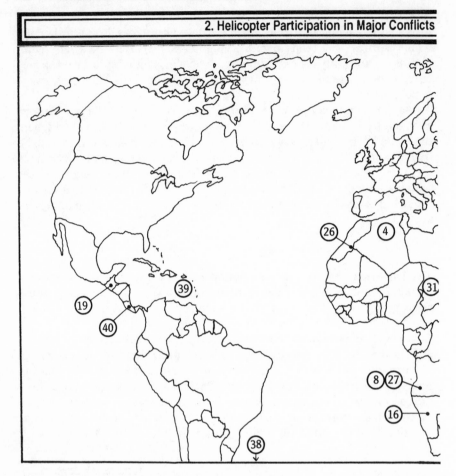

Number	Location	Conflict Dates	Major External Participants
1	Indo-China	1946–54	France
2	Malaya	1948–60	UK
3	Korea	1950–53	China, UK, USA
4	Algeria	1954–62	France
5	Cyprus	1955–59	UK
6	Egypt	1956	France, Israel, UK
7	Vietnam	1959–75	South Korea, USA
8	Angola	1961–75	Portugal
9	India (Himalayas)	1962	China
10	Brunei/Borneo	1962–66	Australia, Indonesia, UK
11	Yemen	1962–69	Egypt
12	Aden	1964–67	UK
13	Mozambique	1964–75	Portugal
14	Kashmir	1965	India, Pakistan
15	Oman	1965–75	UK
16	Namibia	1966–89	South Africa
17	Egypt/Israel/Jordan/Syria	1967	
18	Czechoslovakia	1968	USSR
19	Honduras/El Salvador	1969	
20	China/USSR	1969	
21	India/Pakistan	1971	
22	Bangladesh	1971	India
23	Sri Lanka	1971–	India
24	Egypt/Israel/Jordan/Syria	1973	Iraq
25	Cyprus	1974	Greece, Turkey

Worldwide since the Second World War

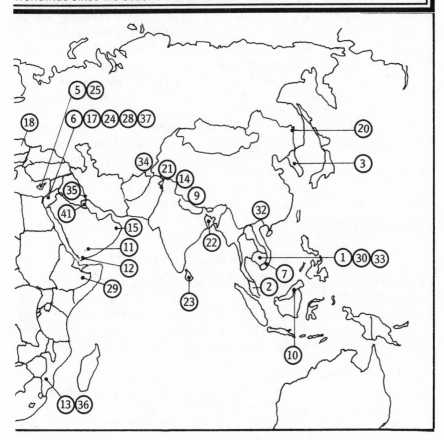

26	Mauretania/Morocco	1975–91	Algeria
27	Angola	1975–91	Cuba, East Germany, South Africa, USSR
28	Lebanon	1975–91	Israel, Syria
29	Ethiopia (Ogaden)	1976–78	Cuba, Somalia, USSR
30	Cambodia	1978–79	Vietnam
31	Chad	1978–88	France, Libya
32	Vietnam	1979	China
33	Cambodia	1979–88	Vietnam
34	Afghanistan	1979–89	USSR
35	Iran/Iraq	1980–88	
36	Mozambique	1980–90	South Africa, Zimbabwe
37	Lebanon	1982	Israel, Syria
38	Falklands	1982	Argentina, (UK)
39	Grenada	1983	USA
40	Panama	1989	USA
41	Kuwait/Iraq	1991	Coalition of 42 countries including Egypt, France, Saudi Arabia, Syria, UK, USA

1. This table excludes civil wars and struggles to gain independence within a state – e.g., Northern Ireland, Somalia, Sudan and Yugoslavia – which have not attracted overt external intervention on one side or another.
2. It also excludes short-lived and less important conflicts, peacekeeping operations, coups and coup attempts.
3. Where there has been intervention external forces have not necessarily been present throughout – e.g., No 7 above where US forces were only present from the end of 1961 to the beginning of 1973.
4. Not all countries in the coalition at No 41 above provided military forces.

armoured vehicles and logistic support were the principal roles for both sides; little evidence of heliborne assaults or even raids behind enemy lines is available. Iraqi 'Hinds' were used as flying artillery, engaging Iranian ground forces with their machine-guns and rockets; Iraq also used missile-armed Aérospatiale Gazelles as tank-killers. Both types sometimes combined to carry out hit-and-run attacks against isolated Iranian positions. The Iranians, on the other hand, occasionally despatched Bell AB 205 or 212 transport helicopters to drop grenades and bombs and machine-gun Iraqi gun positions. Cobras were successful against Iraqi armour, particularly early in the war when air and air defence cover was lacking. Helicopter losses were said to be heavy, partly perhaps because helicopter operations were not always co-ordinated with those of the ground forces. In this war and the Yom Kippur War (1973) between Egypt/Syria and Israel, fighter aircraft were successful in shooting down a number of helicopters. But the reverse is not unknown: in 1984 an Iraqi 'Hind' was reported as having shot down an Iranian F-4 Phantom.

The Falklands War (1982)

On 2 April 1982 Argentina invaded the Falkland Islands and the very next day the British Prime Minister announced that a Task Force would be sent immediately to the South Atlantic. Diplomatic attempts to dislodge the Argentinians failed and the Task Force was thus ordered to eject them from the islands. The campaign was known to the British as Operation 'Corporate'.

The outlying island of South Georgia was captured on 25 April (under Operation 'Paraquat') but it was not until the night of 20/21 May that the landings on East Falkland took place. The next morning two Gazelle reconnaissance helicopters were shot down and a third badly damaged. From then on the 172 helicopters of the Royal Navy, Royal Marines, Army and RAF were not often employed in direct contact with the enemy; naval helicopters naturally continued to carry out anti-submarine and anti-ship patrols and other duties at sea. But shore-based helicopters were more or less confined to combat support and a logistic role, although Scout and Wessex helicopters did fire a handful of anti-tank missiles at buildings and bunkers. With no natural cover on the islands and without an observation sight, it was clear that the Gazelle was not suited to the reconnaissance role; it was thus unable to carry out effectively the correction of artillery fire or the directon of Harrier ground-attack aircraft.

The lack of telephone wires and power lines which make low-level flying in Western Europe so potentially hazardous was welcome but the dearth of natural cover was not. To reduce vulnerability to enemy weapons, speed rather than the usual stealth had to be used. The boggy terrain and lack of roads also made vehicle movement excessively difficult. Heavy demands were therefore placed on all helicopters for the insertion of Special Forces teams, observation posts and small patrols, the carriage of commanders and other personnel, the lift forward of artillery, Rapier surface-to-air missile (SAM) systems, ammunition, fuel and other vital combat supplies, and casualty evacuation. Some of the flying was by night with the aircrew wearing night vision goggles.

The brunt of the load-lifting was undertaken by the single RAF Chinook and the 23 RN Westland Sea King HC.4 helicopters. On the first day of the landings alone, seven Sea Kings lifted nearly 453,600kg (1,000,000lb) of freight and over 500 troops. The ammunition demands of the artillery were voracious and only the larger helicopters could hope to meet them. In the final twelve hours of the fighting, five artillery batteries fired the equivalent of one regiment's training ammunition for four years; 21,000 rounds of 105mm ammunition were flown forward in a desperate effort not to let the guns fall silent too soon. Something of a routine was established: ammunition in, casualties out.

Such was the dearth of helicopters available for the land battle (less than 100, of which 27 were Royal Marine and AAC Gazelle and Scout helicopters, both with a limited payload), and the priority accorded to casualty evacuation and the combat support tasks, that no major heliborne assault was undertaken.

The Argentinians also had about 25 helicopters in the Falklands, consisting of Chinooks, Aérospatiale Pumas, Agusta 109s and UH-1s. They made no impact on the fighting, being used mainly for logistic purposes. Royal Navy Sea Harriers shot down at least three Pumas and a UH-1H, besides damaging others on the ground. The proximity of fighter airfields on mainland Argentina and the presence of a few fixed-wing ground-attack aircraft on the islands posed a continuing threat to the British helicopters, one of which, a Scout, was shot down by an Argentine Air Force Pucará.

Just 25 days after the landings, on 14 June, all Argentinian forces on East and West Falkland formally surrendered. It requires no military insight to appreciate that helicopters were a major factor in the British success. Both in the Ogaden and in the Falklands, their contribution to the land battle did not lie with their firepower but with their mobility and tactical flexibility. Had the ground force commanders not had the means to get troops, artillery and other heavy equipment quickly across what the enemy considered to be impassable terrain, then both these short wars would have lasted much longer and the casualties would have been much greater.

Operation 'Peace for Galilee' (1982)

The invasion of the Lebanon to clear hostile artillery within range of Israeli settlements, and to destroy Syrian and PLO forces further north, was launched on 6 June 1982. Despite their limited number, helicopters featured strongly in this short war, named Operation 'Peace for Galilee'. The twelve Israeli Defence Force (IDF) Cobras and thirty McDonnell Douglas 500MD Defenders, both armed with the TOW anti-tank missile, were in the main committed to the support of Task Force East in its advance into the southern Bekaa Valley. Some 130 missiles were fired and the IDF claimed about 100 hits on Syrian tanks, light armour and other vehicles. IDF helicopter operations were closely co-ordinated with ground units and often based on intelligence gathered by unmannned aerial vehicles. In addition to their attack role, IDF helicopters were used for reconnaissance, casualty evacuation, command and control, and logistic support; in this latter role artillery ammunition was often flown directly to the forward gun positions. Four Cobras were lost, two to enemy fire and two to friendly fire; no Defenders were lost. The Israelis considered small arms to pose the greatest threat to their helicopters, followed by tank main guns. The greatest fear of Israeli tank crews was missile attack, ground- and helicopter-launched, from undetected positions and from any direction.

The Syrians also employed armed helicopters but much less efficiently than the Israelis. Their Gazelles, armed with the HOT missile, managed to destroy a number of Israeli armoured vehicles. Syrian helicopter operations, however, were generally poorly co-ordinated with their own ground forces and sometimes crews were tasked to go out tank-hunting without the benefit first of a full tactical briefing on the current situation. Their success rate was reportedly low. The Syrians lost fourteen Gazelles, some of which were shot down by IDF tanks.

The Gulf War (1991)

In the early hours of 2 August 1990 Iraq invaded Kuwait. 'Hips', supported by 'Hinds' and Gazelles, took part in the assault. The troops they carried quickly seized key installations in Kuwait City while other attack helicopters supported armoured advances along the main roads. As many as a dozen helicopters were shot down and one or two flew into power lines and crashed.

On 7 August President Bush ordered US aircraft and troops to Saudi Arabia to deter a further Iraqi advance into that country. In the succeeding months a coalition of 42 countries, acting in accordance with United Nations resolutions, began to build up their forces as part of Operation 'Desert Shield'. These included a huge number of helicopters of different types – about 2,300. Over 2,000, of which nearly 300 were Apaches, came from the US Army and USMC, others being provided by the Gulf States, Britain (about 100) and France (about 140). In addition to these, there were many naval helicopters in the area, based on ships at sea. During the build-up period desert familiarization and intense training by day and night were undertaken; helicopters also probably flew Special Forces teams into Kuwait to gather intelligence, take prisoners, capture selected items of equipment and carry out acts of sabotage.

Twenty-two minutes before midnight GMT on 16 January 1991, Operation 'Desert Shield' became Operation 'Desert Storm' when the Allies launched their first air attack on Iraq. This attack was not by fighter-bombers but by eight Apache helicopters from the 101st Airborne Division (Air Assault), which penetrated some 90km (56 miles) into Iraq to destroy two key early warning radar sites 110km (68 miles) apart. By putting them out of action a 20km (12.5 miles) radar-free corridor was cleared for the first wave of attack aircraft to hit strategic targets in and close to Baghdad.

Task Force Normandy consisted of two teams, each with four Apaches and two USAF MH-53J Pave Low helicopters for SAR and navigational assistance. The Pave Lows, having provided the Apaches with precise and up-to-date positional data 20km (12.5 miles) south of their targets, peeled off to go to their rendezvous. Another Apache and a Black Hawk were provided for back-up command and control and SAR but stopped at the Iraqi border. Each Apache carried an 870 litre (190 Imp gal; 230 US gal) auxiliary fuel tank, eight Hellfire missiles, 19 × 70mm (2.75in) rockets and 1,100 rounds of 30mm ammunition.

The night was pitch-black but contact using night vision devices was made with the targets at over 12km (7.5 miles) and identification confirmed at more than 7km (4.3 miles). The first Hellfire missiles were launched at over 6,000m from the target, the helicopters providing their own laser designation. Given the lack of opposition, the Apaches were able to move slowly towards their targets at speeds between 25 and 90km/hr (15–56mph) and at heights varying from 30 to 75m (100–250ft). As the range decreased to about 4,000m, 70mm (2.75in) rocket fire was opened and 30mm cannon fire at about 2,000m to complete the destruction. The plan to attack both widely-separated radar sites at precisely the same moment was achieved and both were out of action within four minutes of the attack starting. A few minutes later some 70 American aircraft flew through the gap on their way to Baghdad. Helicopters were used for this mission because they could fly below radar cover at night to reach targets undetected; they could then make repeated attacks until the crews were sure of the sites' destruction and because visual confirmation of success was deemed vital.

Thereafter the precision engagement of ground targets by Apaches and Cobras, often assisted by unarmed OH-58D Kiowa reconnaissance helicopters, became a frequent occurrence. The Kiowas provided laser designation for USAF aircraft, Hellfire-equipped Apaches and USMC Cobras, and for field artillery Copperhead shells. Once the air war had started, Special Forces teams were flown by helicopter deep into Iraqi territory, usually by night, to gather intelligence, search for and destroy Scud launchers, cut communications links, assist in the rescue of downed aircrew and help find and designate targets for attack aircraft. SAR helicopters were on constant standby and on 21 January the first rescue took place when a US Navy A-6 pilot was recovered from behind Iraqi lines by an MH-60G Pave Hawk escorted by two USAF A-10s. As the attack of ground targets proceeded, the war at sea was prosecuted with such vigour that by mid-February the Iraqi Navy had been all but destroyed by Royal Navy, Saudi and US helicopters, including US Army armed OH-58D Kiowa Warriors.

The Iraqi attack on the deserted border town of Khafji on 29/30 January was repulsed with the help of sixteen USMC Cobras firing Hellfire and TOW missiles. This turned out to be the only Allied defensive action of the war. Meanwhile, helicopter cross-border activity continued by day and night, the distance into Iraqi-held territory gradually increasing to 100km (62 miles) or more. The Apaches' videotape gun cameras produced a wealth of information to back up and expand on aircrew reports. Because it proved to be difficult for helicopter crews to spot stationary tanks concealed in dug-outs, they were often redirected to the more visible air defence and artillery sites. Some Iraqi tanks let off smoke pots to try to convince Allied crews that they had already been hit; such a technique and good use of dummy tanks contributed to the difficulty in assessing Iraqi losses. Against mobile radars the USMC AH-1W SuperCobras used the Sidearm anti-radar missile.

On 16 February a battalion of eighteen Apaches attacked targets previously identified by unmanned aerial vehicles. The following day the demoralized state of the Iraqi Army became apparent when about 40 Iraqis surrendered to two Apaches which had attacked a multiple rocket system and a mortar bunker. Also that day helicopter reconnaissance was undertaken for an operating base, named 'Cobra', to be set up inside Iraq when the ground offensive began. Three days later a battalion of more than 450 men surrendered to two Apaches and two Kiowas of the 101st Division when they attacked a bunker complex. Because they were well behind Iraqi lines, Chinooks had to be brought in to fly the prisoners back to Saudi Arabia. Constant Allied helicopter cross-border attacks on artillery, mobile radars, bunkers, tanks and other armoured vehicles served to degrade Iraqi capabilities and seriously undermine their morale while simultaneously raising that of the Allies. Black Hawks with loudspeakers were used to explain how to surrender before bunkers were attacked. By the time the ground offensive started the Allies had total command of the air and had sapped the will of most Iraqis to fight. What Iraqi movement and action there was almost inevitably attracted quick retribution. No helicopters had been lost by the Allies in combat, a testament to the weakness of Iraqi resistance, but twelve were written off due to other causes. No Iraqi helicopters had come far enough forward to engage in ground or air combat, but at least six had been shot down by Allied fighter aircraft.

At 0100 hours GMT on 24 February the ground offensive, 'Desert Sabre', started. The 'mother of all battles', to quote President Saddam Hussein, was at hand. Just 100 hours later it had become the 'mother of all defeats', thanks to a combination of surprise, speed, massive armoured assaults and constant support from the air – the latest example of a blitzkrieg. The rout of the Iraqi Army was achieved by a totally unexpected flanking movement into Iraq well to the west of Kuwait by US, British and French forces, while two USMC divisions and Arab forces pierced the obstacle belt in several places 200km (125 miles) and more to the east. All ground forces were supported by fixed-wing aircraft and reconnaissance and anti-tank/attack helicopters moving with them; British Lynx AH.7/TOW and French Gazelle/HOT added to the destruction of Iraqi armour and artillery. In some instances tanks imploded rather than exploded when they were hit, revealing the fact that they were dummies. Assault and transport helicopters brought ammunition forward and took casualties and prisoners to the rear. To keep pace with the speed of advance, some divisional commanders spent much of the time aloft in their command post helicopters.

An hour after dawn the largest helicopter operation in history took place. Having been chosen and reconnoitred before the ground offensive had started, Special Forces had been inserted to secure 'Cobra' and provide navigational assistance. Six fly-in corridors were used, the Division's Kiowas, Apaches and Cobras leading the way and providing flank protection. The 1st Brigade of the 101st Division, together with some 50 vehicle-mounted TOW systems, two battalions of 105mm howitzers and many tons of ammunition and fuel, were then lifted by 118 Black Hawk, Chinook and Huey helicopters (several of them flown by women) about 100km (62 miles) north of the Saudi border into an unoccupied area of the Iraqi desert to establish the huge 'Cobra' forward operating base. It was a rough circle some 32km (20 miles) in diameter. The assault was virtually unopposed. The second aim of the operation was to use the 'Cobra' base as a staging area for two brigades of the Division to advance north and north-east to isolate the Kuwaiti theatre of operations by severing Iraqi supply lines and cutting off withdrawal routes. Thus, as dusk approached the next day, 66 Black Hawks, carrying some 1,000 men, and escorted by reconnaissance and attack helicopters, skimmed low over the desert towards the valley of the Euphrates. The objective was Highway 8, the main road out of Basra.

It was certainly a novel concept to put the logistic support ahead of the main advance, demonstrating great vision, daring and confidence among Allied planners. It could not have been contemplated, however, without the Allies' air supremacy and the knowledge that the Iraqis had virtually no intelligence-gathering capability. Nevertheless, in the annals of military history, this whole left flanking movement will stand alongside the USMC landing at Inchon in 1950 which transformed the Korean War. The supplies flown in were not only for the helicopters but also for the armoured divisions, to help them maintain their momentum and thus surprise the defenders. Once these forces had passed, the 'Cobra' base was resupplied by road and reverted to a helicopter arming and refuelling point. So far and fast did the helicopters range that the refuelling system was sorely pressed to meet requirements. Apaches often carried auxiliary fuel tanks to increase their range and reduce the need to set up refuelling points even further forward.

By the fourth day, it was merely a case of Allied aircraft, helicopters, tanks and artillery pounding the fleeing Iraqis. On 27 February eighteen Apaches from 2/6 Cavalry of 11 Aviation Brigade carried out a night raid deep into Iraqi territory. The destruction was prodigious: 157 tanks, 108 other vehicles and artillery weapons and 24 bunkers. 'Desert Sabre' had been an unequal contest between the numerically inferior Allies, who were well led, motivated and trained, and had the latest technology air and ground equipment, and a large but demoralized Third World Army with reasonably good equipment but poorly trained in its use; an Army trying to fight the Iran–Iraq war all over again, using linear defensive tactics, rather than a modern air/land, day/night battle.

Once again battlefield helicopters had proved their worth, this time emphasizing their ability to go deep into enemy territory and to operate effectively at night and in bad weather, in both cases to gather tactical information and to destroy targets. Indeed, its pilot's night vision sensor enabled the Apache to fly at night and in weather which grounded most other aircraft. Allied combat losses had been unbelievably low: 223 killed out of a force of over half a million, less than the number killed in the Falklands where only some 28,000 men and women of all three British Service were involved. Helicopter losses overall – from the initial deployment in August 1990 – amounted to 34, with just eight in combat. Iraqi Army Aviation boasted well over 100 combat helicopters, including Gazelles, MBB BO 105s, 'Hinds' and 'Hips' – but they were conspicuous by their absence. Had they been used to guard the Iraqis' open western flank, the Allied encirclement would have been delayed, with unknown repercussions for other aspects of the overall plan. But they did not fight and so there was no opportunity to pit Western helicopters against Soviet-made or even other Western helicopters.

Algeria (1954–62)

The War

In the early hours of All Saints' Day, 1 November 1954, armed bands of Algerian Moslems crept out of the night and attacked a wide variety of targets throughout the country, Government buildings, French Army installations and settlers' farms among them. Cairo Radio announced with undisguised glee that the rebellion had begun and that a Front de Libération Nationale (FLN) had been formed. To start with it did not have the spontaneous support of the Moslem population. But in a campaign of strikes, sabotage and assassination, the FLN, and its military arm, the Armée de Libération Nationale (ALN), quickly grew in size from a total of about 3,000 militant activists to between 30,000 and 40,000 fellaghas (literally combatants, guerrillas) by the end of 1956. As the ALN grew in strength so did its influence spread rapidly. Soon large parts of the country were under its control and it could count on a veritable army of sympathizers. The aim was simply independence from France.

The first rebel actions began in the inhospitable terrain of the Aurès Mountains in eastern Algeria. They then moved to the Kabylia coastal range and later further westwards. As the ALN indulged in hit-and-run tactics, it soon became impossible for the normal security forces to maintain law and order. Complete authority to deal with the situation was therefore handed over to the French Armed Forces, whose policy was to oppose the guerrillas with greater force and whose strength rose within eighteen months from about 50,000 to over a quarter of a million.

Despite the ferocity of the FLN, its massacres of innocent civilians and its use of torture, vengeful French strong-arm counter-measures merely had the effect of increasing popular support for the rebels. In March 1956 Morocco and Tunisia were granted their independence by France, events that were to have important consequences for the struggle in Algeria: sanctuaries, inaccessible to the French but through which aid from other countries could be channelled, were opened up for the guerrillas. The existence of these sanctuaries did much to ensure that the French could not win an outright military victory, despite their efforts to seal off both countries with heavily fortified border defences. These were highly effective in restricting the movement of ALN personnel and arms into Algeria and many rebels' lives were lost in attempts to cross them.

For the first fifteen months or so of the fighting, French troops adopted a largely defensive strategy, carrying out comparatively small cordon and search operations by day where the rebels had struck the night before. But in April 1956 they began a pacification programme which involved 'quadrillage' tactics: major cities and towns were garrisoned in strength while smaller numbers of troops were located in smaller towns, villages and even farms.

At the end of 1956 the FLN, by now strong, highly organized and well equipped, declared that all Europeans in Algiers between the ages of eighteen and forty were legitimate targets: indiscriminate bombings, shootings and other forms of violence became daily occurrences. The challenge was taken up by the French Army's 10th Parachute Division which by early 1958 had more or less restored law and order to the tortured city. By now French troop strength was close to 425,000.

On 1 June 1958 General Charles de Gaulle became Premier in France; on 4 June he flew to Algiers to make a speech that, significantly, omitted the cry that had long been fashionable: 'Long Live French Algeria'. Within a week he had announced that he was going to devise new relationships between France and her overseas possessions. On 21 December he was elected President. Instead of renewing the struggle, it soon became obvious that the French Government's desire to maintain its rule over Algeria was waning. De Gaulle's proposals to solve the problem by self-determination were considered unacceptable by the French population in Algeria (known as the 'pieds noirs') and the Army serving there. Looking to the future, the FLN formed the Provisional Government of the Republic of Algeria in October 1958.

As Moslem public opinion began to swing behind the FLN, French forces renewed their efforts to defeat the ALN once and for all. By 1959 the ALN claimed a strength of 130,000, although the French estimated the total to be about 35,000 regulars and 30,000 auxiliary troops. In a ruthless campaign the French had, by early 1960, largely destroyed or neutralized the ALN, breaking down its units to no more than platoon size. At the end of the war there were probably no more than about 3,000 fellaghas operating inside Algeria. On the other hand, the conduct of the pieds noirs and the French Army (besides, of course, that of the ALN) did not find favour with the French public, or indeed world public opinion. Relations with Metropolitan France deteriorated and the war became, to all intents and purposes, politically unwinnable. Disaffection in Algeria grew and in February 1961 the Organisation Armée Secrète (OAS) was formed by the pieds noirs and some members of the parachute units to fight for 'Algérie française'. The OAS's initial aim was simply to sabotage independence negotiations, but this later evolved into a campaign of wholesale destruction. When, in April 1961, four French generals staged a coup d'état to seize Algiers in defiance of de Gaulle's apparent desire to negotiate a settlement, it became clear that the Algerian problem had to be resolved without delay and before political stability in Metropolitan France was threatened further.

Any latent desire by the French Government to prosecute the war faded rapidly. What the ALN had failed to achieve on the battlefield, the FLN, had been able to win off it, more or less by default; it is a fact, unusual in a guerrilla war, that as the FLN gained popular support the ALN's military strength and success actually declined. On 18 March 1962, after lengthy negotiations, the FLN and the French Government came to an agreement at Evian-les-Bains in France. A cease-fire was to begin the next day and the French were to recognize the right of the Algerian people to decide their own future by means of a national referendum. This was eventually held on 1 July 1962 and an overwhelming majority of Algerians voted for independence.

The Environment

Algeria is a Mediterranean country with a coastline some 1,130km (700 miles) long. It is roughly four times larger than France. The capital, Algiers, and other, then largely Europeanized, cities are situated on this coastline. Ninety per cent of the population of ten million, of whom some nine million were Sunni Moslem and the rest largely of French stock, lived in the narrow coastal plain which provided a stark contrast to the mountains behind. Here rise the Tellian chain of the Atlas mountains and further to the south the Saharan chain. These two rugged ranges, reaching as high as 2,300m (7,550ft) in places and separated by the High Plateau, act as a substantial barrier to movement south into the harsh desert of the Sahara. The Kabylia, in the eastern part of the Tellian chain, are covered by dense forests in some places and are quite treeless in others. The mountains are cut by deep gorges with overhanging cliffs which make cross-country movement on foot extremely difficult and wearying. Thus for any successful military action, helicopter mobility and airborne firepower are virtually indispensable. The valleys are fertile and populated. The western part of the Tellian chain is lower, less rugged but more desolate. Here the mountains are riddled with caves. The Aurès Mountains in the Saharan chain are generally an infertile wilderness and were an excellent place for the guerrillas to locate their camps for the transit to and from Tunisia.

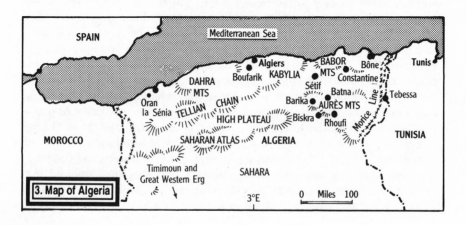

3. Map of Algeria

Except after heavy rainfall dry wadi beds criss-cross the countryside. During the long summer months it is very hot, humid and dry almost everywhere, but in the winter rain and snow fall in the mountains and it is bitingly cold. The weather in the Kabylia can be unpredictable, with storms welling up in a matter of hours. To the south in the Sahara sandstorms can cause the grounding of all helicopters. In the summer temperatures reach 49°C (120°F) at heights of 2,135m (7,000ft) – hot and high conditions that seriously degrade the performance of any type of aircraft.

The French forces were not suited to the environment or to the type of fighting that faced them. Largely organized and equipped for conventional war in Europe, they had to be reorganized and re-equipped to be able to operate in both the narrow and dark alleyways of the towns and the wide open spaces of the desert; often, too, in mountainous terrain where no vehicle could pass. Without their heavy weapons and technological superiority, the French found that the military balance favoured the ALN. The guerrillas' local knowledge of the countryside, their supreme skills at concealment and camouflage, their acclimatization and their quickness of foot and eye outweighed their numerical inferiority and the inadequacy of their weapons which, until the end of 1956, consisted largely of hunting rifles. As one of the ALN's instructions put it: 'The guerrilla must be as elusive as an eel in water, must move like a butterfly in the air and be as alert as a ravenous tiger.' Nevertheless, it was difficult for the guerrillas to co-ordinate their military operations, and their inadequate equipment and training precluded pitched battles with the French – the best source of badly needed weapons.

The conflict in Algeria was essentially an infantryman's war, the key to the military struggle being the degree of mobility and firepower possessed by the combatants. But because the ALN rarely operated in groups of more than 200 men, and usually much less, superior firepower in the form of artillery and heavy weapons was less important than good communications and an effective means of transport. It was soon obvious that the ALN enjoyed a significant advantage in mobility and that the only way that it could be matched, and indeed overcome, was by the use of air power in all its forms.

Air Power

By the end of 1955 the French had come to the conclusion that to defeat the ALN they would have to improve the reaction capability of their forces by means of better intelligence, mobility and firepower. Air power could make the largest contribution to reducing radically reaction times; it could also provide fire and logistic support that hitherto simply could not have been contemplated because of the rugged terrain or the distances involved. Of aviation's five principal roles of intelligence, command and control, the application of firepower, the transport of troops and logistic support, helicopters could undertake a significant proportion.

The Helicopter Build-Up

Only a few Bell 47Gs, bought in Italy, and H-19s (Sikorsky S-55s), borrowed from United States forces in West Germany, were available as the situation deteriorated during the early months of 1955. But on 1 April 1955 Escadrille d'Hélicoptères Légers 57 (57 Light Flight) of the French Air Force, consisting of ten 47Gs and eight H-19s, was formed at Boufarik, some 35km (22 miles) south-west of Algiers. It was to undertake rescue missions at sea and on land and to help maintain law and order in the Constantine and Aurès areas. It was under the command of the 5th Air Region.

On the same day ALAT established Groupe d'Hélicoptères No 2 (Helicopter Group 2) at Sétif, 110km (68 miles) west of Constantine and at an altitude of 915m (3,000ft) above sea-level, with seventeen aircraft; one flight with 47Gs and another with H-19s. This Group was to be commanded for the next six years by Major, later Colonel, Marceau Crespin, a veteran of Indo-China. The first helicopter from the Aéro-nautique Navale – the French Naval Air Arm, known as Aéronavale for short – an H-19, arrived at Sétif on 22 June. Some of these Army and Navy helicopters were then deployed to other locations in small detachments.

On 4 May 1955 two H-19s, based at Biskra, deposited a handful of legionnaires on the summit of the Jebel Chélia in the Aurès massif. A move that might have taken as much as two days by more conventional means was accomplished in twenty minutes. This simple manoeuvre heralded a revolution in French tactical concepts; one that was to be quickly developed as ground unit commanders learnt of the potential of tactical movement by helicopter.

On 1 August 57 Light Flight was re-christened Groupe Mixte d'Héli-coptères 57 (57 Mixed Helicopter Group, 57 MHG). Greater demands were now placed on all helicopters for the carriage of commanders, transport of troops, resupply of remote outposts and evacuation of the wounded. The few helicopters were quickly overwhelmed by the nature and number of tasks given to them. Nevertheless, the tactical benefits offered by only a couple of helicopters was once again demonstrated on 14 January 1956. Acting on information, a plan was drawn up to surprise an important meeting of guerrilla commanders due to take place in the oasis of M'Doukal, some 30km (19 miles) south of Barika; this was where two H-19s, one from ALAT and one from the Aéronavale, were based. A ground force was brought in by vehicle and then took up positions on the northern rim of the oasis but it saw no action, the two H-19 loads of commandos flying in to surprise completely and capture the six guerrilla leaders. As the force was dispersing an order was received to concentrate at Rhoufi where a rebel band had been reported by the pilot of a light observation aircraft. Having been refuelled, the two helicopters flew 120 commandos in a quick shuttle service into ambush positions despite some fire from the rebels. Quick reaction and vastly superior mobility resulted in the French killing or taking prisoner 43 rebels and recovering a large quantity of arms for the loss of four dead and eight wounded.

It was Lieutenant Colonel Marcel Bigeard, Commanding Officer of the 3rd Colonial Parachute Regiment, who was the first to appreciate what the helicopter could do for his men in chasing and ambushing the guerrillas. His first operation, on 22 February 1956, resulted in 43 enemy killed, 96 FLN members arrested and 92 rifles, 24 pistols, documents and other material being captured. The French suffered no casualties.

Because the fledgling French helicopter industry was not able to meet the demands of the French Armed Forces, the French Air Force sent Santini, the veteran from Indo-China and now a captain, to the USA to carry out a one-man investigation into the helicopters best suited to the conditions of the Algerian War. He recommended two types: the Sikorsky S-58 (known in US Army and USAF service as the H-34 and as the HSS-1 by the US Marines) and the Vertol H-21 (the Piasecki Helicopter Corporation had become the Vertol Aircraft Corporation in 1956); the H-21 had the nickname 'Flying Banana' because of its shape. The former was selected by the French Air Force, the latter by ALAT and the Aéronavale. The H-34 had a cruising speed of 160km/hr (99mph) and could carry between ten and twelve combat-equipped troops – although it had seats for fifteen – or a useful load of some 1,935kg (4,265lb). The tandem-rotor H-21 cruised at 163km/hr (101mph) and had a useful load of about 2,268kg (5,000lb); it could transport seventeen troops, although it had seating for twenty.

The lack of agreement as to which helicopter was the most suitable for the prevailing combat conditions led to a series of practical evaluations in the Aurès Mountains and at sea-level near Algiers, starting in July 1956. So far as the Aéronavale was concerned, the results were inconclusive. In terms of pure flying performance the H-34 was superior to the H-21, which proved to be more versatile in the support of ground forces. The Air Force was more concerned with hover out of ground effect, rate of climb, cruising speed and the ability to land in confined areas. ALAT regarded the helicopters in the light of their useful load, the number of stretcher casualties they could accommodate, the speed of troop embarkation and disembarkation and facilities for the ground commander on board to talk to the pilot; ALAT also claimed that the H-21, with its two rotors well above the ground, could land in places where the H-34, hampered by its tail rotor, could not. On the other hand, in rough terrain an H-21 pilot, unable to see his nose wheel, might have difficulty in landing.

Analysis of operations undertaken during the month of July revealed the efficacy of the H-34 compared with the H-19; in 93 flying hours an H-19 carried 1,477 troops while an H-34 lifted 2,900 in 86 flying hours. Even at altitudes of 1,830m (6,000ft) the H-34 could take ten troops.

Both the H-21 and the H-34 were ordered in numbers even before the evaluations began, the first three Aéronavale H-21s and two Air Force H-34s being delivered to Algeria in June 1956. The first H-21 for ALAT was received in August. By this time Escadron d'Hélicoptères Lourdes 1/57 (1/57 Heavy Helicopter Squadron) had been formed and attached to 57 MHG. The Aéronavale H-21s were to be the nucleus of Flottille 31 which formed in July at Alger-Maison Blanche but for the time being were attached to ALAT's Helicopter Group 2. During the next two months these three helicopters flew 600 hours.

The Bell 47G, Djinn and Alouette II were classed as light helicopters, the S-55/H-19 and H-21 as medium and the S-58/H-34 as heavy helicopters. The 47G was an American-designed three-seater, derived from the original two-seat Bell 47 which first flew in December 1945. Like the American H-13 in Korea, it had the ability to carry two stretchers outside the cabin. The cockpit had a plexiglass bubble canopy which gave excellent vision to the pilot and observer. Cruising speed was about 130km/hr (81mph) and range about 350km (218 miles). The Djinn, produced by the French firm SNCASO, used a 'cold jet' propulsion system whereby compressed air was ducted along the rotor blades and expelled through nozzles at their tips without any combustion; directional control was achieved by fitting two fins and a large central rudder in what remained of the engine exhaust flow, no tail rotor being required. The Djinn was a two-seater with a cruising speed of only 105km/hr (65mph) and a range of about 190km (118 miles). Capable of taking two external stretchers, it was a highly manoeuvrable little machine which gradually replaced the 47G in ALAT units.

The Djinn was supplemented in 1958 by the SNCASE Alouette II which broke new ground by being the first helicopter in the world to enter series production with a conventional turboshaft engine. The advantages were numerous. Compared with a piston engine, a turbine engine was much lighter and smaller for the same power output; thus for a given role a lighter and smaller helicopter could be designed. A compact turbine engine could be mounted above the cabin close to the rotor head, thus simplifying the transmission; moreover, such an installation did not absorb cabin space, which has to be more or less under the main rotor for reasons of centre of gravity position. There were other advantages: turbine engines could use a variety of fuels, particularly cheap kerosene, rather than expensive aviation gasoline, and they needed no cooling, which meant that the helicopter could hover at sustained high power. In general, greater ranges, higher speeds and heavier payloads were possible. Even more important, a turbine engine was more reliable and easier to maintain than a piston engine.

Seating a pilot and four passengers, the prototype Alouette II made its maiden flight in March 1955. It had a good performance and with its glazed cockpit afforded good visibility. Cruising speed was 165km/hr (103mph) and range 530km (330 miles). The Alouette II proved excellent as an airborne command post and missile-carrier and for a wide range of general tasks, including casualty evacuation. It was not able, however, to sustain much battle damage.

The Sikorsky S-55/H-19 prototype made its first flight in November 1949, embodying a shape quite unlike that of any previous helicopter. The piston engine was in the nose, above which sat the two pilots. The cabin for passengers or freight was located directly under the rotor so that any variations in the load would only have the minimum effect on the centre of gravity. The H-19 could cruise at 137km/hr (85mph) and it had a range of 650km (404 miles). Although it had space for six stretchers or ten combat-equipped troops, it could usually carry only about four or five troops in Algeria due to the heat and altitude. Although widely used in Korea it was still subject to tiresome unserviceabilities.

With the arrival of more helicopters and new types it became possible to allocate them to the tasks which suited them best. In general, light helicopters were used for the evacuation of casualties close to the scene of the fighting, liaison duties and sometimes observation; the H-19 for the carriage of supplies and of the wounded, prisoners and the dead back to base areas; and the H-21 and H-34 for troop transport, heliborne assaults by day and night and the resupply of troops in action. The two larger helicopters were also useful for recovering other helicopters and light fixed-wing aircraft which had been shot down or crashed for other reasons. The main rotor blades and other items were removed to ensure that the load was within weight limits and not likely to be dangerous to its rescuer. The recovery helicopter would then hover-taxi over the load, hook it up on the end of a sling and gingerly lift it out. Often these damaged helicopters could be repaired and returned to duty.

As the number of helicopters in Algeria grew, staff officers and ground force commanders began to understand the sometimes difficult circumstances under which helicopters operate. The useful load that they could carry depended greatly on the temperature, altitude and distance to be covered. The greater the temperature and altitude the less far it could fly. To cater for this, refuelling sites had to be established and these had to have a firm and level surface and be free of fog, ice and snow, turbulence and strong winds, and obstacles on the approach; above all, they had to be secure – out of range of enemy fire and defendable – and operable 24 hours a day.

Reorganization

By August 1956 it had become clear to the ALN leaders that a more formal countrywide military organization was necessary. Thus six military districts, called 'wilayas', were formed under the command of a colonel; these were further divided into zones (captain), regions (second lieutenant) and sectors (warrant officer). The city of Algiers became an autonomous zone. Regular fighting units were standardized at the same time: the largest was a battalion with up to 350 men and consisting of three katibas (companies) of 80 to 110 men each. A katiba had three ferkas (platoons) of 25–35 men each and a ferka consisted of three fauj (sections) with about ten men each. In 1957 some battalions were enlarged to 600 men and the katibas to 150.

The fellaghas themselves comprised three types of volunteer: Mujaheddin (a regular, a freedom fighter), Moussabiline (an auxiliary) and Fidayine (a terrorist). The Moussabiline's role was to help the Mujaheddin by gathering intelligence and acting part-time as guides, guards and messengers; the Fidayine operated in the cities as bombers, assassins and saboteurs and provided general support to the Mujaheddin. Tactics, however, remained those of the guerrilla: relying on food caches and arms dumps located all over the contested areas, units of whatever size would concentrate, often by night, strike the chosen target and then disperse again into the desert or their hide-outs in the cities. During 1957 the ALN established the 'Base of the East' on the Algerian-Tunisian border and the 'Base of the West' on the Algerian-Moroccan border to organize the flow of men and material into Algeria.

To stop this flow in the east the French erected the Morice Line, a comprehensive electric wire barrier with radar stations, observation posts, artillery emplacements and mines; between the frontier and the barrier aircraft, helicopters and mobile troops patrolled to fragment any fellagha bands before they attempted to cross the barrier itself. Heavy losses were sustained by the rebels as they tried to cross the Line. When these were added to the losses suffered inside Algeria, the ALN leadership concluded that battalions should be broken down into independent katibas which should become the basic fighting unit. Thereafter there was little chance of the ALN emulating the Viet Minh and confronting the French with a situation similar to that at Dien Bien Phu, although this hope took a time to die.

Meanwhile other guerrilla wars and the theories of Mao Tse-tung and General Giap, the North Vietnamese military leader, were studied. The Partisan war in Yugoslavia against the Germans served as something of a model and a few ex-Partisans were infiltrated into Algeria. A serious weakness remained: inadequate transport, the rebels usually having to rely on their own feet, camels and mules. The shortage and lack of sophistication of weapons was also of major concern to the ALN leadership. The inventory was confined in the main to small arms, heavy machine-guns, mortars and bazookas. These were slowly accumulated by capturing them from the French and accepting deliveries from Arab and other states, particularly Egypt and Yugoslavia.

On the French side the increasing number of helicopters and their expanding area of operations soon necessitated further reorganization. Systems for command and control and maintenance had to be devised which would ensure operational flexibility – the capability to respond to any tactical requirement whenever and wherever it arose. In 1956 ALAT began to form aviation troops, some of light fixed-wing aircraft only and some with helicopters as well. Each French Army division in Algeria and geographical zone, of which there were twelve, ultimately had a troop of up to twelve aircraft for routine observation.

On 1 November 1956 the French Air Force disbanded 57 MHG and replaced it with two escadres (wings). 2 Wing at Oran-la-Sénia, under the command of Colonel Félix Brunet, comprised 4/57 Light Helicopter Flight, 3/57 Medium Helicopter Flight and 2/58 Heavy Helicopter Squadron. 3 Wing, commanded by Lieutenant Colonel Canepa, was at Boufarik and consisted of 1/57 Light Helicopter Flight, 2/57 Medium Helicopter Flight and 1/58 Heavy Helicopter Squadron. Since the area served by the 44 helicopters of these two wings was the whole of western Algeria, some of them were deployed, usually in groups of three, to ground units for a period of two or three days, or longer if a big operation was in progress. In February 1957 5/57 Light Helicopter Flight joined 3 Wing and by the end of 1957 6/57 Light Helicopter Flight had also joined this wing, which simultaneously lost 5/57 Flight to 2 Wing.

At the end of 1956 ALAT possessed nineteen light helicopters of three different types, thirteen H-19s, seven Whirlwinds and 29 H-21s; the Aéronavale still had only three H-21s. Such overall numbers were considered far from adequate but steps to relieve the shortfall had already been taken with a further order for H-21s and H-34s; 108 H-21s were delivered to the French Army and Navy during the war. Despite funding difficulties and continuing inter-Service disagreements as to the most suitable helicopter types, the preference was clearly for the larger helicopters.

The Aéronavale also underwent reorganization. On 1 November 1957 the Groupe d'Hélicoptères de l'Aéronautique Navale No 1 (GHAN 1) was established at the naval aviation base at Lartigue, some 27km (17 miles) from Oran. It was eventually to take under command three naval helicopter units: Flottilles 31, 32 and 33. The first to form had been 31F in July 1956 with the H-21C. 33F had formed on 1 June 1957, been equipped with the H-19 and arrived at Alger-Maison Blanche a month later. 32F did not form until January 1958 with the navalized version of the H-34, the HSS-1. These three naval helicopter units were allocated to the Commandos and operated almost exclusively with them as a Marine Commando Group in the westernmost military region of Oran. GHAN 1 only had four commanders during the entire war, Capitaine de Corvette Babot earning the greatest reputation for his style of leadership and innovations in the use of helicopters – the H-21 as a bomber being an example of one!

So, by the spring of 1958 the helicopter order of battle appeared well-founded and the original 35 helicopters had grown in number to over 250 of six different types: Aéronavale, 26 medium helicopters; ALAT, 62 light helicopters and 70 medium helicopters; Air Force, 36 light helicopters, 19 medium helicopters and 44 heavy helicopters.

Armament

For the first year or two of the campaign it had been acceptable for helicopters to fly unarmed – the rebels being inadequately trained and armed – and to land close to the enemy. But as the rebels' rifles gave way to machine-guns and they learned to take account of helicopter movement when aiming, the situation changed. They soon realized that the helicopter was vulnerable, particularly while it was slowing down to land, was in the hover, was on the ground or when it was taking off. The pilot was a good figure to aim at and, given the remarkable marksmanship of most of the ALN, hits on helicopters began to mount alarmingly. In April 1956 three H-19s were shot down in three days during an operation near Tebessa. The first French counter-measures were to use fixed-wing aircraft to precede any helicopter assault, to bomb and strafe likely rebel positions, and to avoid LZs subject to rebel fire. Strafing was usually quite effective but to prevent the rebels recovering in time to fire at the helicopters as they made their approach, the timing had to be precise. Even then there was an inevitable gap between the withdrawal of the fixed-wing aircraft and the arrival of the helicopters. The ALN soon realized this. On some occasions weather or other commitments prevented any use of fixed-wing aircraft. One recourse was to arm a proportion of helicopters and a ratio of one armed helicopter to five transport was considered about right; another was to provide passive protection for the crew and passengers. Both were given bullet-proof vests while the crew also had their seats encased in light armour plate; the H-21 and H-34 had self-sealing fuel tanks.

The most important role for the armed helicopters was to provide fire support for the troop-carrying and resupply helicopters when they were in the vicinity of the LZ. Once the assault troops had disembarked, the armed helicopters remained in the area to engage the rebels and prevent them from escaping or being reinforced. They also flew in support of other missions, such as specific intelligence-gathering, and substituted when possible for fixed-wing aircraft when they were not available. There was usually a dearth of armed helicopters and often other helicopters bringing in reinforcements and supplies to troops in action had to fly within range of enemy weapons without the benefit of armed helicopter support. On 16 March 1958, for example, an ALAT H-21 suffered at least 65 bullet strikes but, fortunately, was able to get back to base. Bullet holes were sometimes repaired with 50mm metal plates with the FLN's star and crescent painted on them!

It was Colonel Félix Brunet who was the driving force behind the new concept of armed helicopters – without, it seems, having the approval of his superiors. Brunet was something of a legend in the French Air Force, having distinguished himself during the Second World War and in Indo-China. Thus he probably felt free to explore tactical innovations with his helicopters, machines about which his superiors knew little. A man brimming over with original ideas, his initial aim was the safety of his aircrew.

The very first armament trials in 1955 involved a soldier, armed with a light machine-gun, lying in a casualty pannier attached to the skids of a Bell 47. This technique did not find much favour, least of all with the unfortunate soldier, and an altogether weightier solution was pursued. The first helicopter to be armed in Algeria in 1956 was an Air Force H-19 which was given a 20mm cannon and two rocket-launchers mounted axially, as well as another 20mm cannon, two 12.7mm machine-guns and one 7.5mm machine-gun mounted in the cabin. Since these weapons, together with their ammunition, weighed more than the useful load of the helicopter, some of them had to be removed. Other combinations were tried, including an eight-tube rocket-launcher below a quadruple bazooka mount which could be swivelled to allow the crew chief to reload it. Eventually one 20mm cannon and two 12.7mm machine-guns were installed on shockless, flexible mounts in the cabin door.

The French had much to consider when contemplating the installation of guns. The overriding factor was the weight allocated to the system. This figure largely determined the gun calibre; the method of aiming, type of mounting, amount and type of ammunition to be carried and ammunition feed also had to be considered. There were three mounting options: fixed to the sides of the fuselage or the skids or even under the fuselage to fire only forwards, door-mounted or in a traversable turret. The first clearly required the helicopter itself to be aligned with the target and this might take precious seconds and in some instances be rather awkward. Nevertheless, quite accurate fire could be achieved. Guns located in the doorways (sometimes called waist or pintle-mounted) required a crewman to fire each one, had a limited arc of fire, were rather heavy and cumbersome and hindered entry to and exit from the cabin. Fire was very inaccurate and to help the gunner at least 50 per cent of the rounds had to be tracer. Turret-mounted guns and their sighting systems were heavier, more complicated and in the early stages of development. Range and lethality were very much a function of the weapon's calibre. As a rule of thumb, the maximum effective range of a 7.62mm machine-gun was 500m, of a 12.7mm gun 1,000m and of a 20mm cannon 1,500m. The larger the calibre the more devastating the effect, but the fewer the number of rounds carried because of their weight and size. The fewer the rounds, the more often the helicopter would have to land to rearm, although extra ammunition boxes could sometimes be stowed in the cabin. Guns brought problems with them such as the ammunition feed, recoil loads which might require muzzle velocities to be reduced and blast overpressures which necessitated airframe strengthening. Rockets, being unguided, were inherently less accurate than guns but produced a heavier weight of fire, particularly when fired in salvos.

The H-19 was soon superseded by the more powerful H-34, the armed version of which was called the 'Pirate'. A team of engineers worked secretly in the back of a hangar at Oran-la-Sénia to install a German MG 151 20mm cannon in the cabin door of an H-34 and 7.5mm machine-guns in the windows. More weapons were soon added. This first armed H-34, nicknamed the 'Corsair' by the ground troops whom it supported during its combat trials, was a formidable piece of flying artillery, its entire payload being absorbed by weapons and ammunition. Forward-firing weapons consisted of one 20mm cannon, four launchers with three tubes each for 73mm rockets, one launcher for 68mm rockets and four 73mm bazookas, reloadable in flight. Firing out of the side through windows and doorways were one 20mm cannon, two 12.7mm machine-guns and one 7.5mm machine-gun. It was soon felt that this one H-34 was somewhat weighed down with armament and consequently lacked manoeuvrability. A standard weapons load was devised for the H-34 Pirates and this consisted of two 12.7mm window-mounted machine-guns on the port side of the fuselage and one on the starboard side, and one 20mm cannon flexibly mounted in the cabin door. There were, of course, exceptions to this standard for specific occasions and circumstances. All H-34s were equipped with fixed fittings for weapons so that any of them could be armed in a matter of ten or fifteen minutes. This gave great flexibility since a transport H-34 could drop its troops and quickly join the fire support team, having been re-roled.

The size and comparative lack of manoeuvrability of the H-21 hampered its effectiveness as a weapons platform, as well as sharply reducing its payload. Nevertheless, a rocket pod containing eighteen 68mm rockets was sometimes attached to both sides of the fuselage and two machine-guns were fixed to the forward undercarriage strut. The preferred weapon, however, was a 20mm cannon, often the MG 151, mounted in the door. There are major drawbacks to sideways-firing guns: the larger side area of the helicopter is offered as a target to the enemy, and the helicopter has to stand off to a flank to fire; here it is vulnerable to enemy troops that have not been detected.

The standard armament for the Alouette II, the only type to be armed more or less permanently, was either 72 × 37mm rockets or four SS-10, or the later SS-11, wire-guided air-to-ground missiles. The SS-11, or AS-11 in the air-launched mode, had a maximum range of 3,000m. Guidance was manual command to line of sight (MACLOS), which meant that the gunner had to manoeuvre the missile on to his line of sight to the target – a technique that required considerable skill. The SS-11 was particularly effective when fired into caves which, because of their position in ravines, were either dangerous, difficult or even impossible to engage with shorter-range cannon or machine-gun fire, rockets or bombs. So keen were the French to arm their helicopters that even the light reconnaissance Bell 47 was sometimes equipped with two SS-10 missiles.

Various gun and rocket armaments were tested by the Aéronavale, including the novel idea of installing a bomb rack by using the fixed fittings of the cargo sling. This rack could take five 113kg (250lb) bombs. The test results were 'interesting', but the idea was not pursued due to the vehement opposition of the Air Force.

Air Force tactics differed from those of the Army. The 20mm cannon was used as the primary weapon as the helicopter orbitted safely at about 460m (1,500ft) out of range of rebel weapons. Nevertheless, specific targets could be engaged with great accuracy. ALAT, on the other hand, preferred to make a more dangerous one-time pass over the LZ, using the H-21's twin axially mounted 0.30in (7.62mm) machine-guns and 37mm and 68mm rockets, of which 72 or 36 could be carried respectively.

Command and Control

Inevitably the system of command and control underwent considerable modification in the light of experience. But by early 1959 a system had evolved that laid emphasis on the dispersion of air power and action at low levels of command – a complete reversal of the traditional philosophy in conventional warfare of the concentration of air power. The French Air Force did not go as far as ALAT in relaxing control of its helicopter units, preferring a degree of centralized administrative control, deployment and technical support. While this policy resulted in generally higher rates of availability, much unproductive flying was undertaken merely to get to the scene of the action.

The 4th Maritime Region, the 10th Military Region and the 5th Air Region were responsible for the administration and support of their own air and ground forces. The Commander-in-Chief, however, exercised operational control, through a Joint Operations Centre (JOC), of the three Army Corps and the three Tactical Air Commands (known as GATACs: Groupement Aérien Tactique) which had their HQs together at Oran, Algiers and Constantine, the country being divided into three Corps areas of the same names, west to east. Under the Corps/GATACs were a total of twelve Divisional Zones and Advanced Air Commands, each working together through a JOC to direct operations in their areas. Divisional Zones were further divided into regimental sectors, of which at one time there were 75. Sector commanders, certainly in the early years of the war, were given a good deal of autonomy and the fellaghas were able to profit from a lack of co-ordination between them. Whenever combined operations were contemplated a joint command post was established and mobile command posts, often airborne, were sent into the field to conduct actual operations.

While the GATACs retained control of the heavy firepower provided by fixed-wing aircraft, they gave to the Advanced Air Commands their own permanent reconnaissance and light attack aircraft. The GATACs also each had a wing or equivalent of helicopters. From about mid-1956 ALAT was assigned to the region of the country east of 3° East, while the Air Force and Aéronavale were given the territory west of this line. Thus 2 Wing and GHAN 1 provided helicopters for the Oran GATAC, 3 Wing for Algiers and ALAT and a small Air Force detachment for the GATAC at Constantine. Under joint control, however, helicopters were allocated to Corps/GATACs or subordinate HQs either side of the line whenever such a requirement arose. In practice, helicopters assigned to Corps/GATACs were usually distributed to zones which, quite separately, had six light helicopters and six light fixed-wing aircraft in a mixed divisional flight. Each command level was informed in advance of how many helicopters would be available to it for the next period or, conversely, how many it would have to supply for a planned large-scale operation elsewhere.

The tactical grouping of ALAT and Air Force helicopters was the Détachement d'Intervention Héliportée (DIH) whose principal task was to deliver combat troops to the scene of the action as quickly as possible. ALAT squadrons were organized into DIHs on a permanent basis and these consisted of six H-21s, one or two H-34 Pirates and a couple of command posts (Djinn, Bell 47 or, later, the Alouette II which was preferred); the latter carried the officer commanding the operation or his representative and his air adviser. This technique quickly found favour and most of the large-scale operations were commanded from the air. It allowed personal and up-to-the minute command and facilitated any change of plans made necessary by unforeseen circumstances.

Air Force DIHs were formed for specific operations and comprised one or two light helicopters for command and control and up to eight H-34s. The DIHs could be concentrated or dispersed whenever required, being supported by the Army unit to which they were attached and their own mobile support detachment. It was intended that they should be able to respond to a call for action within one hour and be able to operate without the facilities offered by fixed bases. One DIH could carry about 60 battle-equipped troops in a single lift, but more than one of these detachments could be used for an operation requiring larger numbers of troops to be landed in the first wave. Army units that enjoyed the support of a DIH soon came to appreciate its value as a means to achieve rapid manoeuvre and mobile firepower.

A smaller tactical grouping was the Unité d'Intervention Héliportée (UIH) consisting of an H-34 Pirate and three trooplift H-34s. UIHs were often deployed away from their parent units for weeks at a time.

Good communications were critical for the success of French operations. The whole of Algeria north of the Sahara was covered 24 hours a day by a VHF net. Requests from ground units or an airborne observer for air support were received simultaneously by the JOC at Corps/GATAC and at every level down to mobile CPs. If, after investigation at division and corps level, a response by helicopters was considered appropriate, then Advanced Air Commanders/Zones would be instructed to issue the necessary orders.

A Change in Tactics

From February 1956 until the end of 1958 the French espoused a policy of territorial control. Known as the 'quadrillage' (literally squaring) system, major towns and cities were garrisoned in strength, with smaller towns, villages and even farms also attracting detachments of decreasing size. Such a policy absorbed huge numbers of troops and left comparatively few for mobile operations. Nevertheless, it proved quite effective in protecting the general public and preventing contact between it and the ALN. It also forced the rebels to step up their activities in the cities – for which the French also had an answer.

During this period, however, French tactics in the rural areas were somewhat unimaginative. Routine foot patrols achieved little and vehicle patrols were sometimes hampered by telegraph poles felled across the road or trenches dug at points which could not be by-passed. In response to a guerrilla action, local French troops would be hurriedly concentrated by whatever means available and, with scant regard for secrecy, would surround the area and search it – by which time the guerrillas had long since gone. Although the number of troops required actually to make contact with a rebel band may have been relatively small, the number needed for the encirclement was usually many times larger, and therein lay the difficulty. In pre-planned search and destroy operations three sides of a chosen area would be occupied while a strong force, acting like a piston within a cylinder, would drive down from the open end. This, too, was largely ineffective. Helicopters were sometimes used in such operations to emplace troops in terrain that was otherwise inaccessible, to act as a blocking force, to serve as an artillery observation post or advanced command post, or to fly in the troops comprising the 'piston'.

Successes were achieved however. In October 1957 a large number of Moslem soldiers, based in the Great Western Erg in the Sahara, mutinied, killed their French officers and went over to the ALN. Three weeks later, in the same area, they killed two oil-drilling teams and their military escort. The French were determined not to let such an outrage go unpunished and deployed Bigeard's 3rd Colonial Parachute Regiment, together with fixed-wing fighters, transports, reconnaissance aircraft and 34 H-34s to Timimoun. After several weeks of searching, a reconnaissance aircraft noticed a bush that appeared to be out of place on a sand dune. Two platoons of parachutists were summoned and they quickly arrived by helicopter. The dissident Moslem soldiers, buried in the sand, were uncovered and killed in the ensuing fight. Ten days later more of the group were found and killed, thanks to the rapid delivery of troops by helicopter and parachute. By this time the climate and desert conditions had taken their toll of men and machines and only seven of the original 34 H-34s were still airworthy.

An interesting sequel to the effect that the ingestion of sand had on engines was Captain Babot's invention of the sand filter. His locally manufactured device did not find favour with HQ staff, who asked the appropriate scientific establishment to produce something more sophisticated. This proved to be so heavy that the H-34's payload/range was badly affected. The operational squadrons ignored it and made their own filters clandestinely in Algeria.

It was not long after the appointment of General Challe, an Air Force general, as Commander-in-Chief of French forces in Algeria in January 1959 that a highly mobile, 20,000-strong tactical reserve of Foreign Legionnaires and parachutists was constituted. Challe believed in dynamic operations to seize the initiative rather than territorial occupation. Although retaining the quadrillage system, he reduced the number of troops committed to it while boosting the strength of the reserve. His aim was to exploit his ability to concentrate superior forces, using elements of his reserve in lightning raids based primarily on hot intelligence. The key to rapid movement was helicopters and Challe asked for more, while at the same time encouraging the development of armed helicopter tactics. The Challe Plan was so successful that the rebels were once more forced to reduce the size of their guerrilla groups, now to ten or twelve men, in the interests of pure survival.

One of the biggest problems facing the French was finding the enemy. One method was to maintain constant ground and airborne patrols. Light observation aircraft daily overflew the same areas at irregular times. The aircrews were thus able to build up a picture of what was normal and what was not. If something abnormal was detected, the procedure was to launch immediately a force, sufficiently strong at least to investigate the situation and prevent any guerrillas escaping, without the need for any reconnaissance or further preparation apart from giving orders. Specifically avoided was the concentration of troops, a sure indication that an operation was afoot and something likely to be detected by the Moussabiline observers or ALN sympathizers. The aim of the French commanders was encirclement by means of total surprise. The key to Challe's strategy was air power and, in particular, helicopters.

To the guerrillas the first indication of an attack was often the appearance of fixed-wing aircraft and the explosion of bombs and shells all around them. This softening-up process might last for about ten minutes. Then, before the guerrillas were able to recover their senses and one minute before landing, a tactical air observer would usually mark the LZ with smoke to identify it and indicate the strength and direction of the wind. Armed helicopters came in next, closely followed by transport helicopters with the Legionnaires and parachutists. The armed helicopters tried to suppress any remaining areas of resistance. At this stage the area was sealed only by airborne firepower. The fighters and bombers strafed parallel to the line of approach of the helicopters on either side of the LZ and subsequently patrolled the perimeter to engage or pin down any guerrillas trying to leave; light aircraft and helicopters helped to detect such movement. At the same time as the first bombs fell, a DIH would embark troops whose job was to secure the helicopter LZ. Once this had been achieved the rest of the force would be flown in and, if necessary, other troops moved by vehicle into blocking positions. If the operation involved as much as a battalion, then it might be directed from the air by the ground force commander and the chief of the command post in whose sector the action was taking place. However, the DIH commander always commanded the actual helicopter landing phase, and it was he alone who decided whether an LZ was safe to use. If rebel fire was too heavy, he would use the alternative LZ or even abandon the mission altogether.

Success depended upon surprise and the ability to insert sufficient troops quickly enough into the area. Such tactics relied on the maximum use of helicopters. Flying some 200–300m apart, they took the attacking troops directly to the LZ, the first soldier exiting when the helicopter was about 1.8m (6ft) above the ground; the last one would be out by the time the wheels touched the ground. Succeeding waves, trucked into different helicopter pick-up points perhaps a dozen kilometres (7½ miles) from the battle area, were collected by the DIH and brought to the LZ. In this manner a battalion of some 480 men could be landed very quickly without the need for any refuelling and, more importantly, without being seen to concentrate for action. If an even quicker build-up of troops was necessary, more troops would drop by parachute between the helicopter waves. Sometimes insertions were made by night despite the problems associated with the lack of navigational aids and formation-keeping.

After the troops had been landed the helicopters were refuelled and readied to provide fire support, evacuate casualties or continue troop lifting. The casualty evacuation system developed during the fighting in Algeria was considered the single greatest factor in maintaining the morale of the French. As well as extracting the wounded, some helicopters were equipped as flying first-aid posts, with doctors and medical attendants aboard. One of these would be deployed to an LZ where first-aid could be given en route to a field hospital or airfield for onward evacuation by fixed-wing aircraft. A further advantage of this system was that it cut out the need for intermediate medical facilities and all that was required to support and defend them.

The following account of a typical operation gives a flavour of the fighting and an indication of how air power was used to good effect. In the Oran Army Corps area near Saida in late 1958 it was discovered that a large band of guerrillas was on the move, and a decision was made to try to encircle it two days later in an area better suited to the French. No unusual reconnaissance activity was permitted while suitable LZs were chosen from maps and aerial photographs. During the afternoon preceding the operation the helicopter crews were briefed, together with the fighter pilots providing support. Well before dawn on D-Day the Commandos arrived at the helicopter pick-up point and were split up into helicopter loads. To distinguish the French from the rebels, who were in the habit of wearing captured uniforms, coloured strips of cloth were worn by the French on their shoulder straps. Once aboard, it was not possible to fasten safety belts due to the bulk of ammunition belts and grenades festooned about each individual.

At 0350 hours the first wave of air assault Commandos departed in their H-34s for the LZs. Precisely one hour later these LZs were bombed by B-26 Invaders and the surrounding area strafed by P-47 Thunderbolts and T-6 Texans. As the last bomb exploded, the H-34 Pirates swept in to rake the LZs with cannon fire and then drop smoke-markers for the troop transport helicopters which were ordered in immediately. The Pirates continued firing at targets around the LZs as the Commandos disembarked and, as they began to deploy, stood by for further opportunity targets. Having dropped their troops, the transport helicopters flew back to their bases; some installed weapons and returned to the scene of the action while others brought in more troops.

As the LZs were bombed, at 0450 hours the ground troops left their camps for the area and by 0900 hours had completely encircled it. A combat air patrol of fixed-wing aircraft was maintained and called in whenever necessary by the command post, airborne in a helicopter, to provide extra fire support for the ground forces. Throughout, the Pirates were criss-crossing the area, searching out the guerrillas and attacking caves and other places the fixed-wing aircraft could not reach. On one occasion they flew below overhanging cliffs to engage rebel machine-gun positions with cannon fire and rockets.

As night fell the costs were counted: two French killed and ten wounded for 197 ALN killed and 60 captured. The technique of not moving the ground troops until the attack had started, relying instead on air power to isolate the area, had paid off handsomely. From later interrogation it transpired that a guerrilla lookout had been positioned just outside Saida with binoculars to watch for any unusual activity or movement out of camp. If any had occurred, the guerrillas would have evacuated the area they were in long before the ground troops could have arrived.

Similar operations were carried out many times but on occasion a completely different technique was used. Once a band of guerrillas had been located, small groups of troops would be airlifted by a DIH onto high ground around the area. They would be resupplied by helicopter; aerial reconnaissance would continue round the clock and light firepower would be at hand, ready to be called in by the commander in his airborne command post. The troops would wait patiently for the guerrillas to exhaust their supplies of food, water and ammunition. With no routes out the exhausted rebels had little chance as they emerged from their hiding places.

Helicopters were also used for the collection of intelligence, not only by visual observation and photographic reconnaissance from the air, but also by more direct means. Up to a complete DIH would land in a selected village and some inmates would be picked at random and flown to the nearest French base for interrogation. Those that did not talk were returned but those that did were detained. Intelligence officers were sometimes flown to the scene of an operation by helicopter when seemingly important documents were discovered, thus enabling a quick follow-up. Thus helicopters played their part in the rapid evaluation and exploitation of intelligence which could not have been achieved in any other way.

While the Aéronavale remained organizationally stable, although swapping its H-19s and H-21s for HSS-1s between late 1959 and early 1960, neither ALAT nor the Air Force escaped further reorganization of their helicopter assets before the war ended in March 1962. In 1960 ALAT had modified Helicopter Group 2 as follows:

- Army Corps at Constantine: HQ Helicopter Group 2 and Groupement 101
- Army Corps at Oran: Groupement 102
- Army Corps at Algiers: Groupement 103

Helicopter Group 2's operational strength was by now 65 H-21s, 21 Alouette IIs and twelve H-19s. ALAT also included 32 aviation troops, fifteen of which consisted of six light helicopters, mainly Djinns but with a few Bell 47s or Alouette IIs, and six light fixed-wing aircraft each.

In March 1961 the Air Force's 2 Wing was renumbered 22 Wing and 3 Wing 23 Wing. Each had four squadrons: light, medium and heavy squadrons and a technical maintenance squadron. Air Force helicopters amounted to about 160 H-34s and Alouette IIs. The Aéronavale had about 35 HSS-1s. The total helicopter strength in Algeria was thus about 380.

Given the size of the operational area and the number of French troops involved in the fighting, this number was quite inadequate. Nevertheless, it was probably the best the French could do, beset as they were with funding difficulties, a very small helicopter inventory to start from and a limited helicopter industry of their own.

Epilogue

Although the Americans used helicopters during the Korean War in some numbers, it was the French who really pioneered their large-scale employment as combat vehicles during the war in Algeria. Helicopter unit commanders, happily unhampered by bureaucratically minded senior officers in Paris and Algeria itself, were given more or less free rein to exercise their initiative. Ideas were tested and, as experience grew, so tactical doctrine became more refined. But it was a joint effort: ground troops and helicopter units working closely together at all levels for their mutual benefit.

There was no established doctrine to start with, only the limited experiences in Indo-China to build on and the knowledge that helicopters with their unique vertical take-off and landing capability could do what fixed-wing aircraft could not. Quick to exploit this capability, the French were nevertheless aware that the helicopter was no substitute for a fixed-wing aircraft, which could fly further and faster and was easier to maintain.

To the French the possession of helicopters offered four major advantages:

● *Surprise.* In the largely infantry war it was generally easier for the guerrillas to surprise the French. The guerrillas could attack at will and subsequently fade into the desert or mountains where French infantry and Commandos found it very difficult to go. The use of the third dimension, however, theoretically enabled French commanders to gain the initiative and achieve surprise both in space and time and strike guerrilla bands when and where they least expected an attack. In practice, however, the French soon discovered that attempting to land a force at an LZ close to which was a well-armed enemy entailed considerable risk; even blanketing the area with intense suppressive fire did not guarantee success. Thus every effort to achieve surprise during planning, assembly and execution was vital.

- *Concentration of force.* Transport helicopters were able to fly in troops rapidly from different bases and build up a numerically superior force which the guerrillas could not match.
- *Flexibility.* By exploiting the mobility of their helicopters the French could take advantage of fleeting opportunities to engage the guerrillas or respond to their attacks over a wide area. Armed helicopters could be engaged on one task yet be on call for another elsewhere.
- *Speed.* Reaction times were minimized. Troops and helicopters could be at the scene of action within minutes. Helicopters were able to cut off by fire guerrillas trying to escape or to come in as reinforcements, or by dropping more troops in ambush.

Until mid-1957 the helicopter contribution to ground operations was conducted in a somewhat ad hoc manner. Only in May of that year was a formal instruction issued. Thereafter, in any operation involving the use of helicopters, a helicopter operations commander was appointed. He was responsible for the plan and its execution. He was assisted by two deputies: a helicopter unit commander who selected the LZs and commanded the airborne and landing phases; and a heliborne unit commander who took over once the troops were on the ground. The helicopter operations commander, often in an airborne command post, controlled the sequence of events and ensured support of the heliborne troops until they had linked up with the ground forces.

Arguably the greatest contribution to the campaign by the helicopter was its undoubted effect on the morale of the fighting troops. The chance of rapid evacuation for the wounded and sick by helicopter did much to build confidence and encourage boldness. But morale, fighting spirit and performance in battle were also enhanced by the tactical airlift of troops: ten minutes in a helicopter could save six to eight gruelling hours on foot or a couple of bumpy hours by vehicle. The troops thus arrived in battle comparatively fresh. Unfortunately, however, owing to the comparatively small number of helicopters deployed in Algeria, the majority of actions and operations had to be conducted without the help of these machines. Nevertheless, the concept of airmobility had been put to the test in combat and found workable – more than that, indeed: worthy of development.

The French quickly learnt that the helicopter had its limitations: even the biggest helicopter could not carry much of a load. At the extremes of heat and altitude flying performance was further degraded. It was clear that combat helicopters require a generous reserve of power to enable them to hover out of ground effect at altitude and in high temperatures, to operate in confined spaces and out of wind, and to give them quick acceleration and deceleration. To operate effectively in the prevailing climatic and topo-graphical conditions all helicopters had to be rugged, robust and able to sustain the minor 'knocks', damage and unserviceabilities that accompany battlefield use. In other words, they needed damp-resistant avionics, engines protected against foreign object ingestion, undercarriages or skids able to accept heavy or rough landings, airframes that could be easily repaired having taken rifle and machine-gun fire, and cargo holds/cabins that were 'soldier-proof'. They had to be easily maintainable.

Every helicopter type was vulnerable to all kinds of guerrilla fire, particularly when at low level and at slow speeds; typically when approaching to land or in the hover. The crew and certain vital components therefore required protection by means of body armour and armour plating. Fuel tanks needed to be self-sealing and it was important that selected systems were duplicated. Nevertheless, the helicopter loss rate was much less than anticipated. From August 1955 to May 1957, for example, ALAT's Helicopter Group 2 suffered 57 helicopters hit but only six lost. During 1959, at the height of General Challe's mobile operations, not a single helicopter was lost to rebel ground fire.

Logistic support in terms of the delivery of fuel and ammunition, the supply of spare parts, and repair and maintenance was quite a burden. To reduce unproductive flying time – the transition from base to the battle area – it was important to locate fuel and ammunition reserves as close to the action as possible. Maintenance procedures had to be as simple as possible and the DIHs when deployed away from base were accompanied by mobile maintenance detachments. The concept of the self-sufficient DIH, deployed away from its parent squadron, worked well. It was generally agreed that ALAT DIH provided a more effective service than Air Force DIH in support of ground operations, a fact put down to the Army crews' greater knowledge and better understanding of the tactics and procedures involved.

The most significant and lasting innovation was the installation of guns, rockets and missiles on some helicopters. Strapping weapons designed for other environments onto an unstable and vibrating platform was little more than an act of faith in the early days. Weapon sighting systems were rudimentary. But even if accuracy left something to be desired, there was logic to it: it is psychologically easier to go forward behind one's own hail of bullets. Furthermore, this suppressive fire did inhibit the guerrillas firing back and it even killed and wounded a few. In fact, the arming of helicopters turned out to be more successful than anyone had dared hope and confounded the sceptics. But even the enthusiasts did not claim that helicopter firepower dispensed with the need for any heavier fixed-wing fire support. The effectiveness of the SS-10/SS-11 anti-tank missile demonstrated the feasibility of firing missiles from helicopters, and was later enthusiastically developed as a means of reducing the imbalance between NATO and Warsaw Pact armoured forces in Europe.

It did not take long for the French to realize that air power could help to redress the odds against them, longer for them to re-learn the vital necessity of co-ordinating air and ground power. Despite being deployed in relatively small numbers, helicopters proved their worth in particular by providing pinpoint troop-lift, by acting as airborne weapons platforms and command posts and by undertaking casualty evacuation, observation and logistic support; a flexible and rapid action capability unmatchable by fixed-wing aircraft or ground vehicles.

In essence, during the French campaign in Algeria the helicopter demonstrated its value as a formidable weapon of war and one that had a major part to play in counter-insurgency operations. The impact of this new technology was every bit as great as the initial participation of fixed-wing aircraft in the guerrilla wars of the 1920s.

Vietnam (1961–73)

The War

The end of the seven-and-a-half-year First Indo-China War between the League for the Independence of Vietnam, otherwise known as the Viet Minh, and the French was sealed by the Geneva Agreement, signed on 21 July 1954, just a few months before the outbreak of the Algerian War of Independence. It provided for an immediate cease-fire and, as a consequence of the French defeat, it signalled the end of French rule over Vietnam, Laos and Cambodia. The Agreement also provided for the latter two countries to become independent and neutral, while Vietnam was divided at the 17th parallel, the Communists under Ho Chi Minh in the North, the non-Communists in the South under the former Emperor Bao Dai; he gave way to Ngo Dinh Diem in October 1955. The Geneva Agreement also stipulated that free elections be held throughout Vietnam by July 1956, but they never took place. The South Vietnamese considered that the elections in the North would not be free and, furthermore, that the South would be swamped by the more populous North; the South Vietnamese pointed out that they were not bound by the Geneva Agreement since they had not signed it.

From mid-1950 the United States had borne the brunt of the French costs of the war, the American attitude being summed up neatly by President Eisenhower in April 1954 when he said: 'The loss of Indo-China will cause the fall of South-East Asia like a set of dominoes.' As the French withdrew, the scene became set for ever-increasing American involvement in an effort to counter growing Communist influence.

It is difficult to fix a date for the start of the Second Indo-China War. Certainly by the autumn of 1957 members of the US Military Assistance Advisory Group had been injured as a result of terrorist action in Saigon and in 1958, by which time Diem had antagonized much of the population due to his dictatorial and corrupt regime, local government officials in South Vietnam had been the subject of frequent terrorist attacks. In July 1959 the Viet Cong, the name given to the Vietnamese Communists, attacked the South Vietnamese Army (known as the Army of the Republic of Vietnam – ARVN) for the first time. Ho Chi Minh now felt able to assume the direction of the war and increasing numbers of Viet Cong, trained in the North, were infiltrated into South Vietnam by means of the Ho Chi Minh Trail, a network of roads, tracks and paths eventually totalling some 19,000km (11,800 miles), which ran through eastern Laos, thus by-passing the defended zone on the 17th parallel.

The situation continued to deteriorate in the South and Diem called for more American assistance, in addition to the funding and military advisers that he had already received. In response, two transport helicopter companies arrived in December 1961 to support the ARVN, and in February 1962 a Military Assistance Command Vietnam (MACV) was established.

A series of Government coups, growing opposition from sections of the population and an inept performance on the battlefield all served to hasten the disintegration of the South. An incident in the Gulf of Tonkin, when two American destroyers were attacked by North Vietnamese torpedo-boats, led to the Gulf of Tonkin Resolution by the US Congress on 7 August 1964. The President was given authority to 'take all necessary measures to repel any armed attack against the forces of the United States and to prevent further aggression'. By the end of 1964 it had become obvious that a Communist victory and take-over could only be averted by the direct intervention of American combat troops.

In March 1965 the first American combat unit arrived in South Vietnam, presaging a massive build-up: from 23,000 at the end of 1964 to more than 165,000 twelve months later. On 8 June 1965 General William C. Westmoreland, Commander of MACV, announced that he now had authority to conduct offensive operations with American troops. Consequently, in 1966, they began to take over this aspect of the war while South Vietnamese troops directed more of their efforts to rear-area security. At much the same time the air war against North Vietnam was intensified. The United States was not alone in supplying troops to help the ARVN; South Korea provided nearly 50,000, Australia 8,000, Thailand and the Philippines over 2,000 each and New Zealand some 500. As the build-up continued into 1968 and American troop numbers approached half a million, it seemed as though the Communists were on the run.

On 30 January 1968 the Viet Cong launched their Tet Offensive, which quickly dissolved any complacency, particularly when it was appreciated that the attacks were country-wide and included the capital, Saigon. The Viet Cong were, however, unable to capitalize on their initial successes and the offensive turned out to be a costly failure. Nevertheless, it heralded a change of emphasis in the American approach to the war. In March General Westmoreland was replaced by General Creighton Abrams, who urged even greater use of heliborne forces to attack the Viet Cong whenever they were found; less effort was to be spent on the slower and more ponderous infantry search-and-destroy operations. More troops were tasked with guarding centres of population at the expense of attempting to control the rural areas.

In January 1969 Richard Nixon became President with the stated aim of ending the American involvement in Vietnam and conducting an honourable withdrawal. This started a few months later as American troops began to hand back their combat responsibilities to the South Vietnamese – one of the first steps towards 'Vietnamization'.

A serious diversion occurred in March 1970. A political crisis in Cambodia resulted in Viet Cong forces advancing on the capital, Phnom Penh. It had been well known for some time that the Ho Chi Minh Trail had been extended to pass through Cambodia and that the Viet Cong had established strongholds and supply bases in that country. In April the United States, South Vietnam and Thailand were asked for help and at the end of the month this was given. Within two months American forces had been withdrawn after a successful operation during which huge quantities of arms and ammunition had been captured. On 24 June 1970 the US Senate repealed the Gulf of Tonkin Resolution. The withdrawal of American troops from South-East Asia continued and by the end of 1971 only 171,000 remained from a peak of almost 550,000.

The following year South Vietnamese forces, supported by American air power, invaded Laos with the aim of cutting the Ho Chi Minh Trail. It did not succeed. Perhaps emboldened by this and the ever-reducing number of Americans and their defensive posture, 15,000 North Vietnamese with 100 tanks crossed the 17th parallel on 30 March 1972 to attack Quang Tri; subsequently other attacks were launched throughout the country and it was not until September that the onslaught was stemmed. By this time, on 11 August, the last American combat unit had been withdrawn.

Peace talks had originally started in May 1968 but it was not until 27 January 1973 that a Peace Agreement was signed by the United States, South and North Vietnam and the Provisional Revolutionary Government of South Vietnam (the Viet Cong). It provided for a cease-fire, the withdrawal of foreign troops and the eventual reunification of Vietnam. The last American troops left in March. It was not long before the first violation of the cease-fire occurred and this led to other more serious ones: the war had been resumed. There was no real resistance to heavy Communist attacks and on 30 April 1975 the South Vietnamese collapsed, surrendering unconditionally.

The Environment

South Vietnam is not a large country and it can be conveniently divided into three main geographical features: the coastal plain, the Central Highlands and the vast Mekong Delta. Roughly 1,000km (620 miles) from north to south, South Vietnam does not exceed 195km (120 miles) at its widest point. Saigon, the capital and since the war known as Ho Chi Minh City, is roughly equidistant from Cambodia and the east coast, some 55km (35 miles) from both. The seaboard itself is about 1,930km (1,200 miles) long and the coastal plain, averaging 20km (12.5 miles) wide, is bounded on the west by the second feature, the Central Highlands. This range of mountains extends from the 17th parallel south to within 80km (50 miles) of Saigon. It rises to well over 1,500m (4,920ft) in many places and most of it is covered in dense jungle. The southernmost third of South Vietnam is less than 150m (500ft) above sea-level and it is through this flat region that the mighty River Mekong flows. The vast delta itself, rarely more than 6m (20ft) above sea-level, consists of a confused system of natural and artificial waterways among rice paddies and tangled vegetation. Despite efforts to channel the flow of water into the paddies, the whole area is subject to flooding. Thus it can be appreciated that the mountainous jungles and swampy lowlands seriously inhibit movement except by air.

Thirty years ago population centres were scattered and poorly connected by the road system, facilitating their isolation by the Viet Cong. The topography influenced the military division of the country which was split into four zones (as shown in Fig. 4). The two northern zones (I and II Corps Tactical Zones) extended from the De-Militarized Zone with North Vietnam to an area about 100km (62 miles) north-east of Saigon. They

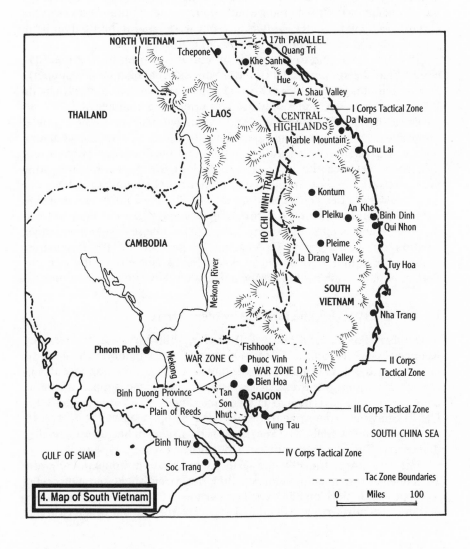

4. Map of South Vietnam

encompassed most of the Central Highlands and their portion of the coastal plain. III Corps Tactical Zone was something of an intermediate zone, stretching from the foothills of the Central Highlands to the northern reaches of the Delta and including the Saigon area. The southern Zone (IV Corps Tactical Zone) comprised almost all the Mekong Delta.

The climate is tropical with high temperatures and humidity most of the year. The rainy season is generally from May to October, although near the 17th parallel it is a month or two later. The north attracts considerably more rain than the south, approximately 320cm (125in) annually whereas 200cm (80in) falls in the Saigon area (compared with London's average annual rainfall of 60cm (24in)). During the winter months (south-west monsoon) the Central Highlands are frequently wreathed in low cloud and heavy rain or fog, any of which can cause the grounding of helicopters. The weather was a key factor in the planning and conduct of operations. Short tropical downpours may have been a nuisance but were less inhibiting than light drizzle and mist which can continue for hours or even days.

Of considerable aid to the British in Malaya had been the fact that that country had been completely isolated from external Communist support. South Vietnam, on the other hand, had a long land frontier in the west with Laos and Cambodia, much of which was undeveloped jungle and ideal as cover for the Ho Chi Minh Trail. An even longer coastline to the east was accessible to intruding small boats, and to the north was the common border with Communist North Vietnam. Ethnically, there were major differences between the two wars. In Malaya the population was split evenly between Malays and Chinese, the terrorists coming almost exclusively from the latter and depending on the Chinese rural population for support. Thus success for the terrorists represented Chinese domination for the Malays and communist misery for the rich Chinese – not an attractive solution for either group. In Vietnam 85 per cent of the population consisted of ethnic Vietnamese, so victory by the North did not constitute domination by an alien ethnic group but an alternative form of government.

The First Helicopters Arrive

In October 1961 General Maxwell D. Taylor, Military Adviser to President Kennedy, went to South Vietnam to assess the situation. The lack of mobility of the ARVN forces struck him forcibly and in response to his recommendations the President agreed to send some support units in addition to more advisers. On 11 December two companies with 33 Vertol CH-21 Shawnees (the same 'Flying Banana' as operated by the French in Algeria) and a few Bell OH-13Es (Bell 47Ds) arrived in Saigon and quickly deployed to Tan Son Nhut, not far to the north-west.

The two units, the 8th and 57th Transportation Companies (Light Helicopter), were in action almost before they could shake out. Operation 'Chopper' took place on 23 December when over 1,000 ARVN parachutists and their US advisers were lifted in 30 CH-21s in a number of waves into a

Viet Cong stronghold only a few miles from Saigon. The Viet Cong were caught off guard by this surprising new development in warfare and offered only token resistance before dispersing. Although an undoubted success, the operation brought to light many operational shortcomings concerning the techniques of loading the troops in tactical sub-units ready to fight on arrival and their speedy disembarkation, ground-air communications, and command and control of both elements of the force (helicopters and ground troops). These early days were a time of rapid learning and trial and error for Americans, ARVN and Viet Cong alike. Lieutenant General John Tolson tells the tale of one CH-21 pilot who, having put down at an LZ, was amazed to see some Viet Cong emerge from the trees and pour their fire into the ground twenty metres in front of him – the happy result of their training where they had been told to 'lead' the helicopter with their fire. He took off again unscathed. Nevertheless, the first US helicopter was shot down on 4 February, although the crew was saved and the helicopter later repaired and flown out.

The CH-21 was vulnerable to virtually any weapon, its control cables and fuel lines particularly so. One story had it that a CH-21 was brought down by a hand-thrown spear! In those early days the Viet Cong would sometimes plant spears at possible LZs and even rig up bows and arrows so that a helicopter's rotor downwash would cause the release of the arrows.

On 26 January 1962 a third helicopter unit, the 93rd Transportation Company (Light Helicopter), arrived off Vietnam and flew direct from its ship to Da Nang in the north. This deployment helped to ease slightly the problem of coverage. But with less than 50 CH-21s, with their limited range, few ARVN units could expect to receive helicopter support. The problem was recognized and during the remaining months of 1962 further units arrived: two more Army helicopter companies, one US Marine Corps squadron (HMM-362) with 24 Sikorsky HUS-1s (similar to the H-34s used in Algeria and redesignated UH-34D Sea Horse in September 1962), the 57th Medical Detachment (Helicopter Ambulance) with five Bell HU-1As and the 45th Transportation Battalion to command the five Army helicopter companies; helicopter maintenance units were also sent in. Deployed to Soc Trang in the Mekong Delta in April in an operation known as 'Shufly', the USMC squadron, now HMM-163 (which had replaced HMM-362), swapped with the 93rd Company at Da Nang in September because the UH-34D was better able to cope with the hot and high conditions in the northern part of the country, the CH-21 being seriously underpowered. In the south its poor performance was less of a liability. This transfer had the effect of concentrating most Army helicopter units in the southern half of the country.

The Huey represented, for the Americans, as big a technological and operational jump forward as the Alouette II had for the French: both had a turbine engine and both were very versatile in the roles that they could undertake. More than any other single item of equipment, the Huey symbolized the Vietnam War. The distinctive 'slap' of its main rotor promised help and its eventual appearance made the Huey the most welcome sight to hard-pressed ground troops.

The arrival of these helicopter units did much for the morale of the ARVN's combat troops. The presence of the five medical Hueys represented little more than a token casualty evacuation capability, particularly since they were based at Nha Trang, 320km (200 miles) north-east of Saigon and far from most US units. The CH-21s, on the other hand, were invaluable, visiting isolated outposts to resupply them and rotate personnel. Heliborne operations at this stage consisted of little more than simple transportation from base to the area of conflict. Nothing more elegant could be contemplated until ARVN troops became more familiar with this new machine.

The First Armed Helicopters

It had not taken long for the Viet Cong to discover that they could fire at and hit helicopters as they landed at their LZs. The initial response was for American crew chiefs to use their own small arms to fire from the open doorways. This wholly inadequate measure soon gave way to something not much better. A 0.30in Browning machine-gun was mounted in the doorway but it had a limited arc of fire, could not fire forward to suppress the enemy as the helicopter made its approach to the LZ and it seriously hindered troop exit. Another way had to be found to protect the CH-21 that did not detract from its troop-lift capability. The answer was to have an armed helicopter to escort it. Slow-flying Army fixed-wing aircraft could not be used since the Army was prevented by law from operating such aircraft in an attack role.

Since June 1956 the 7292nd Aerial Combat Reconnaissance Company (Experimental) had been test-firing a number of weapons, including machine-guns of different calibres and free-flight rockets. In 1959 the USMC had also undertaken weapon trials, including the firing of French SS-11 missiles. These trials did not result in any policy to arm helicopters. So, when the first machines were deployed to South Vietnam they were unarmed. This suited those who believed that American support should be portrayed as non-aggressive, but it was an attitude that could not last for long.

As the situation in South Vietnam deteriorated, an armed helicopter company, named the Utility Tactical Transport Helicopter Company (UTTHCO), was established in Okinawa, Japan, in July 1962. It was equipped with fifteen UH-1As which were armed with one 0.30in M-37C or 7.62mm M-60C machine-gun and seven (sometimes eight) 70mm (2.75in) rockets attached to each skid. In October 1962 the UTTHCO was deployed to Tan Son Nhut, under the operational control of MACV, to support the 33rd, 57th and 93rd Helicopter Companies, mainly in the III and IV Corps Tactical Zones. A month later eleven UH-1Bs were added to its complement; six were deployed to Da Nang in April 1963 to escort Marine UH-34s.

The UH-1B had a more powerful engine which gave a slightly higher speed and allowed a greater weapons load: in addition to the sixteen rockets, a purpose-designed M-6E3 armament system, consisting of two M-60C machine-guns in a hydraulically-operated turret, was mounted on an outrigger on each side of the fuselage. The guns could be aimed by the co-pilot by means of a pantographic sight mounted in the cabin roof. The two M-6E3s moved in concert and could be traversed 10° inboard, 70° outboard, 10° up and 85° down; in other words, when the port system was traversed outwards the starboard system came inwards but ceased to operate on reaching the 10° position. The pilot had a separate sight to fire the rockets and the guns when they were fixed in the forward-firing position. These M-6 'flex guns' offered significantly better firepower than the fixed forward-firing guns of the UH-1A.

Just seven days after its arrival the UTTHCO came under the scrutiny of an organization known as the Army Concept Team in Vietnam. This team had the task of conducting an evaluation into all new ways of fighting the Viet Cong. For the next five months the UTTHCO was to provide all relevant data on actual combat escort missions to enable their effectiveness to be judged. Standing rules of engagement, however, did not allow the armed helicopters to open fire unless they or the helicopters they were escorting were fired on first. About three weeks before the evaluation period ended, on 15 March 1963, this rule was relaxed to allow the Hueys to open fire first if they felt their or the formation's safety was at risk.

It was inevitable that such mundane terms as escort and transport helicopter would soon give way to something more colloquial, if less descriptive. Escort became the meaner and more aggressive 'gunship', often nicknamed 'Hog', 'Heavy Hog' or even 'Frog' depending on the armament carried; transport helicopters were known as 'Slicks' since they were not encumbered with protruding weapons and appeared streamlined.

To assess the effectiveness of the gunship, its vulnerability and that of the 'Slicks' had to be examined during the three critical phases of any operation: transit, when all the helicopters flew at a safe altitude; approach, when they descended to low level several kilometres from the LZ; and finally the actual landing, troop disembarkation and fly-away. Events had already shown that the most dangerous phase was the landing and disembarkation. The presence of gunships quickly resulted in a dramatic drop of 25 per cent in hits on escorted 'Slicks', while those without an escort were now being hit twice as often as before. The message was clear and when USMC UH-34 crews began to ask for Army gunship escort their effectiveness was resolved beyond doubt!

En route to the objective gunships broke off to attack targets that engaged the formation. The procedure was for one helicopter at a time to make a pass while the next one manoeuvred to start firing as soon as its predecessor had finished. A race-track pattern was flown to enable succeeding helicopters to roll on to the attack heading as soon as the one ahead broke left or right. In this way continuous fire was placed on the target in order to protect the attacking gunship during the vulnerable turn away from the target. This practice was considered more effective than a heavier weight of firepower but with gaps between its application. The gunships usually aimed to reach the LZ first to discover, perhaps by drawing fire, if it was occupied and then to lay down suppressive fire. It was thought that this procedure resulted in fewer casualties, despite the fact that surprise was lost. A form of deception was sometimes practised by recönnoitring several LZs. The gunships orbitted the area ready to fire on any pockets of resistance that were identified until all the 'Slicks' had lifted off. To be able to provide accurate fire, the gunships had to fly low, no more than 60m (200ft), and were thus very vulnerable themselves. Nevertheless, during the five-month period during which nearly 1,800 hours were flown in combat support by the UTTHCO, only eleven helicopters were hit and none was shot down.

The vulnerability of the helicopter did not appear to be as serious as some sceptics had been maintaining. Events had shown, at least so far, that the Viet Cong were not very good at hitting helicopters. But even when they did, complete success was not assured. From the American viewpoint, once hit, there were three degrees of damage limitation: first, if the aircraft was shot down, the hope was for the crew and passengers to survive the crash and be rescued; second and better, to break off the mission and get the helicopter down on the ground in a safe area where it could be repaired or recovered; third, and best of all, to continue the mission.

As 1963 dawned the risk to helicopters appeared quite acceptable. On 5 January the State Department announced that the USA would continue to provide the ARVN with helicopter support and reported that: 'In 1962 US Army Aviation units flew over 50,000 sorties in support of operations in Vietnam, approximately half of which were combat support sorties. During the period 1 January to 30 November 1962, 115 US Army aircraft (which included fixed-wing aircraft) were hit by ground fire, only nine of which were shot down.'

Ironically, this announcement was made just three days after the disaster at Ap Bac. Ten CH-21s of the 93rd Company were tasked to lift some 400 ARVN troops and 50 US advisers into an assault on a village about 55km (35 miles) south-west of Saigon, a site thought to harbour a Viet Cong HQ and radio station. No fixed-wing fighter aircraft and only five UTTHCO gunships were available to give fire support. At first all went well, but when the situation began to deteriorate the reserves were directed to an LZ near Ap Bac, a neighbouring village. This area, however, was strongly held by a Viet Cong battalion and when the ten CH-21s approached they met a hail of fire. The fourth CH-21 was shot down and so was another when it attempted to rescue the crew. The gunships made every effort to suppress the enemy fire but without success and two more CH-21s were shot down in addition to one of the gunships. The situation was only relieved when fighters appeared, at which time the Viet Cong slipped away to enjoy the fruits of a memorable victory; their awe for the helicopter had, perhaps, been downgraded to just respect.

One useful lesson for the Americans was that the gunship could not match the firepower of a fighter when it came to taking on a determined enemy in well-prepared positions. Another concerned the availability of ambulance helicopters. Three American advisers and 65 ARVN troops were killed and many more wounded. But the 57th Medical Detachment was too far away to be used. Just two weeks later it was ordered to redeploy to Saigon and promised five more-capable UH-1Bs to replace its UH-1As. The UH-1B became operational in March, but still with only five helicopters it was quite impossible for the 57th to cover the whole of South Vietnam from Saigon; one aircraft was therefore detached to Pleiku and another to Qui Nhon to cover the II Corps Tactical Zone, while the three Saigon aircraft looked after III and IV Corps Tactical Zones. The humble 'Slick' would continue to bear the main burden of casualty evacuation.

Towards the end of 1963 the Viet Cong, as they became more accomplished at directing their fire at moving aerial targets and began to build up their stocks of 12.7mm heavy machine-guns, gained the confidence to try to draw helicopters into carefully planned ambushes. Having sited a number of heavy machine-guns to cover anticipated approach and exit flight paths, they would start an action which they hoped would result in the despatch of 'Slicks' and gunships to the scene. This worked well in practice and many helicopters were hit, although few were shot down.

South Vietnamese ground tactics, often with American helicopter support, consisted mainly of 'search and destroy' operations. These were largely unsuccessful and extremely frustrating, given the time and effort spent on them. The presence of the helicopter certainly increased mobility, local firepower and flexibility for the Allies, but it did not have a major effect on the fighting once the ground troops achieved contact. It did, however, inhibit the Viet Cong and force them to plan their actions very carefully in advance, particularly with regard to air defence, exploitation after a successful attack and their withdrawal routes.

Helicopter weapon systems received continuous attention and in May 1963 the XM-3 armament sub-system became available in South Vietnam. Attached to both sides of the fuselage in place of the M-6E3 and separate rocket tubes, the XM-3 consisted of two pods of 24 rockets each which could be fired simultaneously, singly or in ripple up to the full total of 24. During 1964 and 1965 other weapon systems were introduced. The XM-16, consisting of the standard M-6E3 sub-system together with two XM-158 seven-tube rocket pods, became the basic gunship armament for the next few years; maximum effective range of the 70mm rockets was 2,500m. The M-5 used the M-75 automatic grenade-launcher, mounted in a traversable turret in the nose, to fire 40mm rounds out to about 1,500m at a rate of 220 rounds per minute. With an M-5 the UH-1B/C was called a 'Frog', with an XM-3 a 'Hog', and when armed with both an XM-3 and an M-5 a 'Heavy Hog'.

Proposals to get some Marine gunships generated considerable opposition within the Corps. Nevertheless, some UH-34s were armed during late 1964 with a pod of eighteen rockets on each side and two M.60s on the starboard side, an installation called the TK-1 (Temporary Kit-1).

Changes in Organization

In the spring and early summer of 1963 major changes to the helicopter order of battle were instituted. The newly arrived 52nd Aviation Battalion took over command of all US Army Aviation units in the I and II Corps Tactical Zones from the 45th Battalion which was redesignated the 145th Aviation Battalion. In May the 114th Aviation Company (Airmobile Light), complete with its three platoons of UH-1Bs, arrived. A month later the 8th, 33rd, 57th, 81st and 93rd Transportation Companies (Light Helicopter) were redesignated the 117th, 118th, 120th, 119th and 121st Aviation Companies (Airmobile Light) respectively. By now the UH-1A and the CH-21, both underpowered, were well on the way to being replaced by the UH-1B in these companies.

A further step forward was the arrival in May of four Sikorsky CH-37 Mojave medium-lift helicopters to assist in the recovery of downed aircraft. They could handle far heavier loads than the CH-21; indeed, they could lift that helicopter once it had been partially stripped down. The CH-37 was an ugly and cumbersome machine with large fan-cooled piston engines housed in nacelles at the end of stub wings, the unfortunate result of being designed just a few years too early to benefit from the advent of the turbine engine. The clamshell doors underneath the cockpit admitted up to three Jeeps or a 105mm howitzer and crew, or 26 troops or 24 stretchers. Some 5,000kg (11,023lb) could be lifted as an underslung load. The CH-37 had a range of approximately 235km (146 miles) with its maximum payload and could cruise at 185km/hr (115mph).

Examination of the results of the UTTHCO evaluation led to organizational changes. It had been concluded that between five and seven gunships could protect up to 25 'Slicks' and it was therefore decided to reorganize the helicopter companies as far as possible to recognize this fact. Consequently, each company was split into two platoons of eight UH-1B 'Slicks' each and given, as they became available, an armed platoon of eight UH-1B gunships; one reserve Huey, to make 25 in all, was put into the service platoon. The 'Slicks' were limited to the carriage of eight ARVN troops while the gunships carried no troops at all besides their crew of four. Using the same type of helicopter for different roles naturally caused problems. The UH-1B was not designed as a gunship and with the installation of weapons, and usually flying at maximum gross weight, its manoeuvrability and speed suffered. The 'Slicks' consequently had to reduce their transit speed to allow the gunships to keep up with them. If the formation was attacked en route and the gunships had to react, then they could not catch up again unless the formation reduced its speed still further.

This was clearly unsatisfactory and something would have to be done. Hostile fire during transit was, as a rule, to be ignored. The important thing was for the gunships to be available with a full ammunition load at the LZ to support the critical approach and landing phase of the assault.

Another organizational, and tactical, innovation was the establishment of an 'Eagle Flight' in some companies. It consisted typically of one armed Huey command post with the US aviation commander and the ARVN troop commander aboard, seven 'Slicks', five gunships and one further Huey for casualty evacuation. It was really a task force, usually on the ground but occasionally airborne, on call to undertake missions against targets of opportunity. Its main attribute was its ability to react quickly and thus achieve surprise. If a target proved to be too large for just one flight, other Eagle Flights could reinforce it. By November 1964 every helicopter company in South Vietnam had formed its own Eagle Flight. Besides its tactical advantages, it also did much to improve collaboration at unit level between ARVN troops and their supporting American helicopter crews – a lesson that was to be exploited later with the formation of true airmobile (or air assault) units.

The Build-Up Continues

By the end of September 1964 there were some 260 Army helicopters in South Vietnam. The vast majority were Hueys with a few Mojaves, OH-13 Sioux and OH-23 Ravens making up the balance. In addition, the USMC had a squadron of 24 UH-34s. This strength permitted the deployment of a US Army Aviation company or USMC squadron in support of every ARVN division, with some assets left over for each Corps Tactical Zone. As well as the helicopters the US Army had nearly 150 fixed-wing aircraft in the country.

At the end of 1964 US helicopter units were deployed as follows:
- *I Corps*: USMC HMM-365 Squadron
- *II Corps*: 52nd Aviation Battalion (in support of both I and II Corps) with 117th and 119th Companies
- *III Corps*: 145 Aviation Battalion with 68th (formerly UTTHCO), 118th, 120th Companies and Company A of the 501st Aviation Battalion (which had only arrived in December)
- *IV Corps*: 13th Aviation Battalion with 114th, 121st Companies and Company A of the 502nd Aviation Battalion (also newly arrived)

As the Americans took stock of the overall situation they made the assessment that the Viet Cong controlled between two-thirds and three-quarters of South Vietnam. American losses were mounting as advisers and helicopters became more involved in the fighting. On the other hand, the Viet Cong were increasing in strength despite their heavy losses and were more often prepared to stay and fight rather than rely on simple hit-and-run tactics. Evidence was to hand that, to a major degree, the Viet Cong were trained, led and supplied by North Vietnam and that thousands of North

Vietnamese troops were integrated into Viet Cong units. If anything, their tactics and techniques were developing faster and more effectively than those of their opponents.

Allied weaknesses with regard to airmobility and the vitally important adjunct of combat intelligence were recognized. There was more to airmobility than simply loading troops into helicopters and carrying them to an objective; that was little more than airportability. Airmobility, or indeed air assault, involved a much more complex process, embracing much careful planning based on sound and up-to-date intelligence and reconnaissance, the setting of attainable objectives, the assembly of helicopter units and ground troops, the disposition of troops to helicopters, the selection of one or more LZs, the co-ordination of support from gunships, artillery and fighter aircraft, the maintenance of the force in the target area or plans for its withdrawal, and arrangements for aeromedical evacuation. The process ended with the briefing of all taking part and rehearsals if necessary.

Even then this was merely the next rung up the ladder. It was probably the best that could be achieved with ground troops who had only been given sporadic instruction and practice in the use of helicopters. It was far short of a true airmobile or air assault capability. That was yet to come. If the Allies were to regain the initiative and avert defeat, a quantum jump in the effectiveness of equipment, training, battle procedures and techniques, and morale was imperative. The time had come for American combat troops to be brought into the struggle.

The Arrival of US Combat Units

On 8 March 1965 the 9th Marine Expeditionary Brigade arrived at Da Nang. Its principal task was to provide security for the air base but it was also no stranger to offensive operations. In its support it had two squadrons of UH-1Es which undertook tasks as diverse as transport, reconnaissance, armed escort, casualty evacuation and command and control. As a gunship the UH-1E was less heavily armed than the UH-1B, having a pair of M-60C machine-guns on outriggers on either side with a seven-tube rocket pod attached below them. Later a TAT-101 chin turret with two M-60Cs was also installed. The arrival of these new Marine squadrons, under the operational control of the 1st Marine Air Wing, brought an end to the single-squadron Operation 'Shufly'.

The air base at Bien Hoa, just north of Saigon, was equally susceptible to Viet Cong attack. Thus on 5 May the first US Army combat unit, the 173rd Airborne Brigade (Separate), an independent brigade with one artillery and two infantry battalions, arrived in South Vietnam to guard it and the airfield at Vung Tau. It was soon joined by the 1st Battalion of the Royal Australian Regiment and a New Zealand field artillery battery. Airmobile training began immediately and on 28 June elements of the brigade were committed, together with ARVN units, the Australians and the New Zealanders, to the largest heliborne operation yet undertaken in South Vietnam. At least 144 Army fixed-wing aircraft and helicopters, including 77 'Slicks', were involved; eight days later the 173rd returned to the same area in a similar assault. Both operations were judged a success, not only in terms of anti-Viet Cong action but also with regard to airmobile techniques.

An early lesson learnt concerned force structure – and this was only possible because of the vision of some American commanders (although perhaps generated by trials in the USA) and the luxury of having at least enough helicopters to permit such an endeavour. For its first three months the 173rd Brigade drew its helicopter support from the 145th Aviation Battalion but in September a helicopter company, A Company (Airmobile Light) of the 82nd Aviation Battalion, was put under its operational control and co-located with it. The advantages were numerous and immediately obvious. This resubordination resulted in a common purpose and the consequent determination to work together. Personnel got to know each other well and this led to a greater respect for each unit's specialist skills and the support it needed in combat. More training was possible and so airmobile techniques became more sophisticated and refined.

While the brigade benefited enormously so did the helicopter company, the first in Vietnam to be equipped with the more capable UH-1D Huey. In comparing the three months of attachment with the earlier three months of merely being in support, the company flew 165 per cent more combat sorties, while the average number of hours flown monthly by each pilot decreased by 24 per cent and average aircraft utilization decreased by 23 per cent. Even more important was the fact that a battalion of the brigade could be moved anywhere in its tactical area of operational responsibility within two hours. Without an attached company such a move took two or three times as long.

The 1st Cavalry Division (Airmobile)

As a result of a study into airmobility by the US Army in 1962 (known as the Howze Board and described briefly in the final section of this book), it was recommended that an air assault division, an air cavalry combat brigade and an air transport brigade should be established. In January 1963 a plan was issued for the formation, organization, training and testing of the division, subsequently named the 11th Air Assault Division (Test), and the 10th Air Transport Brigade; approval to test an air cavalry brigade at the same time was not given. Both the division and the brigade, inevitably, were under-strength in manpower and equipment. The tests were nevertheless thorough and the results sufficiently convincing to warrant further development of the concept.

Although established to test airmobile concepts in a European environment, the division inevitably fell under the shadow of the Vietnam War. On 1 July 1965 it was announced that the 1st Cavalry Division (Airmobile) (see Fig. 5) would be activated as a combat-ready formation of the US Army.

Under the command of Major General Harry W. O. Kinnard (who had been the commanding general of the 11th Air Assault Division), it was ordered to deploy to Vietnam in September. The division was to absorb the assets of the 11th Air Assault Division (Test) and the 2nd Infantry Division and have nearly 16,000 officers and men. Its 428 helicopters (Fig. 6), nearly five times the number in an infantry division, and six Mohawk surveillance aircraft were its primary equipment; on the other hand, its 1,600 ground vehicles, most of which were Jeep-sized, were just about half the number held in an infantry division. A fundamental change in combat philosophy had been achieved. For the first time in military history an Army formation was to place primary reliance on aircraft for all major functions of land combat rather than on ground vehicles and weapon systems.

By 3 October the division had consolidated at An Khe in Binh Dinh Province, its helicopters based at the 112 hectares (275 acres) heliport carved out of semi-jungle and known as the 'Golf Course'. It was given an area of responsibility of some 58,550km² (22,500 sq miles) with each brigade having its own area; the 1st Air Cavalry Squadron was given a roving reconnaissance mission throughout the divisional area but in particular in the western highlands in which were located several Special Forces camps.

The 1st Cavalry Division embodied the concept of airmobility by means of four organizational-tactical pillars. Equipped with reconnaissance helicopters, gunships and 'Slicks', the purpose of the air cavalry was to find targets and maintain contact with the enemy. The role of the assault helicopter battalions was to lift the infantry into LZs to bring the contact to a successful conclusion. These troops were backed by airmobile howitzer battalions and gunships to provide intimate fire support. The concept was

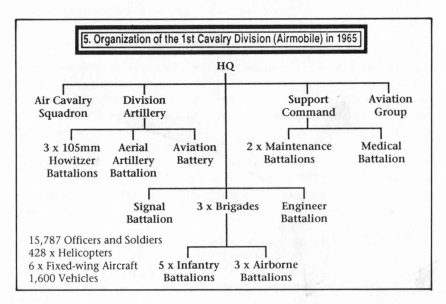

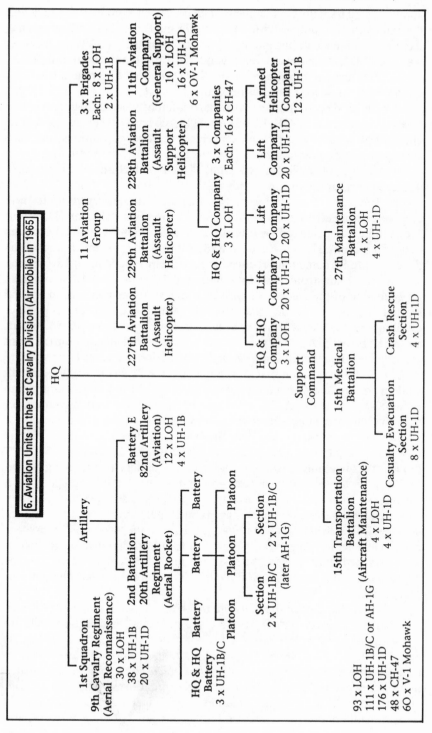

6. Aviation Units in the 1st Cavalry Division (Airmobile) in 1965

HQ

1st Squadron
9th Cavalry Regiment
(Aerial Reconnaissance)
30 x LOH
38 x UH-1B
20 x UH-1D

Artillery

Battery E
82nd Artillery
(Aviation)
12 x LOH
4 x UH-1B

2nd Battalion
20th Artillery
Regiment
(Aerial Rocket)

HQ & HQ   Battery   Battery   Battery
Battery
3 x UH-1B/C   Platoon   Platoon   Platoon

Section   Section
2 x UH-1B/C   2 x UH-1B/C
(later AH-1G)

11 Aviation
Group

3 x Brigades
Each: 8 x LOH
2 x UH-1B

227th Aviation   229th Aviation   228th Aviation   11th Aviation
Battalion   Battalion   Battalion   Company
(Assault   (Assault   (Assault   (General Support)
Helicopter)   Helicopter)   Support   10 x LOH
Helicopter)   16 x UH-1D
6 x OV-1 Mohawk

HQ & HQ   Lift   Lift   Lift
Company   Company   Company   Company
3 x LOH   20 x UH-1D   20 x UH-1D   20 x UH-1D

HQ & HQ Company   3 x Companies
3 x LOH   Each: 16 x CH-47

Armed
Helicopter
Company
12 x UH-1B

Support
Command

15th Transportation   15th Medical   27th Maintenance
Battalion   Battalion   Battalion
(Aircraft Maintenance)   4 x LOH
4 x LOH   4 x UH-1D
4 x UH-1D

Casualty Evacuation   Crash Rescue
Section   Section
8 x UH-1D   4 x UH-1D

93 x LOH
111 x UH-1B/C or AH-1G
176 x UH-1D
48 x CH-47
6O x V-1 Mohawk

completed by transport helicopter logistic support to supply the troops and the helicopters in action with ammunition, fuel, food and other requirements. The essence of airmobility as practised by the 1st Cavalry Division was the ability to operate over a wide area, to commit large number of troops and their fire support very quickly to the scene of action and then to sustain them there for as long as needed.

The division was equipped with four different types of helicopter. The smallest was the Bell OH-13S Sioux light observation helicopter which could carry a pilot and two passengers in cramped conditions, or more usually just a pilot and crew chief armed with a light machine-gun, at a cruising speed of 130km/hr (80mph). The Bell UH-1B, already widely deployed, was the gunship – although slower than the 'Slick' it had to escort. The UH-1D was the primary transport and could carry up to nine combat-equipped troops in addition to the crew at 185km/hr (115mph). Troop lifts were planned on the basis of seven combat infantrymen per helicopter, although fuel could be traded for one or two extra men; high-density altitudes sometimes reduced the number to six. Standard armament was the M-23 consisting of a pintle-mounted 7.62mm M-60D machine-gun on each side of the fuselage. Apart from the M-23 another reason for the reduction in lift capability was the additional weight of armour plate, totalling some 205kg (452lb), for seats, crews' flak vests and the pilot's and co-pilot's breast plates. Yet more armour plate was demanded for the nose to provide protection during nose-high flares prior to assault landings.

The CH-47A Chinook had a payload of 4,590kg (10,120lb), or 33 passengers, and a cruising speed of 212km/hr (132mph). In the mountains of South Vietnam it could initially lift only 3,175kg (7,000lb); the reduction in useful load was due partly to the extra weight of weapons, ammunition, a gunner and armour plating. The more capable CH-47B and C models followed, the latter in 1968 with more than double the payload of the A model and the ability to seat 44 troops in a high-density arrangement. On one memorable occasion towards the end of the war 147 refugees were carried in a single lift. As well as carrying troops and supplies, the Chinook was frequently used to undersling 105mm guns from one position to another. The arrival of the Chinook posed a new problem: how to prevent customers succumbing to the temptation to fill up the huge cargo hold – and thus probably exceed the payload limit. These four aircraft types represented the four technical pillars of airmobility and made the concept practicable.

Although not part of the division, the 478th Aviation Company (Heavy Helicopter) deployed with it. It possessed the largest helicopter of all: the Sikorsky S-64 Skycrane (CH-54A Tarhe), which first flew in May 1962. It could lift 9,072kg (20,000lb) underslung and this meant that it could take as a single load a 155mm howitzer – which the Chinook could not – besides other heavy and bulky items such as bridging, bulldozers, damaged aircraft, ammunition pallets and fuel bladders. Various pods could be attached under the tailboom. One type of pod was equipped as a surgical operations room, another as a communications centre which the division used as a key part of its Forward Command Post. The Skycrane's most unusual load, however, was a 4,536kg (10,000lb) bomb with an extended nose fuse and dropped by parachute. It was used to clear surface vegetation without making a crater and so produce an instant LZ. Two further Skycrane companies, the 273rd and 355th, deployed to South Vietnam later to join the 1st Aviation Brigade.

An organizational innovation was the inclusion of an aerial rocket artillery (usually known as ARA) battalion within the division's artillery – the 2nd Battalion, 20th Artillery (Aerial Rocket). Its three gun batteries consisted of three platoons, each of two sections. A section had two UH-1Bs armed with the XM-3; towards the end of 1968 these UH-1Bs were replaced by AH-1G Cobras carrying four XM-159 pods with 76 70mm (2.75in) rockets in all. Initially each battery also had four UH-1Bs mounting six French SS-11 anti-tank missiles (in US service designated AGM-22B as part of the M-22 missile system) instead of the XM-3. These missiles were intended for use against specific hard targets, such as armoured vehicles, pillboxes, bunkers and other strongpoints. The occasions for the use of missiles were rare, however, and it was decided to modify these helicopters to carry just two missiles and between 24 and 36 rockets.

ARA batteries were usually put under the operational control of artillery battalions, with platoons and sections deployed to fire support bases. At least one section per battery was held on alert, ready to respond immediately to calls for fire support. ARA took over when ground artillery could no longer reach the target and it was therefore used for area targets; gunships, on the other hand, usually engaged point or at least fairly compact targets. In addition to its primary role of direct fire support, ARA also carried out armed reconnaissance and escort duties and was adept at suppressing LZs before the 'Slicks' arrived. Specifically tasked to apply fire, ARA could bring a greater weight of firepower onto a target more quickly than a gunship unit. Nevertheless, it was recognized that even ARA firepower would not be sufficient for the destruction of large enemy groups, whether on the defensive or when attacking Allied forces; fixed-wing aircraft, including perhaps Boeing B-52 bombers, would then be necessary.

Within three weeks the division was to become embroiled in the Battle of the Ia Drang Valley, a bitter struggle which lasted more than a month and which would probably have been lost had it not been for the crucial part played by the division's helicopters. After their unsuccessful attempt to besiege the Plei Me Special Forces camp 40km (25 miles) south-west of Pleiku, the three North Vietnamese Army (NVA) regiments involved withdrew westwards. The 1st Brigade, with continuous support from the Air Cavalry Squadron, was ordered to find and destroy them. On 1 November an officer from the squadron spotted suspicious movement a few kilometres west of Plei Me camp and troops were brought in by helicopter with gunship support. Again, the NVA withdrew temporarily, leaving the Americans to find an important hospital complex.

On 9 November the 3rd Brigade relieved the 1st and continued the attempts to bring the NVA to battle south of the River Ia Drang. On 14 November the leading companies of the 1st Battalion, 7th Cavalry, were flown unopposed into LZ 'X-Ray' by the 229th Aviation Battalion. The LZ was large enough to take eight UH-1D 'Slicks' simultaneously. But by the time the fourth company arrived, indirect fire on the LZ was intense, the enemy was closing in and it was no longer possible to get all the 'Slicks' in; eight were waved off. Nevertheless, by nightfall a company of the 2nd Battalion, 7th Cavalry, had managed to fly in, the perimeter had been secured, supporting mortar and artillery fire had been registered and arrangements had been made to accept helicopters by night. Due to sniper fire on the tree line, some approaches had to be made without lights, the helicopters being talked down until a torch was switched on at the last moment. Nevertheless, the helicopters did get in with supplies and all the wounded were evacuated. The next day the NVA put in further attacks that were so fierce that they prevented the fly-in of another company.

To help in solving the major problem of identifying the perimeter for the supporting tactical fighters, artillery and ARA, all infantry platoons were ordered on one occasion to throw coloured smoke grenades. Eventually the NVA pressure slackened and more troops could be flown into the beleagured LZ and into areas surrounding it. The battle was effectively over, although several skirmishes were yet to take place.

The lessons for the division were numerous, but supreme was the realization that without helicopter support the infantry would have been overrun. With them it had been possible, most of the time, to deploy reinforcements where and when they were needed, to bring in supplies and evacuate wounded. The Americans were thus able to strengthen their force by air more quickly than the NVA could on foot; the removal of casualties by air also lightened the burden of caring for them, and freed more men to fight. The maintenance of a secure LZ and the approaches to it were crucial; if supporting fire was to be brought down on its perimeter to counter NVA close-quarter combat tactics, known as 'hugging', then some means of marking the perimeter was essential. Tactical fighters, ARA and tube artillery could be brought down very close to the infantry positions and could be applied simultaneously to the same target provided that forward air controllers (FACs) and artillery observers worked together. It was quite feasible for the helicopters to fly under artillery trajectories. The use of pathfinders to control the arrival and departure of helicopters from the LZ by day and night removed a burden from the battalion's command post.

Within days crew fatigue had become a concern: six to eight flying hours a day under combat conditions and in often difficult weather and at night was normal, ten hours or even more not unusual. During this battle a few pilots flew as many as 40 hours in a three-day period. Finally, helicopters had once again proved less vulnerable than might have been expected: 59 had been hit by enemy fire – three while on the ground – but only four had been shot down and of these three were recovered.

The Battle of the Ia Drang Valley proved to be something of a turning point as Allied offensive action forced the NVA and the Viet Cong onto the defensive. In early 1966 the 173rd Airborne Brigade, ably supported by what was becoming its 'own' aviation battalion (the 145th), and the 1st Cavalry Division undertook a series of successful actions.

During one of these, Operation 'Masher-White Wing', the Chinook demonstrated its prowess for the first time in underslinging artillery and transporting ammunition from one fire base to another to provide the necessary fire support for dispersed infantry units. Quite often these fire bases were in mountain locations unreachable except by helicopter. The movement of this artillery was an important adjunct to the concept of airmobility. While helicopters had helped to redress the balance between ever more effective firepower and mobility, the danger arose, particularly in Vietnam, that airmobile troops might out-distance their supporting ground-based firepower unless it too had similar mobility; hence the use of the Chinook and Skycrane to move the guns. Fortunately not every day was like the one when a battery of 105mm guns, together with their crews and ammunition, was moved by Chinook to 36 different locations in a single 24-hour period.

The 1st Aviation Brigade

By early 1966 the feeling was growing that the maximum benefits were not being derived from the helicopter force, due to the different types of helicopter units, their dispersed locations and their idiosyncratic methods of operation which inhibited the change of their subordination from one ground formation to another. To achieve the desired standardization and flexibility of command, it was decided to form the 1st Aviation Brigade under Brigadier General George P. Seneff. On 25 May 1966 the brigade was activated and assumed command of all US Army Aviation units that were under the control of MACV and not organic to the divisions; the helicopters of the 1st Cavalry Division, therefore, did not join this brigade, and nor did the aviation battalions of the two US infantry divisions (the 1st and 25th). The 4th, 9th, 23rd (Americal) and 101st Airborne Divisions arrived later and each had its own Army Aviation assets. The divisional aviation battalions varied in their organization but typically comprised an HQ and HQ company, two assault helicopter companies, an air cavalry troop and some other helicopters supporting specific divisional units.

The new arrangement did not find universal favour as many officers feared initially that the centralization of aviation support was in fundamental opposition to the long-held belief that decentralization to as low a level as feasible was the best way to employ Army aircraft. Their anxiety was abated when it was learnt that operational control was to remain with the supported ground commander.

The two major tasks confronting General Seneff were to deploy his aviation assets in the most effective way and to develop standard operational procedures. To meet the requirements of ground units without their own aviation assets, or to reinforce units with organic aviation, a combat aviation battalion HQ could be placed in direct support to control all helicopter assets, such as medium- or heavy-lift helicopters, 'Slicks' and gunships, or air cavalry that might be allocated to that unit for a specific operation or for a certain period of time. Territorially, where possible, an assault helicopter company was co-located with each American brigade and, later, South Korean brigade. Within the 1st Aviation Brigade two Combat Aviation Groups – the 17th and the 12th – were formed to command helicopter units in the II and III Corps Tactical Zones respectively (the USMC was responsible for I Corps Tactical Zone).

While this reorganization was comparatively simple to accomplish, General Seneff was faced with a problem that was not subject to a quick solution: a chronic shortage of pilots and technicians. As the brigade formed, some aviation companies had field grade officers assigned to pilot posts; one company was reputed to have 30 majors out of a strength of 50 pilots. By the end of Fiscal Year 1966 it was anticipated that the US Army would need, world-wide, 14,300 pilots but that only 9,700 would be available; the situation was forecast to worsen in 1967 with only 12,800 pilots to meet a requirement for 21,500. All that could be done was to increase pilot training in the USA, shorten the time between Vietnam tours and accept the burden in country by allowing pilots to fly more hours: 100 a month became normal and 120 not unusual. A 'Slick' pilot could expect to fly between 1,200 and 1,400 hours in a twelve-month tour, a gunship pilot perhaps 1,000. Inevitably fatigue among pilots and technicians led to an increased accident rate.

The USMC experienced similar difficulties, although the numbers involved were smaller. By 1 July 1968 only 4,045 helicopter pilots were available to fill 5,010 posts.

1966

By the end of 1966 the number of US troops in South Vietnam totalled 385,000 and helicopter strength amounted to 1,515. During the year 153 helicopters had been lost in combat, out of 255 combat losses since 1961. The first UH-1C gunships for the Army had arrived and these offered an increase in payload of 350kg (772lb), greater fuel capacity and higher speeds compared with the UH-1B. These features helped to narrow the gap between 'Slicks' and gunships. In March the USMC had received the first of its turbine-powered Boeing Vertol CH-46A Sea Knights, destined gradually to replace its piston-engined UH-34s, and by the end of the year four squadrons were operating. The CH-46 had a tandem rotor and a large cargo hold with a ramp at the rear. It could accommodate 26 troops or lift some 2,995kg (6,600lb) internally, or up to 4,536kg (10,000lb) as an underslung load. However, the addition of machine-guns and armour reduced the lift capability to less than 20 troops and the CH-46A suffered initially from technical difficulties. An improved version, the D model, with more powerful engines, new rotor blades and thus better hot and high performance, began to arrive in South Vietnam in November 1967.

The M-21 armament sub-system had begun to replace the XM-16. Designed for the UH-1C, instead of four M-60C machine-guns, it had two M-134 7.62mm six-barrelled Miniguns with double the rate of fire at 2,000 rounds per minute each. When either gun reached its inboard limit, it stopped firing and the other gun automatically doubled its rate of fire to compensate. The two XM-158 rocket pods were retained as part of the M-21.

During the massive Operation 'Junction City', begun on 22 February 1967, 249 helicopters of 12 Combat Aviation Group lifted eight battalions into an assault in conjunction with the only parachute assault of the war. The objective was War Zone C, a Communist stronghold on the Cambodian border north-west of Saigon. As the fighting continued into March and April, heliborne troops were used to surround the enemy and block their escape routes. The 9th Viet Cong Division was badly mauled but War Zone C was not subjugated. The result for both sides was a return to lower-scale guerrilla warfare from the largely conventional actions of 'Junction City'.

The Americans are adept at improvisation and the year 1967 was to see more examples of their skills and the introduction of the first genuine attack helicopter, the AH-1G HueyCobra.

The HueyCobra

Appreciation of the shortcomings of the Huey gunship had led to proposals for a purpose-built gunship. Design of such a machine started in 1964 but it was not until March 1966 that a contract was awarded for the development of the Lockheed AH-56A Cheyenne, known as the Advanced Aerial Fire Support System, to meet the requirement. A technologically high-risk project, progress soon slowed while costs rose and it became clear that many years would be required to bring the machine into operational service. But the Army had an immediate need for a new gunship and could not wait for the Cheyenne. Fortunately Bell had undertaken research into an attack helicopter based on the proven dynamics of the UH-1. In particular, the Model 540 'Doorhinge' rotor system, used on the UH-1C, was ideally suited to the new helicopter. Bell were therefore able to offer an interim gunship more or less off-the-shelf. The AH-1G, or Cobra as it quickly became known, had a fuselage only 0.91m (3ft) wide and a frontal area some 60 per cent less than that of the UH-1. The pilot sat above and behind the gunner, who also had his own set of flying controls; to permit free movement of the floor-mounted flexible sight, his cyclic control was effected by means of a sidearm controller mounted on the starboard side of the cockpit. Observation from both cockpits was obviously far better in this tandem-seat helicopter, which was also more manoeuvrable and faster than the UH-1, having a cruising speed of 240km/hr (150mph) and a diving speed of 350km/hr (220mph). All this contributed to improved survivability, which was further enhanced by selective armour protection and self-sealing fuel tanks.

The Cobra first flew on 7 September 1965 and on 13 April 1966 110 production versions were ordered by the US Army. On 1 September 1967 the first Cobra reached South Vietnam. The early models were armed with a traversable TAT-102A (Tactical Assault Turret) under the nose which contained a GAU-2B/A 7.62mm Minigun; later versions had the XM-28 armament sub-system incorporating either two Miniguns or two 40mm grenade-launchers or one of each. The gunner's trigger controlled the two rates of fire for the Miniguns, 1,600 or 4,000 rounds per minute; 400 grenades a minute could be fired. The stub wings each had two pylons which could each carry either the XM-159 nineteen-rocket pod, the XM-158 seven-rocket pod, the XM-18 fixed gun pod containing an M-134 Minigun and 1,500 rounds (on the inboard pylons only), or the XM-35 Vulcan six-barrelled 20mm cannon which had a range of 2,500m and fired at 650–850 rounds per minute. For those Cobras carrying one XM-35 on the port inboard pylon, the other three pylons usually mounted XM-158 pods. The Cobra was certainly a deadly snake.

By the end of September the 1st Platoon of what was by now the 334th Armed Helicopter Company – with a direct descent from the UTTHCO (July 1962), the 68th (August 1964), the 197th (March 1965) to September 1966 when it was renumbered the 334th – had received its Cobras. Its crews were soon able to appreciate the quantum jump forward in capability. This, of course, necessitated changes in tactics and procedures, as well as adaptation on the part of the crews: no longer could they rely on the help of door gunners, nor hear the sounds of incoming hostile fire because of the enclosed individual cockpits. Despite the natural desire to replace all gunships with the Cobra, this was simply not possible and the UH-1C gunship continued to equip a number of units right through to the end of the war.

Another new helicopter to arrive in South Vietnam at much the same time as the Cobra was the Hughes OH-6A Cayuse – more generally known as the 'Loach', a name taken from its role of LOH (Light Observation Helicopter). Armed with either an XM-27 system, containing an M-134 Minigun, on the port side of the forward fuselage, or an M-60-equipped door gunner on the starboard side, it represented a major increase in reconnaissance capability over the underpowered and slow OH-13 and OH-23. The Cayuse was to become the principal reconnaissance helicopter with the air cavalry in Vietnam. In 1969 the OH-58A Kiowa arrived as the intended replacement for the OH-6A but found little favour. It lacked the same excellent crash survivability features, hover performance and tail rotor control.

An eventful year, 1967 had seen the tide swinging in favour of the Allies. To a large degree this had been possible because of the helicopter. The number of US Army helicopters had risen by 1,000 to over 2,600, of which some were dedicated Cobra attack helicopters. Statistics on helicopter vulnerability were revealing: one aircraft hit by hostile fire every 1,147 sorties, one shot down every 13,461 sorties and one actually lost every 21,194 sorties. Obviously the helicopter was not as frail as some had predicted.

Armed Chinook

In addition to its more obvious tasks the Chinook was pressed into action both as airborne artillery and as a bomber. In a special programme three of four A/ACH-47A Chinooks, known as 'Go-Go-Birds' or 'Guns A-Go-Go', were delivered to South Vietnam in May 1966, the fourth in August. They were modified to incorporate some armour protection for the eight-man crew and to carry weapons: a 20mm cannon with 800 rounds and a pod with nineteen 70mm (2.75in) rockets on each side of the fuselage, and an M-5 40mm grenade-launcher with 600 rounds under the nose. Either a 0.50in (12.7mm) machine-gun with 700 rounds or a 7.62mm machine-gun with 3,000 rounds could be installed in four fuselage windows, two on either side, and one on the tail ramp – 360° coverage was thereby achieved. In its bombing role 208-litre (46 Imp gal; 55 US gal) drums containing tear gas or, on occasion, napalm were simply rolled down the ramp onto such targets as underground fortifications which were resistant to more con- ventional methods of attack. The napalm was then ignited by fire from the escorting gunships.

The 220km/hr (137mph) speed and heavy firepower of the 'Go-Go Birds' outrivalled any other gunship. Operating either singly or as a pair, they had a range of weapons suitable for most targets and could sustain their fire for longer periods. For most of its time in Vietnam the 1st Aviation Detachment of A/ACH-47A Chinooks flew under the operational control of the 1st Cavalry Division's ARA battalion. But the loss of three of the four helicopters, the sheer productiveness of the Chinook as a medium lifter and the arrival of the Cobra put an end to this particular innovation in February 1968 after 21 months of considerable excitement and success.

1968

The year 1968 opened dramatically. On 31 January the NVA and the Viet Cong began their Tet Offensive during which they attacked 28 of South Vietnam's 44 provincial capitals, as well as a host of other cities and military bases. Tan Son Nhut and Bien Hoa air bases, the US Embassy and the MACV complex in Saigon were among the first to be attacked and penetrated. It was partly due to the actions of armed helicopters, particularly the Cobra, that these bases did not fall; the fighting prevented fighters from taking off from either air base. During the Battle of Hue in the north there were days when only helicopters could fly in the appalling weather which at times restricted cloud bases to little more than 30m (100ft).

One of the episodes of the Vietnam War to attract the full gaze of the world's attention was the continuing siege of the USMC base at Khe Sanh – planned by the NVA perhaps as an American 'Dien Bien Phu', to sap the US will to continue the war. Helicopter air assaults by the 1st Cavalry Division from platoon-size up to battalion were a major feature of the relief operation, 'Pegasus'. Indeed, every battalion committed to the operation was brought in by helicopter. A key element in its success was the reconnaissance and area-surveillance carried out by the division's air cavalry squadron. Even before the 1st Cavalry Division had been able to exploit the relief of Khe Sanh, it was extracted to prepare for Operation 'Delaware-Lam Son 216' to start four days later. The 1st Cavalry Division and the 101st Airborne Division were to carry out an airmobile assault into the A Shau Valley, supported by a ground advance by the 1st ARVN Division. The valley, lying between two high mountain ranges in the south-western part of I Corps area, was only 10km (6 miles) from the Laotian border. It had been held by the NVA for two years and during that period had been developed into a major supply base and terminus for the infiltration of personnel into South Vietnam. Care had been taken to provide it with protection against possible air attack.

On 19 April the first air assaults took place in comparative calm, but then the heaviest anti-aircraft fire of the war so far greeted subsequent waves: 23 helicopters were hit and ten were lost. By the end of the operation 21 had been lost and many more damaged. Nevertheless, the heavy air defences, coupled with the adverse weather which inhibited flying operations, were unable to prevent a successful outcome to 'Delaware': the concept of airmobility had passed a stiff test. Yet the importance of up-to-date intelligence on enemy strengths and locations and the destruction or neutralization of enemy air defences around LZs was abundantly clear.

So successful had the 1st Cavalry Division been as an airmobile force that in June the order to convert the 101st Airborne Division into an airmobile division was issued. In December 1967 the main part of the division had joined its 1st Brigade, which had been in South Vietnam since 1965. To give the division more helicopters necessitated some changes to the 1st Aviation Brigade, which by this time had about 2,000 aircraft. The main units of the brigade at this time were four combat aviation groups which had the following helicopter units:

- *12 CAG*: 3/17 Air Cavalry Squadron (ACS) (equivalent to a battalion), 11 Combat Aviation Battalion (CAB), 145 CAB, 210 CAB, 214 CAB, 269 CAB and 222 Combat Support Aviation Battalion (CSAB), totalling three air cavalry troops (equivalent to a company) and twenty companies: fifteen assault, four assault support and one heavy.
- *16 CAG*: 14 CAB and 212 CAB with six companies in all: four assault and two assault support.
- *17 CAG*: 7/17 ACS, 10 CAB, 52 CAB and 268 CAB with three troops and nineteen companies: fourteen assault, four assault support and one heavy.

● *164 CAG*: 7/1 ACS, 13 CAB and 307 CAB with three troops and six companies: five assault and one assault support.

Thus the 1st Aviation Brigade had under its command 38 assault helicopter companies, eleven assault support helicopter companies, two heavy helicopter companies and nine air cavalry troops. The most common organization for an assault helicopter company was two transport platoons with ten UH-1D/Hs each and a gunship platoon of eight UH-1B/C or AH-1G Cobras; three more UH-1s were available for the company HQ. An assault support helicopter company had two platoons of eight CH-47 Chinooks each and a couple of OH-6As for command and control and other tasks. An air cavalry troop aimed to have eleven gunships, ten observation helicopters and six 'Slicks'.

In addition to the four CAGs the brigade included 58 Aviation Battalion, 201 Corps Aviation Company and 478 Heavy Helicopter Company, all independent units, and seventeen fixed-wing aircraft companies.

While this brigade was considerably larger than the air forces of many countries, it was not alone in having helicopters. As well as the additional 800 or so helicopters in the two airmobile divisions, the USMC operated a further 340 in the I Corps Tactical Zone, the USAF approximately 60 and even the USN had about 45 in Helicopter Attack (Light) Squadron 3, known as the 'Seawolves', with four detachments based ashore and three aboard tank landing ships and in a detachment called the 'Sealords'. In due course the number of detachments rose to nine, all but one being based ashore in the vicinity of the squadron HQ at Binh Thuy.

HA(L)-3 was formed in April 1967 out of a small detachment, with a handful of unwanted US Army UH-1B gunships, which had arrived in South Vietnam in July 1966. Its principal roles were reconnaissance and fire support for US naval and ARVN forces operating in the Mekong Delta. The squadron's strength gradually increased and by the beginning of 1970 the 'Sealords' were operating the only eight UH-1Ls, a utility version of the UH-1E, ever built. The 'Sealords' were used for logistic tasks, command and control, and the insertion of the Navy's elite SEAL (Sea-Air-Land) Special Forces teams, while the 'Seawolves' provided gunship support.

USMC helicopters operating in I Corps Tactical Zone in support of the 1st and 3rd Marine Divisions and the Americal (23rd US Army) Division were organized in a different way from the Army's. The 1st Marine Air Wing initially commanded two Marine Air Groups, the 16th at Marble Mountain, Da Nang, and the 36th at Chu Lai. In late 1967, however, the 36th moved to Quang Tri and joined III Marine Amphibious Force. The 16th and 36th were not organized in the same way but in general terms each had: two heavy squadrons with eighteen Sikorsky CH-53 Sea Stallions each; four medium squadrons with 21 UH-34Ds each, later replaced by CH-46 Sea Knights; and two light squadrons with 24 UH-1E Hueys each.

The first four CH-53s had arrived in January 1967 and soon proved their worth in many different roles. As an assault transport the CH-53A could accommodate 38 combat-equipped troops; in the casualty-evacuation role there was space for 24 stretchers and four medical attendants; and as a cargo helicopter it could lift 9,072kg (20,000lb) as an underslung load. Within its first twelve months of operations it had recovered nearly 400 downed aircraft. The more powerful D model, which first appeared in 1969, could take 64 troops in a high-density seating arrangement.

The UH-1E was similar to the Army's UH-1B but modifications included a rotor brake, different radios and aluminium construction to reduce corrosion by salt. As a gunship the UH-1E was eclipsed by the Cobra, the first four of which for the USMC arrived in South Vietnam in April 1969. At the end of that year the 24 Cobras in country were consolidated in HML-367.

Submerged by the huge fleet of American helicopters, but not to be forgotten, was the Vietnamese Air Force fleet which was built up to some 600 Hueys and Chinooks by the beginning of 1973; few UH-34 Choctaws remained by this time. This force was supposedly responsible for the evacuation of ARVN casualties and the general support of ARVN forces, but in practice American 'Dust-Off' helicopters undertook the major burden.

The North Vietnamese also operated some Soviet-built helicopters: the 'Hound', 'Hook' and 'Hip'. As far as is known they undertook no assault tasks, being confined to general utility, liaison and logistic support duties. The large 'Hooks' were sometimes used to undersling fixed-wing fighters from secret storage sites to their airfields which were frequently attacked by US aircraft.

Air Cavalry

Air cavalry units were indispensable for reconnaissance, surveillance and security. Their value as both intelligence-collectors and as a guard force had been recognized by giving each infantry division's armoured cavalry squadron and the 11th Armoured Cavalry Regiment an air cavalry troop. In addition, as noted previously, the 1st Aviation Brigade had three air cavalry squadrons (Fig. 7), each equivalent to an aviation battalion, and each of the two airmobile divisions had one squadron. An air cavalry troop was a potent reconnaissance force with, typically, an aero scout platoon of ten observation helicopters, an aero rifle platoon with six 'Slicks' and four rifle squads, and an aero weapons platoon with nine gunships; the troop HQ had another two gunships.

The platoons were often split into teams and colour coded. A white team comprised two observation helicopters which were used variously for reconnaissance, the direction of fire from artillery and tactical fighters, providing navigational help to troops on the ground and for radio relay. A blue team provided a rapid-reaction force of some 30 infantrymen to provide immediate reinforcements to ground troops needing their help, to guard aircraft shot down and rescue the crew, and to exploit contacts. Two gunships made up a red team to supply immediate direct aerial fire support. War is never that simple and it soon became clear that different groupings for reconnaissance missions suited different air cavalry squadrons; some had one or two gunships and one observation helicopter, while others had two of each and a 'Slick' for the rescue of downed aircrew. Such groups were known as pink or hunter-killer teams.

An air cavalry squadron could retain its standard organization but was flexible enough to be able to change to four specialized troops: for example, all aero weapons platoons could amalgamate into an aero weapons troop, aero scout and aero rifle platoons similarly joining up. Fuel and ammunition requirements were a daunting logistic problem for the air cavalry. Based on a planned aircraft availability rate of 80 per cent and each of these 22 aircraft flying five hours a day, an air cavalry troop would consume some 24,225 litres (5,330 Imp gal; 6,400 US gal) of fuel. The ammunition requirement embraced different calibres of machine-gun ammunition (e.g., 75,000 rounds of 7.62mm, 20,000 rounds of 20mm, 350 × 70mm rockets and 3,000 × 40mm grenades).

Based on the principles of avoiding decisive engagements but always maintaining contact with the enemy and trying to exploit it, ground operations involving the air cavalry usually progressed through a number of phases. Success often depended on rapid development of the situation. Constant practice soon produced very slick procedures whereby a battalion of over 500 men could be in action within four hours of the first report of a sighting.

The first phase was intelligence, either collected by the unit itself or acquired from other sources, as to the presence of an enemy force. Air reconnaissance would follow to check the contact and see whether action

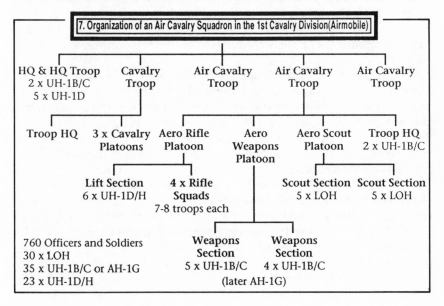

7. Organization of an Air Cavalry Squadron in the 1st Cavalry Division(Airmobile)

HQ & HQ Troop — Cavalry Troop — Air Cavalry Troop — Air Cavalry Troop — Air Cavalry Troop
2 x UH-1B/C
5 x UH-1D

Troop HQ — 3 x Cavalry Platoons — Aero Rifle Platoon — Aero Weapons Platoon — Aero Scout Platoon — Troop HQ 2 x UH-1B/C

Lift Section 6 x UH-1D/H — 4 x Rifle Squads 7-8 troops each — Scout Section 5 x LOH — Scout Section 5 x LOH

760 Officers and Soldiers
30 x LOH
35 x UH-1B/C or AH-1G
23 x UH-1D/H

Weapons Section 5 x UH-1B/C — Weapons Section 4 x UH-1B/C
(later AH-1G)

by ground forces was indicated. If so, the air cavalry troop commander would fly in his blue team to develop the situation and try to tie down the enemy until the reinforcements from the battalion in whose area the action was taking place could arrive. When these exceeded company size control would be relinquished by the air cavalry. If there was no strong ground reaction force on standby, the air cavalry role was limited to little more than aerial reconnaissance and there was little scope for the use of initiative and aggression; promising contacts with the enemy might thus be wasted.

Experience in other guerrilla wars had shown that daily flights over the same areas by the same crews were the best way of detecting the enemy: crews became so familiar with their areas that anything different stood out. Looking through the jungle canopy, and not at it, was a skill that took time to acquire. It demanded courage on the part of the crews of the observation helicopters because they had to fly at between 3m and 10m (10–33ft) above the tree tops at speeds no greater than about 50km/hr (31mph) if they were to see anything of use: movement, smoke, something glinting, a newly felled tree over a stream, communications wires, antennae, a man-made shelter, debris, even just footprints. Often the enemy gave away their position by opening fire. A smoke or white phosphorus grenade was dropped to mark this. The observation helicopters could then leave the area to the gunships which had been circling above, the lead at 245m (800ft) and the trail at 365m (1,200ft), ready to open fire. The aim of pink teams, therefore, was to search a given area on nearly a daily basis to look for the unusual, to detect any enemy presence, fix the position and report back to the local battalion tactical operations centre. A blue team, supported by a red team, could be on the scene quickly to follow up the contact in the classic 'find, fix and destroy' operation. An artillery battery was usually on call for indirect fire support, the helicopters adjusting the fall of shot as necessary. If the blue team could not cope then other assets, including more infantry, artillery and fighter aircraft if necessary, were brought in in a procedure referred to as 'pile on'.

In this case the command and control helicopter, carrying perhaps the battalion or even brigade commander and orbiting at a safe altitude to observe all activity below, would conduct the whole orchestra of red, white, blue and pink teams, artillery from local fire bases and fighter support. The 'Slicks', having picked up the on-call infantry company in the brigade area of operations, would approach low over the jungle canopy, their supporting gunships on the flanks spewing rockets and 40mm grenades at the tree line round the LZ; door gunners would contribute enthusiastically to the torrent of fire and noise as the 'Slicks' descended into the LZ. Although it was rarely easy to find a separate touchdown spot for each 'Slick', the aim was for all of them to land and depart simultaneously so that enemy fire would not be concentrated on just one or two helicopters. They might not land, just hover low enough for the infantry to leap out and sprint for the relative safety of the tree line. More and more 'Slicks' would trundle across the LZ as yet more infantry disembarked. Once the LZ was declared secure, perhaps a few Chinooks would lumber into sight, dangling 105mm howitzers, to set up a new fire base. The gun on the ground, the strops would be jettisoned, the helicopters land to one side and the crews heave out the ammunition.

Air Assault

Many air assaults encountered little or no opposition, but in the planning process it was always assumed that the enemy would be present. Suspected enemy strengths and dispositions, and the terrain, usually dictated whether detailed reconnaissance and a preparatory bombardment from the air and by artillery would take place. Tactical surprise was not necessarily lost when a preparatory bombardment was made. The usual procedure then was for the artillery and air strikes to finish when the 'Slicks' were between one and two minutes from landing. As the last explosions died away, the gunships would come in to blast any specific targets not suppressed and to 'sanitize' the area around the LZ. Hard on the heels of this gun run came the 'Slicks'.

The command and control Huey was a vital element in any air assault operation. Different radios for the command group – the ground force commander, the aviation commander and the artillery and Air Force fire support co-ordinators – were available. Its members needed to be able to communicate with their higher HQ, the ground troops, the supporting artillery, ground observers and FACs directing fighter aircraft. The helicopter formation leader used the standard on-board FM and VHF radios for his purely aviation needs.

Operation 'Silver City' was mounted by the 173rd Airborne Brigade in the Phuoc Vinh area of War Zone D, north of Saigon, between 9 and 22 March 1966. Captain Wally Steward of Company A, temporarily detached from the 82nd Aviation Battalion to become part of the 173rd Airborne Brigade, describes the initial assault by the 'Cowboys', his company's call-sign, and other aspects of the operation:

'Detailed orders for the operation, including the allocation of crews to aircraft, were given during the evening of 8 March and followed higher-level briefings attended by the company commander and his operations staff. The company was to provide ten UH-1D "Slicks" with two escorting fire teams of two or three UH-1B gunships as its contribution to the air assault of two battalions into an unsecured LZ. First light operations were preferred because of the lower temperature which allowed more troops to be carried in each aircraft as well as giving more time for consolidation on the ground before nightfall.

'The morning of 9 March began with breakfast well before dawn. Weapons were then drawn and the helicopters pre-flighted by torchlight in the Corral, the "Cowboys'" "home plate". As usual, taking great pride in their "own" aircraft, the crew chiefs and door gunners were there first, well before the allotted time of some 30 minutes before take-off. Dawn was breaking when the order to "crank" was given by "Lead" – Cowboy 6, the company commander. There was the normal frantic scramble when one UH-1D would not start and had to borrow a battery from a neighbouring aircraft; this was carried over and plugged in, being returned following a successful start-up. The "Falcons", the company's gun platoon, were going through a similar routine in their own locaton, a few hundred metres away near the perimeter where the permanently armed UH-1Bs would be left pointed outwards for safety reasons.

' "Commo check Fox Mike" came over the radio a few minutes later. We checked in by the chalk number allocated at the briefing the evening before. Checks on the other radios followed. The scheduled take-off time arrived and we followed "Lead" out of the Corral, anti-collision beacons flashing in the early dawn, to form up in trail formation – line astern – and make our way to the pick-up point to join the other helicopter companies making up the battalion lift. "Horse Thief", the company maintenance officer and his staff in a UH-1 crammed with quick-change assemblies and other items with which to effect rapid field repairs, brought up the rear. It was scarcely daylight when all five participating companies of "Slicks" were drawn up in the concentration area, ready to load the first wave of six troops per aircraft.

'Meanwhile, to the north, the LZ preparatory bombardment – prep – was about to begin. Spread over some 30 minutes, this commenced with all in-range artillery, on a fire plan, striking likely enemy locations around the LZ; when the light level was good enough USAF tactical fighters, directed by an airborne FAC, continued the prep.

'By now, the airmobile operation was well under way with the command and control ship from the 145th Aviation Battalion high overhead, monitoring the progress of the lift elements as they called at the sequence of reporting points. Other battalion level assets, also airborne, included the "Dust-Off" helicopter ambulance and the "Hill Climber" CH-47 ready to recover any downed aircraft as soon as it had been rigged for sling loading after realization that a quick repair was impracticable.

'With one minute to landing, a single white artillery phosphorus shell signalled the end of the prep. Fire teams from the 197th gunship company swept in to confirm the effectiveness of the prep, and to identify and suppress with machine-gun and rocket fire any possible pockets of resistance.

'The adrenalin began to flow as we descended from our 2,500-feet en route altitude towards the LZ in the staggered trail formation to be used for the landing. Since my company was in the lead, the door gunners on the outside of the formation prepared to give suppressive fire during the final approach and landing. As the company levelled and decelerated for the landing, "Suppress" came over the company frequency and the M-60s burst into life as fire was directed at likely enemy cover in the tree lines around the LZ.

'A little further out, at the edges of the LZ, the "Falcons" now overhauled the decelerating formation to provide further suppressive fire with both 70mm (2.75in) rockets and their M-60s as the "Slicks" touched down; for obvious reasons the door gunners stopped firing as the infantry scrambled out. A few seconds later, all troops safely on the ground, "Lead" called lifting and the "Cowboys" exited the LZ, to be followed some 30 seconds later by the next lift company. Timings were critical and the eagle eye of the command and control ship maintained a close watch, chiding lift elements which were slow in unloading and clearing the LZ. Within minutes the whole of the first wave had disembarked safely and all the "Slicks" were on the way back to collect the next wave. We spent nearly four hours in formation that morning, including refuelling, before returning to the Corral.

'Besides other air assaults "Silver City" required routine but intensive resupply tasks to be flown. One "Cowboy" "Slick" was about to depart from an LZ in tall jungle when a fire fight broke out. The 2nd Battalion, 503rd Infantry, had been approached during the night by a regimental-sized Viet Cong force which then pressed home an attack in the early morning. The door guns from the UH-1D on the ground were pressed into immediate action. All available artillery was brought to bear and USAF F-100s provided intimate close air support. Ammunition began to run low in the battalion area. It was not practical to stop the supporting fire but "Cowboy 570" managed to find a safe route in, locate the coloured smoke and bring the helicopter, with a pre-packaged underslung load of ammunition, to a hover. "Drop it and get the hell outa here" came over the FM from the company below and over the crescendo of noise from the small arms fire, the crash of artillery and bomb explosions. That someone on the ground in a much more serious predicament could show such concern for the "Slick" crew was an example of the mutual respect which had developed between the Army aviators and those whom they supported, neither of whom, I suspect, would have willingly traded places.'

By the end of 1968 it had become clear that success on the battlefield could be correlated with the effective use of Army Aviation assets by any division, whether it be airmobile or infantry. It was found, by 9 Division in the Mekong Delta for example, that combat efficiency in terms of higher enemy losses and lower American losses was achieved when an air cavalry troop and an assault helicopter company were put under the operational control of each of its three brigades on a daily basis – an arrangement that was only possible when the extra assets were made available by the 1st Aviation Brigade. Before this was effected, contact with the enemy had been sporadic and, when made, often fruitless. Army Aviation units were sometimes split into day and night teams to maintain pressure on the enemy. In 9 Division night search teams usually consisted of a command and control helicopter and a light fire team of two gunships and a Huey able to fire flares; if a night raid was to be undertaken this team was augmented by two or three 'Slicks' to carry the infantry.

Night Vision Equipment

As may be imagined, efforts to produce night vision equipment were not neglected. In September 1965 the Helicopter Illumination System was evaluated. To start with, it was based on seven landing lights taken from Fairchild C-123 transport aircraft and mounted in the cabin of a UH-1B gunship. After trial and tribulation the Nighthawk became the standard equipment; it comprised a very much more powerful xenon searchlight with both infra-red and white light, a night observation device (a starlight telescope) and an M-134 Minigun installed in a UH-1D or H. Flying at between 215m and 305m (700–1,000ft), the Nighthawk was escorted by two gunships which attacked any target detected by the searchlight in the infra-red mode or with the night observation device.

To illuminate camp perimeters and other targets simple flares were dropped. In November 1969 the 1st Cavalry Division was issued with three INFANT (Iroquois Night Fighter and Night Tracker) systems for evaluation. The INFANT, incorporated in a UH-1H, consisted of a low light level TV with an infra-red searchlight integrated with the M-21 armament subsystem on both sides of the fuselage and two receivers in the nose. After the trials four INFANT platoons of UH-1Ms were formed. Other experimental devices, such as a moving target indication radar, were also tested on both the Huey and Cobra.

Cobra Tactics

The Cobra proved itself during the year even while new tactics were being developed for it. To take maximum advantage of its flying performance and firepower required new ideas which had to be tested in actual combat. In simple terms, the end requirements were to be able to place the Cobra's ordnance on the target without the helicopter itself being hit. Both could be achieved by starting the attack run from a greater height than the UH-1 gunships and steepening the dive angle. The higher the Cobra was before starting its attack, the safer it was; the steeper the dive angle, which rarely exceeded 30°, the more accurate the fire. Also to be taken into account was the fact that the higher the Cobra was, the more easily it could be seen and more time was therefore available for the enemy to get ready to fire at it. By the end of 1968 most Cobra pilots could match the machine-gun accuracy of their UH-1B colleagues and put their rounds 50m from their own ground troops; it was commonplace for rockets to be placed as close as 70m. When 'hand-to-hand' fighting was in progress these distances were reduced sometimes to as little as 10m. The Cobra had the option of varying its attack speeds and usually made a point of not attacking over the heads of Allied ground troops but rather at an angle of 90° or so. Accuracy of fire depended greatly on the gunship crews' knowledge of the exact locations of the ground troops, friendly and enemy; since at least 1966 it had been a standard operating procedure for friendly troops to mark their positions

► Artillery spotting trials were undertaken in Britain in 1935 using licence-built Cierva C.30 autogiros, designated the Avro Rota I in military service. [*Via M. J. Hooks*]

► An RAF R-4B Hoverfly I. The R-4 was the only American helicopter to fly on operations during the Second World War. [*Museum of Army Flying – MAF*]

▼ The Sycamore took part in operations in Cyprus, Kenya, Malaya and during the assault on Port Said in November 1956. [*MAF*]

▲The H-5D had more than twice the power of the R-4 and could carry a pilot, a medical attendant and two stretcher casualties in external panniers. [*US Army Aviation Museum – USAAM*]

▼Helicopters offered much quicker and gentler evacuation than vehicles. H-13 Sioux crews saved many hundreds of lives by flying the seriously wounded to MASH units. [*USAAM*]

▲Two casualty evacuation H-23 Ravens and an H-13E at an operational base in Korea in 1951. The H-23 was also used by the French in Indo-China. [*USAAM*]

▼A HRS-1 lowers a 114mm rocket-launcher into position close to the front line in Korea, August 1952. [*Marine Corps Historical Center – MCHC*]

▲The XH-40 prototype first flew on 22 October 1956. The US Army specified an ability to carry a 363kg (800lb) payload over a radius of 185km (115 miles). [*USAAM*]

◀Six Whirlwinds from HMS *Ocean* head towards Gamil Airfield, near Port Said, Egypt, on 6 November 1956. [*MAF*]

◀This landing pad in Borneo is too small for this Wessex to get all its wheels down so the pilot has to hold the tail wheel off the ground. [*Westland*]

▲▶Below the fuselage of this Mi-4 'Hound' is a 12.7mm machine-gun pod. The outward appearance of the 'Hound' is strikingly similar to that of the HRS-1/H-19 Chickasaw.

▶Troops offload fuel and supplies from a Westland Scout in the Radfan Mountains in 1966. [*MAF*]

◀ Mi-8 'Hip Cs' took part in the Soviet invasion of Czechoslovakia in 1968. Although transport helicopters, they can carry a variety of weapons. This pair are carrying four 16-shot 57mm rocket pods each. [*Author*]

▶ USMC helicopters participating in Operation 'Desert Storm'. From right to left: an AH-1W TOW-armed Cobra, a UH-1N Huey and a CH-46 Sea Knight. [*Major S. Slade*]

◀ The rugged Scout proved invaluable in the Falklands War in 1982. [*MAF*]

◀ AH-64 Apaches quickly demonstrated their effectiveness by day and night, often well behind Iraqi lines, during Operation 'Desert Storm'. [*McDonnell Douglas*]

▶ AAC Gazelles undertook a variety of tasks but remained unarmed. [*Major S. Slade*]

◀▲Both ALAT and the Aéronavale operated the Vertol H-21. Despite its size it was powered by a single piston engine. [*SIRPA/ ECPA, France*]

◀The French Air Force selected the H-34. Although

lighter than the H-21 it had a more powerful piston engine. [*SIRPA/ ECPA, France*]

▲The two-seat Djinn was a useful observation and utility aircraft, distinguished by its

unique propulsion system. [*Aérospatiale*]

▼The versatile Alouette II was able to undertake many different roles including armed escort. [*SIRPA/ECPA France*]

◀The crew chief of this H-34 is reloading his 73mm bazooka before realigning it along the helicopter's axis. Below is a seven-shot 68mm rocket pod. [*Colonel V. Croizat*]

◀An H-34 at Oran-la-Sénia with five pods of seven tubes each for 73mm rockets and a 20mm cannon in the starboard cabin door. [*Colonel V. Croizat*]

►Even the three-seat Bell 47G could be armed with two SS-10 anti-tank missiles. [*Colonel V. Croizat*]

▼An H-34 approaches to pick up troops. [*SIRPA/ECPA, France*]

◄Troops of the 3rd Colonial Parachute Regiment leap from an H-34 during Operation 'Timimoun' on 21 November 1957. [*SIRPA/ECPA, France*]

▼◄A patrol commander jumps from an H-21 of Flottille 31F near Saida. With no tail rotor it could land safely in undergrowth which would have prevented any other helicopter from landing. [*SIRPA/ECPA, France*]

▲The UH-1A could be distinguished from the later UH-1 by its shorter main rotor mast. [*USAAM*]

▼The four 7.62mm guns of the XM-16 system (two on either side) could be fired off the line of sight by the gunner while the pilot fired the 70mm rockets. [*Captain W. Steward*]

◀A UH-1B with the starboard 24-tube rocket pod of an XM-3 system and an M-75 40mm grenade-launcher in the nose together denote a 'Heavy Hog'. [*Captain W. Steward*]

▲Infantry await pick-up by UH-1D 'Slicks'. By relocating the fuel tanks, the UH-1D had a larger cabin than the 'B model and could accommodate nine combat-equipped troops and a crew of three. [*Captain W. Steward*]

◀The HR2S was designed to meet a USMC requirement for an assault helicopter to carry 23 battle-equipped troops. In US Army service it was designated the CH-37 Mojave. [*USAAM*]

▶A Chinook underslings a Cobra. The unpleasant effect of the Chinook's strong rotor downwash can be appreciated. [*Captain W. Steward*]

◄Usually referred to as the Skycrane despite its official name of Tarhe, the CH-54's ability to carry a wide variety of heavy loads made it invaluable. [*Author*]

►Cobra crews aimed to put their rocket fire within 65m of their own troops and within 35m in an emergency. [*USAAM*]

►A CH-46D Sea Knight of the 1st Marine Air Wing takes off from An Hoa on 11 July 1968. [*MCHC*]

◄A Skycrane of the 478th Aviation Company (Heavy Helicopter) carries a 4,536kg (10,000lb) bomb. The extended fuse ensures that detonation will occur just above the ground to achieve the maximum blast effect. [*USAAM*]

►The UH-1C was designed specifically to fill the gunship role while the Cobra was being developed; 749 were built. This one is armed with the M-21 system: an M-134 six-barrelled 7.62mm Minigun and an XM-158 rocket pod are visible on the port side. [*USAAM*]

◀The narrow frontal aspect and wide chord of its main rotor blades are distinctive features of the Cobra. This one is armed with two 19-tube XM-159 70mm rocket pods and two XM-18 six-barrelled 7.62mm Minigun pods on the wing pylons. In the TAT-102A under the nose is an M-134 Minigun. [*Captain W. Steward*]

▶ The OH-58 Kiowa was intended to replace the Cayuse but it proved to be underpowered, less effective and less rugged. It was therefore used mainly for general tasks. [*USAAM*]

▼The OH-6A Cayuse became the primary reconnaissance helicopter. Its port-mounted XM-27 system consisted of an M-134 Minigun and 2,000 rounds. [*Captain W. Steward*]

▶An A/ACH-47A has its M-5 grenade-launcher serviced at An Khe in September 1966. Other weapons visible are an XM-159 rocket pod and, above it, an M-24A 20mm cannon; protruding from the cabin windows are two traversable 12.7mm cannon. All these weapons are duplicated on the starboard side. A fifth 12.7mm cannon is mounted on the rear-loading ramp. With these weapons and their ammunition the A/ACH-47A had a radius of action of some 185km (115 miles). Note the flat armour plates under the nose and on the rotor pylon. [*USAAM*]

◀A USMC CH-53A Sea Stallion lifts an underslung load at Vandergrift on 4 October 1968. In the background can be seen a Marine CH-46. [*MCHC*]

▶Two UH-1Ds of the 82nd Aviation Battalion make an approach to LZ 8 during Operation 'Silver City' in March 1966. [*Captain W. Steward*]

▶The UH-1H was similar to the 'D model but had a more powerful engine. [*USAAM*]

◀A red team of two Cobras came from the aero weapons platoon of an air cavalry troop. [*Captain W. Steward*]

▶The UH-1B with TOW missiles proved decisive against NVA tanks. Note the missile sight on the port side of the nose. [*MAF*]

◀Every effort was made to recover downed aircraft. Note the gunner on the rear ramp of this Chinook as it underslings a Huey. [*USAAM*]

▶At least one 'Dust Off' helicopter usually accompanied assault missions. [*USAAM*]

▶In addition to its usual armament of a 12.7mm nose gun, and 57mm rockets and 'Swatter' anti-tank missiles on the wings, the Mi-24 'Hind A' had a cabin for eight troops.

▼No more than about 40 Mi-6 'Hooks' were ever deployed despite their ability to lift up to 12,000kg (26,455lb).

▲Like the 'Hind D' the 'E' model has a reshaped front fuselage section. In both, a four-barrelled 12.7mm turreted gun replaced the nose gun of the 'A' model. The distinctive missile rails of the 'E' model denote 'Spiral' rather than 'Swatter' missiles. [*R. Senkowski*]

▼This 'Hip H' has a full suite of protective devices. At top right is an IR jammer. To the right of the '50' is a decoy flare-dispenser and above it an engine exhaust gas-diffuser. Behind the soldier holding his hat, part of the cockpit armour plating is visible. [*Via R. Senkowski*]

▲A 'Hind E' armed with two 80mm rocket pods and a 'Spiral' missile on each wing tip. The diffusers are conspicuous. [*Via R. Senkowski*]

▼The wingman of a pair of 'Hind Es' photographs his leader as they patrol a military airfield. [*Via R. Senkowski*]

◄Spetsnaz troops walk away from a 'Hip H'. Beyond it is an SAR 'Hip H' with a large red cross below the diffuser. [*Via R. Senkowski*]

◄Prior to an operational mission. Dress regulations seem to have been ignored, footwear in particular being left to individual choice! [*Via R. Senkowski*]

▲As well as the standard survivability equipment visible on this 'Hip H' are: triangular-shaped 'Slap Shot' IFF antennae under the nose and tail fin, a Doppler radar box under the tailboom, a gun camera box below the second porthole from the left, a rescue hoist above the cabin door and a 12.7mm gun in the nose. [*Via R. Senkowski*]

▼The only difference between the 'Hind E' and 'F' is the latter's fixed twin-barrelled 30mm cannon in place of the 12.7mm turreted gun. Below the cannon is the sight for the 'Spiral'. [*Author*]

◀The crew chief of a 'Hip H' fires a 12.7mm machine-gun through a porthole. Note his parachute.

▶The gunner of an AH-1Q Cobra in the front cockpit launches a TOW missile during evaluation tests in 1973. [*Bell*]

◀The crew of a 'Hind E'. The two pilots have AKSU-74 5.45mm sub-machine-guns strapped to their right thighs: there is no stowage space in the cockpits for them and in the event of evacuation the pilots will have both hands free and not have to worry about taking their weapons with them. [*Via R. Senkowski*]

▶An AH-64 Apache with a prototype Longbow radar atop the mast and a Hellfire missile on one of the wing pylons. The in-service designation will be AH-64D. [*Martin Marietta*]

◀An SS-11 mounted on an AAC Alouette II in 1963. [*Author*]

◄The first Tiger prototype during an early test flight in May 1991. Unlike most attack helicopters the pilot sits in the front cockpit. [*Eurocopter*]

◄The armed OH-58D Kiowa Warrior with a mast-mounted sight/sensor system is a highly developed

version of the Vietnam-era OH-58A. [*Bell*]

▲A mock-up of the RAH-66 Comanche, the next US Army combat helicopter. Note the fantail rotor and retractable weapons bays; although a twin-barrelled gun is shown here, production aircraft will have

a triple-barrelled gun. [*Boeing/Sikorsky*]

▼The single-seat 'Hokum' is to be Russia's next attack helicopter. It uses the traditional Kamov co-axial, contra-rotating rotor system which obviates the need for a tail rotor. [*Kamov*]

▲The Mi-28 'Havoc', like the 'Hokum', is expected to have a much better manoeuvre performance than the 'Hind'. [*Author*]

◀The Horizon radar stowed on a Puma. In flight the radar hangs below the fuselage. [*Author*]

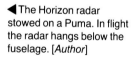

◀AAC Lynx launch their TOW missiles. [*Westland*]

with smoke grenades, the gunship crew identifying the colour. Such a procedure made it more difficult for the enemy to produce similarly coloured smoke at the same time.

Meanwhile, the build-up had continued and reached over 3,350 US Army helicopters by the end of 1968. Some of these had been the latest model of Huey, the UH-1H. With more power than the UH-1D, it had a greater payload which showed to good advantage in hot and high conditions. It soon replaced the UH-1D for casualty evacuation. The other benefits it offered included cockpit instrumentation for night and adverse weather flying and greater reliability.

Cambodia

In January 1969 Richard Nixon became President of the USA and quickly brought the concept of 'Vietnamization' to the fore. This was a two-pronged concept: strengthening the ARVN, so that it could assume a greater responsibility for the prosecution of the war, and extending the so-called pacification programme in South Vietnam. Plans for the withdrawal of some US units were prepared.

Three months earlier the 1st Cavalry Division had been ordered to move to III Corps Tactical Zone with its main HQ at Phuoc Vinh to oppose NVA and Viet Cong forces operating out of their sanctuaries in Cambodia. Throughout 1969 the division's war of attrition against supply trails leading out of Cambodia inhibited enemy operations and uncovered base camps and supply dumps. However, it was quite obvious that these dumps were themselves being fed by much larger supply depots across the border in Cambodia – out of reach for years due to a political edict. But in March 1970 General Lon Nol assumed control of the Government in Cambodia after a successful coup. The North Vietnamese reacted violently and Lon Nol asked for help. The rule preventing attacks across Vietnamese borders was relaxed and a limited incursion into Cambodia was authorized.

It was during this same month, March 1970, that the number of US helicopters in South Vietnam reached its highest total: more than 4,350, of which over 3,900 belonged to the Army. Of this latter figure some 2,400 were Hueys, 780 OH-6 LOHs and 470 Cobras. The balance was made up mainly of Chinooks and Skycranes. But withdrawals were already imminent; indeed, within the next fourteen months all Marine helicopter units had gone, nineteen months before the cease-fire was signed.

Helicopters were the key element of the plan to invade Cambodia. The 1st Cavalry Division was to make a series of heliborne assaults into the 'Fishhook' area, a part of Cambodia that jutted into South Vietnam, while ARVN and American ground units thrust towards the same area. Air cavalry units would have a major role to play in carrying out reconnaissance, screening the advance and then searching for and attacking targets of opportunity. 'Fishhook' was thought to house the control centre for all Communist military and political actions in South Vietnam. It was believed to be a HQ and communications centre with an adjoining hospital and administrative elements.

Early on 1 May USAF B-52 bombers began Operation 'Toan Thang 43' (Total Victory), preceding a heavy artillery bombardment and the dropping of two 6,804kg (15,000lb) bombs with extended fuses to produce two LZs in the jungle. Aerial reconnaissance and the attack of opportunity targets by the 1st Squadron, 9th Cavalry, followed and when the first air assault forces landed just 2½ hours after the last B-52 bomb had exploded, resistance was light. On this first day small supply dumps were found, but further impetus was given to the operation on 3 May when A Troop of the 1st Squadron found the first large weapons dump from the air. Even better was to come the following day when B Troop found a huge complex to the north-west of the area. Ground troops were inserted on 5 May and quickly unravelled an area, later nicknamed 'The City', some 3km (1.9 miles) square containing a massive assortment of living quarters, medical and training facilities, workshops and storage bunkers, together with vast quantities of food, ammunition and explosives. Other depots were discovered elsewhere, all yielding similar material, including communications equipment and wheeled vehicles.

While the operation had achieved many of its aims, it had produced a quite unexpected reaction in the USA. This became of such concern to President Nixon that he ordered all invading forces to be withdrawn from Cambodia by the end of June. Nevertheless, the results of the operation were impressive and had seriously weakened the NVA and Viet Cong. In addition to inflicting heavy losses on the enemy and capturing huge quantities of war material and food, the Allies had learnt much about the NVA's logistic system. Once again, helicopters had been decisive in taking the battle to the enemy, in making possible the search of areas much larger than ground units could have covered and in attacking fleeting targets that ground forces could not have reached. Vietnamization and the withdrawal of US troops could proceed; in fact, four of the ten US divisions had gone by the end of the year.

As a result of a study into the efficacy of some of his aviation assets, particularly the use of Cobras in the escort role, the new Commanding General of the 1st Cavalry Division, Major General George W. Putnam Jr, lately commander of the 1st Aviation Brigade, ordered two air cavalry troops to be formed out of the two armed helicopter companies in the 227th and 229th Assault Helicopter Battalions and supplemented by more LOHs from other divisional units. Shortly afterwards, during the late autumn of 1970, the 1st Cavalry Division was given operational control of another air cavalry squadron, the 3rd Squadron, 17th Cavalry. Now with two and two-thirds air cavalry squadrons which were given the support of the division's ARA battalion, Major General Putnam had to all intents and purposes an Air Cavalry Combat Brigade as envisaged by the Howze Board eight years earlier.

Operation 'Lamson 719'

'Lamson 719' is probably the best known operation of the entire war and possibly the least well understood. During the autumn of 1970 it became ever clearer that the incursion into Cambodia had done little to deter the NVA and Viet Cong from continuing the war, although it had temporarily wrested the initiative from them and succeeded in inhibiting operations for a while. However, it now appeared that Cambodia itself was becoming a target for the North Vietnamese; in addition, enemy efforts were in hand to rebuild bases in that country opposite III and IV Corps Tactical Zones. Certainly, during the dry season between October and the following April, the Ho Chi Minh Trail was going to be busy. To regain the initiative and cut off Cambodia completely, the best place to interdict the Trail would be in South Laos. It was therefore decided to carry out a cross-border attack on the North Vietnamese supply depots on the Ho Chi Minh Trail in southern Laos in February 1971. The aim was threefold: to destroy the depots, disrupt the lines of communication and defeat local NVA forces.

The planning and execution of 'Lamson 719' was subject to factors not present before. There were two particularly important constraints. Due to a US Congressional ruling, no US troops or advisers were allowed on the ground in Laos, the only American assistance being confined to air and artillery support from bases within South Vietnam. This was therefore to be a true test of Vietnamization. The second important difference compared with previous operations was that the target area of some 35km (22 miles) by 60km (37 miles) was well protected by nineteen anti-aircraft battalions equipped with larger-calibre weapons than hitherto met: 23mm, 37mm and 57mm. Together with some 12.7mm heavy machine-guns, these weapons were deployed around potential LZs as well as to protect important storage sites and vital ground. The defences were further reinforced by sections of 10 – 12 men, armed with a couple of machine-guns, rocket-launchers and an 82mm mortar, who, changing their positions daily, were able to dominate most of the LZs, pick-up points, fire bases and other ARVN positions. In addition to the air defences elements of five divisions, twelve infantry regiments, a tank regiment with the amphibious PT-76 light tank and the T-34 medium battle tank, and an artillery regiment were present. Total NVA strength was estimated at 13,000 combat troops and 9,000 support troops.

Against this large conventional force the battle effectiveness of helicopters was going to be put to a severe test. ARVN forces consisted of the equivalent of three divisions, an armoured brigade and three Ranger battalions. The US 101st Airborne Division's 101st Aviation Group of 2nd Squadron, 17th Cavalry, with four air cavalry troops, and three aviation battalions, was given the operational control of other aviation units from the 1st Aviation Brigade and a medium helicopter squadron from the USMC to provide the necessary support.

The weather was also a major planning factor since participating helicopters would have three areas of operation: the heliports on the coast, to which most of the helicopters returned each night; the forward staging area at Khe Sanh; and in the air over Laos itself. Fog and heavy rain during the mornings sometimes precluded flying or made it difficult and dangerous.

'Lamson 719' began on 30 January 1971 with activities within South Vietnam to secure Khe Sanh, Route 9 and the Laotian border areas. The actual attack into Laos began on 8 February with a ground advance across the border along Route 9 supported by the airlift of troops into positions both north and south of the road; some of these were to be fire bases to protect the flanks of the advance. The initial objectives were taken and the advance progressed slowly, but by the middle of the month it had become bogged down due to stiffening resistance. This was exacerbated by worsening weather which often precluded fixed-wing fighter support and forced the helicopters to fly along valleys when the hills on either side were wreathed in cloud. Thus the choice of routes to fire bases and LZs became restricted and comparatively easy for the NVA and Viet Cong to predict. ARVN fire bases were a prime target for the enemy and on 25 February one was overrun by T-34 tanks; others had to be evacuated. By the end of the month it had become clear that the main supply route into Laos could not be kept open on a secure and permanent basis while simultaneously maintaining the advance towards Tchepone, one of the communications

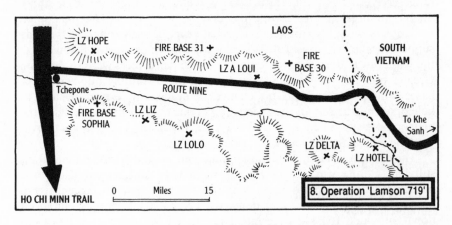

8. Operation 'Lamson 719'

NVA	ARVN	USA/USMC
Elements of:	1 infantry division	101st Aviation Group
5 divisions	1 Airborne division	2nd Squadron, 17th Cavalry
12 infantry regiments	1 Marine division	1 squadron USMC medium
1 tank regiment	3 Ranger battalions	transport helicopters
1 artillery regiment	1 armoured brigade	
19 AA battalions		
general support troops		
engineer transport		

hubs of the NVA supply complex. The ARVN commander, Lieutenant General Lam, decided that he should therefore use his aviation assets to attack Tchepone.

Between 3 and 6 March ARVN troops made heliborne assaults into three LZs along the south side of Route 9, which permitted one fire base to be established within range of Tchepone. A battalion assault into LZ 'Lolo', however, cost eleven helicopters shot down and 44 hit by hostile fire. On 6 March two ARVN battalions were put into LZ 'Hope' north-east of the town, which was then captured without much ado. This heliborne assault was one of the largest of the war, involving about 120 'Slicks' escorted by dozens of gunships and fixed-wing fighters. Yet, despite the strength of the enemy's air defences, the number of helicopters in the air, and the transit distance of 65km (40 miles), only one 'Slick' was shot down and fourteen damaged. This was almost certainly due to the massive preparatory bombardment by B-52s and tactical fighters, and the efforts of the supporting air cavalry.

The capture of Tchepone did nothing to relieve NVA pressure which, in fact, increased. General Lam therefore decided that, having achieved most of his aims, it was time to end the operation and withdraw his troops from Laos before the worsening weather further inhibited flying operations. A concerted enemy effort was now made to hinder this withdrawal. Anti-aircraft weapons were concentrated on anticipated fly-in routes and around fire bases, and intense fire was directed at any helicopter that came within range. Nevertheless, the extraction of many troops, particularly those unable to break contact with the enemy, went ahead by helicopter. Helicopters were also tasked for armed reconnaissance and to provide support for the fire bases. 19,724 sorties were flown during the first week of the withdrawal, during which time at least 25 helicopters were shot down. Greater pressure than ever was applied to the dwindling number of fire bases which by now had no chance of evacuation except by air; 40 helicopters were used for the evacuation of one of these bases and 28 of the helicopters were hit by hostile fire. By 25 March the operation was over with the bulk of the troops back inside South Vietnam.

The operation had not been an unqualified success and Vietnamization still had a long way to go. But the helicopter had proved itself in a particularly hostile environment. 'Lamson 719' had certainly been costly in terms of helicopters lost and damaged. Over 200,000 sorties had been flown, of which 164,442 were into Laos. In all, 107 helicopters had been lost (a loss rate of about 15 per cent) and more than 600 damaged, some beyond repair. It should be remembered that the majority were combat sorties, often into areas of heavy anti-aircraft fire, sometimes large calibre and radar-directed; over half the losses were sustained by 'Slicks' during approaches into, or departures from, LZs under aimed fire. These losses were due partly to the ARVN's failure to keep the enemy away from the perimeters of LZs and pick-up points, thus allowing them to take up firing positions close by.

The appearance of significant numbers of tanks caught the Allies unawares. The gunships had no effective weapon with which to engage them. The Cobra attacked using a combination of 70mm (2.75in) flechette rockets at maximum range and followed these up with HE and white phosphorus rockets. The latter necessitated closing to within 1,000m of the tank and thus coming within range of its 12.7mm machine-gun and probably other weapons in the area. The XM-35 20mm cannon was used when fitted, but this too demanded closure with the target. Gunship crews were not too keen to attack tanks and preferred to hand them over to fighter aircraft; but the lesson was learnt that some kind of modern heliborne anti-tank weapon was needed without delay.

The most effective use of the aviation assets available was achieved by daily joint planning with air and ground commanders and staffs. At a lower level route planning assumed life or death proportions: routes were chosen which linked friendly positions (in case of forced landings due to bad weather, malfunctions or hostile fire), which used certain terrain features for navigational purposes and which avoided known or suspected enemy positions. Whenever possible, transit altitudes were generally 1,220m (4,000ft) or higher, followed by a rapid descent and nap-of-the-earth (NOE) approach into the LZ. Tight formations used in previous operations gave way to loose trail formations since most LZs were very small and could only cope with one or two helicopters at a time. Brand-new LZs were preferred to used 'secure' ones since surprise was more easily achieved and escorting gunships could fire at will.

Helicopter against Tank

'Lamson 719' was the last major heliborne operation carried out by US forces. During the remaining months of 1971, while US units, notably the 1st Cavalry Division and most of the 101st Airborne Division, were being withdrawn from South Vietnam, helicopter support continued to be given to the ARVN.

The appearance of Soviet-built tanks during 'Lamson 719' had been taken to heart and on 24 April the first of a new generation of anti-tank missiles arrived at Tan Son Nhut. It was the TOW missile – Tube-launched, Optically tracked, Wire-guided. Two UH-1B gunships were modified for this weapon system which included a telescopic sight unit in the helicopter's nose. Crews were advised to open fire at targets at a maximum range of 3,000m (actual maximum range of the missile is 3,750m) at an altitude of 915m (3,000ft) – so that they were out of small arms range – and at a flying speed of between 90km/hr (56mph) and 150km/hr (93mph).

On 28 April the two UH-1Bs flew north to be in position to participate in an expected attack on Kontum. Just in time, because on 2 May a TOW missile was fired in anger for the first time. It destroyed its target, a captured American M-41 tank. Three PT-76 tanks were also despatched that day by the team of two UH-1Bs, two escorting Cobras and a UH-1H command and control helicopter. On 26 May a fresh assault against Kontum was made. During the battle that day 21 missiles were fired and ten tank kills claimed, besides other point targets destroyed. Five of the tanks were the more modern Soviet-built T-54.

The 'TOW campaign' lasted until 12 June, during which time 81 TOW missiles were fired in action and 57 targets (including 24 tanks, armoured personnel carriers, artillery and wheeled trucks) destroyed. Simultaneously the six UH-1M gunships armed with the SS-11 fired 20 missiles against just three tanks: a T-54 and a PT-76 were destroyed and a PT-76 damaged. These experiences encouraged the US Army to equip a new version of the Cobra with eight TOW missiles once the war was over. The TOW system proved to be a significant improvement on the SS-11, which had not been used against the tanks in Laos.

'Lamson 719' saw the introduction of a shoulder-launched surface-to-air missile, the Soviet SA-7. It made no impact on that operation but when it reappeared in June 1972 it proved quite effective: some Cobras were lost to it and its very presence forced helicopters to fly much lower, which brought them into the envelope of anti-aircraft and machine-gun fire. Some areas became temporarily 'no-go'. The SA-7 also concentrated some minds on measures to counter these heat-seeking missiles; subsequently attempts were made to suppress the infra-red signature of helicopters, particularly by shielding the engine exhaust and deflecting the gases upwards into the rotor downwash.

'Dust Off'

No account of helicopter operations in Vietnam would be complete without paying credit to the casualty evacuation crews whose exploits became a by-word for courage and resourcefulness. Such US Army crews used the radio call-sign 'Dust Off'. It was chosen by the commander of the 57th Medical Detachment in 1963 from a list of unused call-signs in the Signal Operations Instructions book for US Forces in South Vietnam.

One of the most important original roles for the UH-1 Huey had been casualty evacuation with a specification to take four stretchers internally. Although significantly better than the H-13 in this role – in terms of speed, endurance, stretcher load and the fact that the wounded could be carried internally and therefore cared for by a medical attendant – the early Huey models lacked the power to undertake their full load under all conditions in South Vietnam. Indeed, in I and II Corps Tactical Zones, for example, the A and B models could not always take even two stretcher cases in addition to the crew of four (aircraft commander, pilot, crew chief and medical attendant). The UH-1D was little better although it had the space to take six stretchers or nine walking wounded. Within these limitations the casualty evacuation role was carried out most effectively. Yet it was only when 25 of the more powerful UH-1Hs arrived at Long Binh with the 45th Medical Company (Air Ambulance) in July 1967 that a comprehensive service could be provided from battlefield to operating table. The UH-1H had the much more powerful T53-L-13 engine (developing 1,400shp compared with the 770shp of the derated L-1A of the UH-1A), which nevertheless consumed less fuel. The UH-1H also had flight instruments for night and adverse weather flying and a Decca navigation system.

Because of the jungle terrain the ambulance helicopters could not always land to pick up their casualties, so various devices were installed to lift them out from a high hover. It was not until May 1966, however, that an electric personnel rescue hoist, able to take a load of 272kg (600lb), was first used. Attached to a hook on the end of a 75m (246ft)-long cable could be any one of an assortment of rescue harnesses such as a 'jungle penetrator', a collapsible seat to which a lightly wounded casualty was strapped or, in the case of the seriously wounded, a Stokes litter, which was essentially a wire basket. After the arrival of the UH-1H, a trial showed that, hovering out of ground effect in a temperature of 35° C (95° F) in the Central Highlands, a UH-1D could lift 83kg (183lb) while a UH-1H could take 482kg (1,063lb); thus the UH-1D could take one light casualty while the UH-1H could hoist out five. By the end of January 1968 the last UH-1D air ambulance had been converted to a 'Slick' and transferred to an assault helicopter battalion; all US Army helicopter ambulances were now UH-1Hs.

A hoist evacuation was one of the most dangerous types of mission to fly. Gunship escort was rare and practically all evacuation missions were flown by a single helicopter. In accordance with the Geneva Convention, 'Dust Off' helicopters were unarmed and marked with large red crosses. This did not stop the NVA and Viet Cong firing at them as though they were combat helicopters. On arrival at the pick-up point, the helicopter had to remain in a high hover, vulnerable to enemy fire, for many minutes. Above trees or vegetation, it had nowhere to land in the event of a serious technical malfunction or if incapacitated by hostile fire; furthermore, in such circumstances its conditions of height and no speed did not allow a safe auto-rotative landing even if somewhere to land was close by. Flying skills were at a premium because the hoist and the crew chief operating it were to one side of the aircraft, thus adversely affecting lateral stability. The problem was heightened by the fact that sometimes the hover had to be in a crosswind or downwind. Two pilots were normally carried so that during a lengthy extraction they could swap control of the aircraft. 'Dust Off' crews were expected to fly in very bad weather and at night, and the aircraft commander would act as navigator and co-pilot.

At the beginning of 1965 only the 57th and 82nd Medical Detachments (Helicopter Ambulance) with ten UH-1Bs were in South Vietnam, but during the year the number of medical helicopters deployed there rose dramatically. With the 1st Cavalry Division came the 15th Medical Battalion, which included an air ambulance platoon consisting of a casualty evacuation section with eight Hueys and a crash rescue section with four. In September the first medical company (air ambulance) with 25 UH-1Ds arrived to support operations in the II Corps Tactical Zone under the command of the 43rd Medical Group. It was followed before the end of the year by two more medical detachments (helicopter ambulance). In March 1966 the 44th Medical Brigade took command of most of the US Army medical units in South Vietnam, including the medical groups deployed in the various Corps Tactical Zones. These groups in their turn commanded the air ambulance companies and detachments, but not the divisional air ambulance platoons of the 1st Cavalry and the 101st Airborne Divisions. These two platoons used the call-sign 'Medevac'. Later some divisions were supported by a single medical detachment (helicopter ambulance), although the 9th Division in the Delta was supported by a medical company (air ambulance).

The medical companies and detachments were usually tasked either to support all units in a specific area or to provide direct support to an individual unit for a certain operation. Casualties were classified as urgent (those requiring immediate evacuation to save life or limb), priority (those with serious but not critical wounds) or routine. The medical man on the ground decided the classification while the ground commander advised the incoming 'Dust Off' crew of the security of the LZ. Inevitably, in both cases, casualties were sometimes overclassified and LZs said to be more secure than they turned out to be.

The number of helicopter ambulances peaked at about 140 in 1969. About 75 per cent of them were available to fly when tasked and in 1969 each of these averaged four missions a day. Of the US Army's 120,000 personnel wounded in action, more than 100,000 were evacuated by helicopter; some of these of course were carried by 'Slicks'. If casualties were sustained during an air assault, for example, succeeding waves of 'Slicks' would pick up the wounded from earlier waves once the incoming troops had disembarked. Ambulance helicopters also transported some 750,000 other Allied military personnel and Vietnamese civilians.

Only personal sidearms and the occasional M-79 grenade-launcher were carried for self-protection. Vulnerable, with a distinctive rotor 'slap' that alerted the enemy to their approach and flying in the most dangerous parts of the combat area, it was inevitable that the loss rate was higher than for any other role. It was calculated that air ambulance losses were 3.3 times higher than the loss rate for all other roles, and 1.5 times higher than that for other helicopters on combat missions. Of the approximately 1,400 air ambulance pilots who flew during the war, some 220 were killed or wounded by enemy fire and a further 270 died or were injured as a result of crashes, often at night or in bad weather when engaged on evacuation flights. An air ambulance helicopter was hit once every 311 sorties, but when a hoist was used this average was reduced to a hit every 44 sorties.

Nevertheless 'Dust Off' and 'Medevac' activities saved many lives, reduced the mortality rate and did much to contribute to morale. The standard of selfless and courageous service was set early on by one of the first commanders of the 57th Medical Detachment (Helicopter Ambulance), Major Charles Kelly. Setting an example that was to be followed by 'Dust Off' crews for the rest of the war, his exploits and determination to rescue the wounded at all costs earned him the sobriquet 'Mad Man' Kelly.

A 'Dust Off' Medal of Honor

Dense fog greeted the dawn of 6 January 1968 at Chu Lai, a coastal city in the south of I Corps Tactical Zone and the base for the 54th Medical Detachment (Helicopter Ambulance). The weather the night before had prevented the successful evacuation of two wounded South Vietnamese from a reconnaissance camp in the mountains to the west. After another failure that morning Major Patrick H. Brady volunteered to try. As 'Dust Off 55' reached the mountains, the visibility became so bad that the tips of the rotor blades could not be seen by the crew, but the rotor downwash thinned the fog just enough for Brady to be able to hover-taxi along a track to the camp. At least the lack of visibility prevented aimed enemy fire, but it also caused Brady to miss the LZ and land hazardously between the outer and inner defensive perimeters. The worst was over; having collected the wounded, 'Dust Off 55' climbed into the overcast and delivered them to hospital.

No sooner had that mission been completed than Brady and his crew were off again, this time to the Hiep Duc Valley where a company of the US 198th Light Infantry Brigade had taken 60 casualties during the night. On this sortie Brady flew through cloud before letting down through a misty hole and continuing low-level. Again the dreadful visibility surprised the enemy and Brady was able to sneak into the company area. Having loaded some wounded, he took off on instruments for fire base 'West' where there was an aid post. Here he briefed three other crews to follow him back to the company under siege, but in the event they could not handle the weather or the blanket of fire that greeted them. Only Brady managed to get in, this time and twice more; in his four trips he pulled out 39 wounded, eighteen of them stretcher casualties.

Having refuelled, 'Dust Off 55' was next sent south-east of Chu Lai to rescue US troops whose LZ was in direct view of enemy machine-gunners. His helicopter hit on its low-level approach into the LZ, Brady turned his aircraft to face away from the most intense fire and hover-taxied backwards towards it and where the wounded lay. This drew so much fire that it was too dangerous to load the casualties, so Brady took off and orbitted the area until asked to return. Again the fire was intense and again Brady put the bulk of his aircraft between the enemy and his cockpit, hovering backwards towards the wounded. This time they were embarked successfully and Brady escaped without further trouble.

It had been a busy morning but more requests for 'Dust Off' support were to come in. A US platoon had been entirely killed or wounded in an ambush, also south-east of Chu Lai. Ignoring advice to wait until the enemy had broken off contact, Brady, having exchanged helicopters, flew to the spot without delay and landed in a minefield close to the casualties. As the firing raged around the aircraft and shrapnel from an exploding mine 5m (16ft) away tore holes in it, the wounded were bundled on board and flown out to safety. Twice more that day Brady flew vital 'Dust Off' missions, bringing his total of evacuees to 51. For these exploits he was awarded the highest American decoration for valour, the Medal of Honor.

Search and Rescue

The US Navy, over water, and the Air Force, over land, had always been responsible for SAR. Although such work was on a smaller scale than the day-to-day evacuation of battle casualties by Army helicopters, US Navy and Air Force helicopters achieved lasting recognition during the Vietnam War for their daring rescues of downed airmen, both north and south of the 17th parallel. Until the end of 1965 a variety of largely inadequate helicopters, insufficient in number, carried out rescue missions very much on an ad hoc basis.

On 8 January 1966, however, a much more formal arrangement was instituted when the 3rd Aerospace Rescue and Recovery Group was established to co-ordinate the activities of three USAF rescue squadrons: the 37th at Da Nang, the 38th at Tan Son Nhut and the 39th at Tuy Hoa, together with detachments at the majority of USAF bases in South Vietnam and Thailand. The 40th Squadron was established at Udorn Air Base, Thailand, later, bringing the total number of aircraft, fixed- and rotary-wing, to over 70.

In due course the standard composition of a SAR Task Force became a Lockheed HC-130P Hercules command and control and air-to-air refuelling aircraft, two rescue helicopters and four Douglas A-1 Skyraiders; sometimes FACs in light fixed-wing aircraft also participated in rescue operations. Initially, the helicopters were Sikorsky HH-3Es, a variant of the ubiquitous S-61, quickly named the 'Jolly Green Giant'. It had a range of about 1,000km (620 miles), a cruising speed, fully loaded, of 232km/hr (144mph), a payload of 2,268kg (5,000lb), limited armour protection and defensive armament, a rescue hoist with 76m (250ft) of cable and, installed later, a telescopic flight refuelling probe. Despite these attributes it did not compare with the Sikorsky HH-53B, specifically designed to meet the needs of the war; the first two were delivered to Udorn in 1967. Known as the 'Super Jolly Green Giant', this helicopter had better armament (three GAU-2B/A Miniguns, the same as the Army's M-134), a cruising speed of 278km/hr (173mph), at least three times the payload, space for 24 stretchers and four medical attendants or 38 passengers, and a range limited only by the crew's endurance because of the helicopter's airborne refuelling capability.

Downed aircrew were usually located by means of the homing beacon they carried in their survival vest. As the rescue team arrived in the area, the survivor would be instructed to fire a flare to indicate his precise position and the A-1s would then move in sharply to provide suppressive fire all around him. As they did so, one of the helicopters would fly in to pick him up while the other remained out of harm's way, ready to come in if something went wrong and the crew of the first rescue helicopter had to be recovered as well as the survivor.

The location and rescue of downed aircrew were usually given top priority. This was much appreciated by all aircrew and also by the enemy who often tried 'come-on' tactics using captured equipment. A great many brave men were lost trying to rescue others; indeed, there were a number of instances when more men were lost than rescued. The attrition rate of aircraft was high. One of the best known cases involved an F-4 Phantom crew shot down over Laos. In two and a half days 336 sorties were flown in an attempt to rescue the two men. In the event, only the weapons operator was brought out but only after five A-1s and five HH-53s had been badly damaged and one of the rescue team killed.

The Recovery of Downed Aircraft

Following the Korean and Algerian Wars it was appreciated that the recovery of helicopters that had been shot down or forced to land would repay handsome dividends. Even if they could not be repaired to fly again, components could be removed for use as spare parts. In May 1963 four Army CH-37 Mojaves arrived in South Vietnam and were quickly pressed into service to take over from the CH-21s whenever possible; the first Marine CH-37s arrived in September 1965. They did not have enough power to lift the heaviest loads and were retired when the much more capable Chinook, Skycrane and CH-53 arrived; the Skycrane was powerful enough to lift a stripped-down Chinook. At the other end of the scale, even the UH-1 recovered some of the lighter helicopters. In all, the staggering total of some 12,000 fixed- and rotary-wing aircraft from all the Services were recovered during the war; of these some 5,600 were US Army helicopters. The Chinook alone retrieved about 6,000 aircraft. Approximately 10,000 were returned to service.

The End

The 27 January 1973 cease-fire was continually broken by the ARVN, NVA and Viet Cong in their frantic attempts to gain as much territory as possible. Becoming progressively weaker, the ARVN was unable to cope when the NVA launched a massive onslaught at the end of 1974.

The final act in the war in April 1975 saw the return of USMC helicopters to Saigon to evacuate remaining US and some Vietnamese personnel and fly them to ships out at sea. Emotional scenes of people trying to scramble aboard the helicopters landing on the roof of the US Embassy were shown around the world. Finally, in the early morning of 30 April, the last one left. The helicopter, so much a symbol of the war, had been in at the death.

Epilogue

If any one thing characterized the Vietnam War it was the ubiquitous helicopter. Unquestionably it was the ground forces' greatest asset. Deployed in huge numbers, US helicopters offered an unparalleled degree of flexibility to the ground forces in their provision of firepower and mobility. So great was their contribution to the Allied effort that there is little doubt that their presence prevented a rapid and humiliating US defeat and significantly delayed the eventual Communist victory. Not surprisingly, the temptation to use helicopters proved very great – almost to the extent that operations were considered inadvisable without helicopter support. When bad weather intervened and prevented such support, this dependence had the effect of impeding tactical operations.

The helicopter is not a substitute for the infantryman. Infantry and Special Forces patrols, operating covertly for days or even a week or more, can often achieve much better results with the use of stealth and cunning than a more direct approach with aerial fire support and daily resupply by helicopter. The tactical disadvantages were recognized early on but were frequently disregarded. Lieutenant General Tolson quotes the remarks of an Australian officer during an after-action analysis of an air assault by the 173rd Airborne Brigade into War Zone D in July 1965: 'I would like someone to make an assessment to what extent do we lose the initiative by the excessive use of helicopters. By the use of them, the enemy can determine where you are and the strength you are in.' On the other hand, dummy insertions were sometimes made, causing a weary enemy to cover many a mile looking for non-existent troops.

Nevertheless, the difference between the First and Second Indo-China Wars, in the opinion of many, was the presence of the helicopter. It was widely believed that the French were defeated in the First Indo-China War because they found it difficult to move between their defensive enclaves and carry the fight to the Viet Minh. Their inevitable reliance on laborious ground movement, moreover, made them susceptible to ambush. US forces, by and large, had much greater freedom of movement, often travelling by helicopter. Thus they were much less open to ambush. Administratively, the American viewpoint was that the delivery of ammunition, food, water, cigarettes, mail and other amenities contributed greatly to the maintenance of morale, which was heightened by the thought that, if wounded, evacuation by helicopter would follow quickly.

While gunship fire support, and indeed close air support from tactical fighters, was often indispensable, its indiscriminate use sometimes backfired. The doctrine practised from quite early on by the British in Malaya and Borneo, where air power was subordinate to ground forces operations and every attempt was made to avoid civilian death and destruction, was not transferred to Vietnam. The temptation to apply fixed- and rotary-wing fire power in Vietnam was overwhelming, but the fact that it might not have been wholly appropriate, given the nature of the enemy, his weapons and the environment in which he operated, seems rarely to have been considered carefully enough.

The American concept of airmobility was not originally developed for the Vietnam War but principally for a sophisticated battlefield in Europe. Its aim was to permit the concentration and dispersion of forces under the threat of nuclear weapons. That it worked so well in mountainous jungle and swampy flatlands, in tropical downpour and high humidity, is a tribute to those who conceived and executed the concept. Indeed, proof of the American confidence in the concept came when General Westmoreland elected to use air assaults by the 1st Cavalry Division to relieve Khe Sanh under the unblinking gaze of the world's press.

The value of the air cavalry for reconnaissance and security was quickly appreciated. To exploit its full potential, however, it was recognized that immediately available reaction forces were necessary to follow up enemy contacts. Reconnaissance without reaction was wasteful. Thus, blue reaction and red fire teams were established to support white reconnaissance teams which were then free to continue surveillance and not become embroiled directly in the ground action. In the same way, 'Eagle Flights' and larger airmobile forces were ideal in being able rapidly to exploit unexpected and minor brushes with the enemy, who might otherwise have been able to fade away and avoid battle. Sometimes these contacts grew into major operations.

Where the Americans made advances on the French experience in Algeria was obviously in scale but also in being able to put their helicopters to greater use: widespread command and control and radio relay, almost unceasing surveillance allied to immediate attack, more sophisticated casualty evacuation, the deployment of artillery by air, the rapid insertion of large numbers of reinforcements, massive resupply and the comprehensive recovery of downed aircrew and aircraft. Darkness did not bring these operations to a halt. It was often said that the night belonged to the Viet Cong. This may have been partly true, but helicopter night operations helped to mitigate this advantage by putting pressure on the enemy, as well as giving a degree of protection to the helicopters.

Where, arguably, the Americans did not make full use of their helicopter power was in their efforts to win the hearts and minds of the South Vietnamese. Given the huge number of helicopters deployed throughout the country, more help could have been given to villagers in distress, notably more infrastructure and medical aid, and in the simple distribution of their pay to minor Government officials and small ARVN units in far-flung outposts, many of whom were in considerable arrears. Not only was this bad for morale but such a state of affairs sometimes resulted in these people seizing food from the local villagers without payment. The author spent many flying hours in Borneo distributing pay packets and medicines to the locals in addition to the occasional evacuation to hospital.

No operation can be expected to succeed without effective command and control, and airmobile operations were no exception. It was quickly discovered that the leader of a helicopter formation conducting an air assault could not control all the various contributing assets. Another helicopter, completely separate from the formation, was necessary to carry the operational commanders and, if ARVN, their senior US advisers; also an operations officer, an air liaison officer to organize tactical fighter support and an artillery officer to co-ordinate fire support. Often occupying the co-pilot's seat would be the officer nominated to command all the aviation elements involved in the operation. Flying out of harm's way and in secure voice communication with the ground commanders, the command group aboard the command post helicopter could observe the proceedings and conduct the operation like an orchestra. The art of command at battalion level was continually refined as ground troops, supported by air cavalry, artillery and tactical fighters, were employed together as a matter of routine.

Two important tactical lessons were prominent among a host of minor ones: air assault flight profiles and helicopter vulnerability. While the NVA and the Viet Cong were equipped mainly with small arms and light-calibre weapons, helicopters could safely transit at an altitude beyond the range of these weapons but in full view of the enemy; a high degree of security could be maintained by the careful selection of LZs which at the appropriate time often received a preparatory bombardment. But when the enemy started using heavier-calibre weapons and even surface-to-air missiles, during 'Lamson 719' for example, such tactics resulted in unacceptable losses. Operating in direct view of the enemy was simply too hazardous. The corollary was not to 'harden' the aircraft, although this was a useful measure, but to fly out of sight of the enemy – at very low level, at night, in restricted visibility, and by circuitous routes avoiding known enemy locations. In this way the unique capabilities of the helicopter in the low-speed regime could be properly exploited to surprise the enemy.

As the French had already discovered, the helicopter was not a vehicle that was easy to destroy. It could take a surprising number of hits without suffering catastrophic structural damage. Nevertheless, helicopter losses were enormous: 4,869, according to the Comptroller, Officer of the Secretary of Defense, attributable to the following causes:

	All Services	US Army
Combat Losses:	2,587	2,246
AA and small arms fire	2,373	2,069
Fighter aircraft	2	1
SAMs	7	6
Attacks on helicopter bases	205	170
Operational accidents:	2,282	2,075
Total:	4,869	4,321

The intensity of combat and number of sorties flown had a direct bearing on statistics. In 1967 1st Cavalry Division flew 977,983 sorties, had 688 aircraft hit but lost just 36 of them – a loss rate of one aircraft per 27,166 sorties. During the first six months of 1968 the division flew 407,806 sorties, had 271 aircraft hit and lost 66 – a loss rate of one aircraft per 6,179 sorties. This latter period encompassed heavy fighting during the Tet Offensive, the relief of Khe Sanh and the strike into the A Shau Valley.

Between January 1966 and December 1971 over 36,150,000 sorties were flown by US helicopters in South Vietnam. 2,094 helicopters were lost to hostile action and 2,209 to other operational causes (for example, accidents due to pilot error, technical malfunctions, mid-air collisions, etc). The combat loss rate during these six years alone was one helicopter every 18,193 sorties and to all causes one helicopter every 8,210 sorties. To the US Army's losses the UH-1, unsurprisingly, contributed the most: 1,211 lost to hostile action and another 1,380 in operational accidents. The fact that, very roughly, one loss in two was not due to combat points probably to the fatigue and stress suffered by air and ground crew. Tactics to increase combat effectiveness and improve survivability are under constant study; but attention needs to be paid to finding ways to reduce non-combat losses.

Aircrew, although the most vulnerable part of the man/machine combination, were by no means always lost with their helicopters. Some pilots managed to get themselves shot down more than a dozen times but CW 2 Steve Hall of the 176th Assault Helicopter Company may have set a record by being shot down and losing his helicopter four times in a single day, 20 September 1969. 'Slicks' were more attractive targets than gunships. For one thing they were less manoeuvrable and therefore easier to hit; they had more personnel on board, and infantry at that; and their return fire was much less deadly than that of gunships.

As the French had previously discovered, surprise is an important factor in any air assault although preparatory bombardments might cause its loss. Coming into a 'hot' LZ to disembark or extract troops is a very high-risk venture and not to be undertaken unless the risk is considered acceptable and co-ordinated support is available from all types of fire – fighter, artillery, gunship and any local ground-based weapons. Once surprise has been lost it is difficult, but not impossible, to sustain an airmobile operation for long, particularly if faced by a determined enemy who is intent on counter-attack, as was the case during 'Lamson 719'; Operation 'Masher-White Wing' proved the reverse when continuous contact was maintained with the enemy for 41 days. The security of LZs and fire bases is paramount. Airmobile or other troops must be deployed to guard them.

The advent of the purpose-designed gunship, embodied in the Cobra, stands out as one of the equipment innovations of the war. Despite the fact that the UH-1B and C were considered as no more than temporary gunships, they rendered useful service and were still operating at the end of the war. By then, however, the Cobra had filled the gap left by the unsuccessful Cheyenne and proved itself far superior as a responsive, hard-hitting weapon system, and one that could provide more intimate fire support to the ground forces than its predecessors.

The Vietnam War spawned a wide variety of helicopter weapons. Gunships required a weapon that could deter enemy personnel from firing at the 'Slicks' and for this quick-firing machine-guns and cannon proved suitable. For larger-area targets, soft-skinned vehicles, bunkers and similar targets, a rocket, or in some cases a grenade, was preferable. The 70mm (2.75in) unguided rocket was usually adequate. Door gunners in the 'Slicks' with pintle-mounted machine-guns were credited not only with effective defensive fire but also with achieving many enemy kills. Innovation was encouraged and led to such weapon systems as the 'Mad Bomber', where mortar bombs were dropped through two wooden chutes mounted in the cabin of a Huey, and the Chinook 'Go-Go Bird'. While the grenade-launcher did not long survive the end of the war, the experiences of 'Lamson 719' ensured the continuing development of anti-tank guided missiles. The relative failure against NVA tanks emphasized the urgency of making good a potential weakness in the European theatre where the Warsaw Pact tank threat was immeasurably larger. NATO did already have a few anti-tank helicopters armed with SS-11 missiles before 'Lamson 719' but the numbers were derisory. One year after 'Lamson 719' work on a new attack helicopter programme was begun, the AH-64 Apache eventually winning a competition and entering service a decade later.

Organizationally, the exploits of the two airmobile divisions, the 1st Cavalry and the 101st Airborne, proved that divisions with their own helicopters in sufficient numbers and of wide capability could achieve an initial shock impact and thereafter sustain the momentum that divisions less well endowed could not. The airmobile divisions were tailored to find the enemy, hold them in position and then destroy them. The constituent parts of the divisions were closely integrated, living, working and fighting together. They understood each other's strengths and weaknesses, what they could do and what they could not. The divisional commander had a priceless asset: his own helicopters, over 400 of them. He did not have to bid for them and could make his plans secure in the knowledge that he would get whatever helicopter support he wanted whenever he wanted it.

For the infantryman in the airmobile divisions there was never the feeling that he was fighting on his own. There would always be air cavalry overhead, gunship and ARA fire support, aerial resupply and, if the worst came to the worst, medical evacuation by air.

Some of the tactics and lessons of Vietnam apply to general war but some do not. In Europe and the desert, for example, the environment cannot be compared in terms of terrain, climate and the varying hours of daylight and darkness; while the enemy is likely to have different types of equipment and standards of training. In Vietnam the helicopter flew regularly over enemy-held territory and was opposed most of the time by light-calibre weapons. In general war the majority of helicopter operations, even now, will be conducted over friendly territory and the principal targets will be armoured fighting vehicles, not personnel. But time has not stood still and the experience gained in Vietnam has been used wisely. Continuous development, evaluations, trials and exercises have followed to ensure readiness for action in any theatre – the best way to prevent war.

Afghanistan (1979–89)

The War

In the early hours of 27 December 1979 Western capitals were notified by the Soviet Union that it was responding to an appeal by the Afghan Government to help repel 'external aggression'; limited forces would be used and as soon as the situation had been restored Soviet forces would be withdrawn. In fact, on Christmas Day two Soviet motor rifle divisions had crossed the River Amu Darya (Oxus) into Afghanistan on two routes. It was later reported that at much the same time a Spetsnaz (Special Forces) unit had attacked the Darulaman Palace in Kabul and killed President Hafizullah Amin. On 28 December it was announced that Babrak Karmal, head of the Parcham faction of the People's Democratic Party of Afghanistan (PDPA) and then in exile in the USSR, had taken over as President of the Revolutionary Council, General Secretary of the PDPA and as Prime Minister.

In April 1978 a revolution had taken place. The Afghan Government had been overthrown and replaced by the PDPA with its Marxist credentials. The already close relationship with the USSR was then strengthened and at the end of the year a Treaty of Friendship was signed. Soviet civil and military aid – advisers, tanks, aircraft and helicopters – was sent into Afghanistan.

Throughout 1979 opposition to the new Afghan Government's policies and left-wing ideology spread. It was unco-ordinated, however, being regional, tribal, ethnic and religious in nature; but there was general agreement that the Government was atheistic, intent upon the suppression of Islamic life and interfering too much in tribal affairs. Resistance was proclaimed to be a holy duty for all Moslems. Sporadic guerrilla (Mujaheddin) raids were launched against small Afghan Army posts and the country's infrastructure, but attempts to attack various towns were beaten back by armoured forces with air support. Nevertheless, it was clear by late autumn that the Government was steadily losing the ability to control the country outside the main cities. Doubts began to surface in Soviet minds as to whether Amin's Communist regime could survive. If it could not, a radical Islam-orientated regime might assume power and this could have serious repercussions for stability in Soviet Central Asia, given the rise of Islamic fundamentalism in the wake of Ayatollah Khomeini's seizure of power in Iran in February; furthermore, a Treaty of Friendship with the Soviet Union would be seen to be of little value if the Afghan Government was allowed to fall.

In August 1979 a team led by Army General Ivan Pavlovsky, Commander-in-Chief of Soviet Ground Forces and a veteran of the invasion of Czechoslovakia in 1968, and Army General Aleksei Epishev, Chief of the Main Political Directorate of the Armed Forces, was sent on a two-month visit to Afghanistan to assess the situation. The Soviet Army newspaper *Krasnaya Zvezda (Red Star)* claimed ten years later (18 November 1989) that the decision to invade was taken at an informal meeting between General Secretary Brezhnev, Foreign Minister Gromyko, KGB Chairman Andropov, Defence Minister Ustinov and two others – certainly not by the full Defence Council. According to that article and to Army General Valentin Varennikov quoted in the monthly magazine *Ogonyok* (in March 1989), the decision to invade was opposed on purely military grounds by many senior officers, including the Chief of the General Staff, Marshal of the Soviet Union Nikolai Ogarkov.

Although the main Soviet invasion had started on 25 December, the units involved were not the first into Afghanistan. As early as 7 July 1979 an airborne battalion had been deployed secretly to Bagram Air Base, 50km (31 miles) north of Kabul, to protect it; it was joined by elements of another in December. On 20 December these troops secured the Salang Pass, the crucial choke point on the road linking Kabul and the Soviet Union. Starting on Christmas Eve, a Soviet airborne division was flown into Kabul while other troops landed at Shindand and Kandahar. Including some 4,000 Soviet advisers, about 12,000 Soviet troops were therefore already in, or on their way to, Afghanistan before the two motor rifle divisions crossed the border.

Within a week of the invasion Soviet troops totalled at least 50,000 and by the end of February 1980 about 80,000 in six divisions. This force was known as the Limited Contingent of Soviet Forces in Afghanistan (LCSFA) and given the military designation of 40th Army. It received substantial logistic support from the adjacent Military Districts, principally the Turkestan. Its equipment included heavy armour and artillery, and it was supported by fighters and helicopters. The 40th Army was only strong enough to protect the main urban areas and provide a measure of security along the roads linking them. The Russians could not contemplate emulating the French quadrillage system or the widespread American deployment in South Vietnam. If they wished to carry the fight to the Mujaheddin and attempt to regain control of the countryside, then a much larger force would be needed. They could not rely on the Afghan Army which had already suffered grievous losses through combat casualties and mass desertions and was no longer an effective fighting force.

During 1980 a further 5,000 to 10,000 Soviet troops were brought in and the inexperienced reservists who had participated in the invasion were replaced by regular troops. These measures barely affected Soviet options. Action was now taken to improve airfields and lines of communication, and build barracks and storage facilities, all indications that the Soviet presence was not going to be short-lived.

In March 1980, during a large operation in the eastern provinces, it became apparent that Soviet equipment and tactics, designed for a European battlefield, were not suited to the terrain, climatic conditions or Mujaheddin tactics. In particular, tanks could not manoeuvre in the mountains and had little value except as defensive strongpoints; motor rifle troops were reluctant to get out of their vehicles and fight on foot, and thus became easy targets. Some tank, air defence and missile units belonging to the invading divisions were therefore replaced by more infantry and helicopters. Given that Soviet troop strength never even reached 120,000, it would seem that an early decision was taken not to emulate the Americans in South Vietnam and escalate the fighting, but to try to achieve better results with more suitable tactics, better trained troops and more appropriate equipment.

The early introduction of Soviet domestic policies added up to creeping 'Sovietization' of the Afghan way of life, at least in the urban areas. This did nothing to increase popular support for the Karmal regime. Indeed, resistance grew although hampered by a lack of co-ordination between the six principal Mujaheddin groups. Serious shortages of modern military equipment also restricted their capabilities and effectiveness. Politically, the Mujaheddin were virtually bankrupt, having little to offer but a rejection of the PDPA Government and its Marxist ideals.

As Tunisia and Morocco had provided sanctuary for the fellaghas fighting against the French, and Cambodia and Laos safe havens for the North Vietnamese and Viet Cong, so Pakistan soon found itself inundated with refugees from Afghanistan (as did Iran to a lesser degree) and as a base in which the Mujaheddin groups could locate their HQ to plan their operations, organize their supply lines, and rest and recuperate.

On the death of Leonid Brezhnev, the Soviet leader, in May 1982 Yuri Andropov assumed power and he was succeeded in February 1984 by Konstantin Chernenko. Both new leaders appeared reluctant to raise the stakes in Afghanistan for fear of the extra manpower and financial costs and the probable further loss of influence world-wide. By the end of 1983 the war had become one of attrition with both sides trying to show that the other could not win. The result was a frustrating and debilitating stalemate with no prospect of either side gaining the upper hand militarily or of the regime expanding its internal power base or popular support.

Soviet troop strength had risen to about 115,000 by the end of 1984 with perhaps a further 35,000 or more giving assistance from the Turkestan and Central Asian Military Districts. The Afghan Army could barely muster 35,000. These allied forces were numerically inadequate to defeat the Mujaheddin, estimated to be 200,000–250,000 men, although in 200 to 300 groups with conflicting aims and unable to combine long enough to inflict any lasting damage on Soviet and Afghan forces. The war was thus fought more at the provincial rather than regional or even national level.

Soviet and Afghan troops were still largely committed to guarding Kabul and the other major cities and protecting convoy traffic supplying them with food and raw materials. A more offensive task, mainly for Soviet forces, was to attack Mujaheddin bands who threatened the lines of communication and their infiltration routes across the Afghan-Pakistan border. To offset the Mujaheddin's superior ability to move across difficult country and their knowledge of the terrain, the Russians stepped up their use of mines and probably chemical weapons; helicopters and airmobile infantry in the shape of Spetsnaz, parachute and air assault troops bore the brunt of the more mobile warfare.

In an effort to increase pressure on the Mujaheddin while minimizing Soviet casualties, intensified use of air power was made in support of ground operations. It was also believed by the Russians that they could destroy support for the Mujaheddin and inhibit their operations by bombing villages thought to be sympathetic and destroying crops and water supplies. This policy certainly had the effect of depopulating many rural areas and reducing material support for the Mujaheddin. But the Karmal regime's attempts at pacification (local truces, holding large meetings (jirgas) to discuss complaints against local government officials, etc) were doomed to failure because of its continuing strong-arm terror tactics and the incompetence and venality of the PDPA. At best the Government had control over no more than about 20 per cent of the population.

On 11 March 1985 Mikhail Gorbachev became the Soviet leader. Hints of a reassessment of Soviet policy surfaced in his report to the 27th Party Congress in February 1986 when he described Afghanistan as a 'bleeding wound'. Although not perhaps a Soviet 'Vietnam', the costs in financial terms, casualties and international prestige were nevertheless becoming prohibitive. In July 1986 Mr Gorbachev promised to withdraw six Soviet regiments (these included one tank and three air defence regiments, the latter having been quite superfluous since the Mujaheddin had no aircraft) by the end of the year as evidence of his desire to reach a political settlement rather than a military one. In December the new PDPA leader, Major General Mohammed Najibullah, who had taken over from Karmal in May, announced a plan for national reconciliation and declared a six-month unilateral cease-fire. The conditions attached to the plan, however, were quite unacceptable to the Mujaheddin who quickly rejected it and the cease-fire.

A change in Soviet tactics was apparent in 1986. Rather than trying to stop the flow of weapons across the border from Pakistan, bombing civilian targets and reacting to Mujaheddin operations, a more offensive posture was adopted. The aim now was for élite troops to seek out and destroy Mujaheddin strongholds and their supply and infiltration routes. Spetsnaz and heliborne troops undertook a series of operations in the areas bordering Pakistan. They were generally limited in scale and not completely successful, partly because the greater exposure to direct combat led to higher casualties and, without any increase in manpower, the Russians were unable to retain occupation of the areas they had captured. 1986 was also the year that the Mujaheddin received their first Western shoulder-launched surface-to-air missiles, which were to have a profound effect on the course of the war.

For the Russians 1987 proved to be a dismal and discouraging year. As the Americans stepped up the supply of sophisticated weapons and non-lethal aid such as radios, clothing and medical supplies, Mujaheddin resistance to the Government stiffened. By now they had received a fair quantity of heavy weapons and had learnt that co-operation between their rival factions was vital if the war was to be prosecuted with any real chance of success. This co-operation and a greater degree of professionalism forced the 40th Army once more onto the defensive.

Such was the military situation that Mr Gorbachev was faced with a difficult decision. It was becoming more and more apparent that the LCSFA could not contain the Mujaheddin. The policy of 'national reconciliation' was showing no signs of success. Heeding the American experience in Vietnam, the Russians were not keen to pour in more troops and strengthen their presence. Furthermore, Mr Gorbachev now appeared to believe that domestic factors within the USSR and Soviet interests world-wide had become more important than the Soviet involvement in Afghanistan. The time had arrived to staunch the 'bleeding wound'.

In February 1988 Mr Gorbachev announced that Soviet troops would begin to withdraw from Afghanistan on 15 May provided that the USA and Pakistan did not interfere. But the adverse situation had forced a change in Soviet policy: the withdrawal no longer depended on the formation of an Afghan Government of national reconciliation. After eight years supporting the Communist Government at great cost, the Soviet leader was now, in effect, leaving it to its fate.

The withdrawal began on schedule and by 15 August half of the 40th Army was back inside the USSR. There was then a pause in the withdrawal schedule, until January 1989. On 15 February the last convoy crossed the River Amu Darya into the Soviet Union, the last man to leave being Lieutenant General Boris Gromov, the Commander of the 40th Army.

The Environment

Afghanistan, with an area of 650,000km^2 (250,000sq miles), is not a big country compared with its neighbours but two and a half times the size of the UK. Landlocked, it has only one natural border, the River Amu Darya, to the north of which lies Soviet Central Asia. The western border with Iran wanders through very desolate terrain until it meets the Pakistan frontier in the south-west. The immensely long border with Pakistan then goes east for some 520km (320 miles) before turning north-east and snaking its way through the mountains up to the Wakhan Corridor, where there is an 80km (50-mile) common border with China. None of these borders has deli-neated tribal areas, the nomadic people being no respecters of international agreements.

The Hindu Kush Mountains are the most important geographical feature and constitute an almost impenetrable barrier to ground movement;

they also pose major problems for helicopters. Starting in the Pamirs in the Wakhan Corridor, where some peaks exceed 6,000m (20,000ft), this enormous range runs mainly south-west until it reaches a point about 160km (100 miles) north of Kabul where it then opens out like a fan. The main range, rarely reaching above 5,000m (16,400ft) runs due west while spokes lie to either side. The Hindu Kush divide the country into three regions. In the north, fertile foothills slope down to the plains which extend to the Amu Darya. The central part of the country consists largely of high mountains bisected by deep and narrow valleys. On the eastern frontier passes cut through the mountains, the most famous being the Khyber Pass linking Peshawar in Pakistan with Jalalabad. The Salang Highway, with its long road tunnel, is a strategic route through the Hindu Kush linking Kabul with the Soviet Union. The south and south-west is a region of high plateaux and sandy deserts. Only the River Helmand delta in the south-west and the area along the Amu Darya are below 600m (2,000ft).

About 90 per cent of Afghans live in the cities and towns, the remainder being village farmers or nomads and herdsmen. The cities are usually based on rivers which have debouched out of the mountains and into the plains. Kabul, the capital, is situated at about 1,800m (6,000ft). To the west it is dominated by the Kuh-e-Baba mountains and to the north by the Hindu Kush. Kandahar controls the routes through the deserts of the south, which then connect with those passing round the western side of the Hindu Kush;

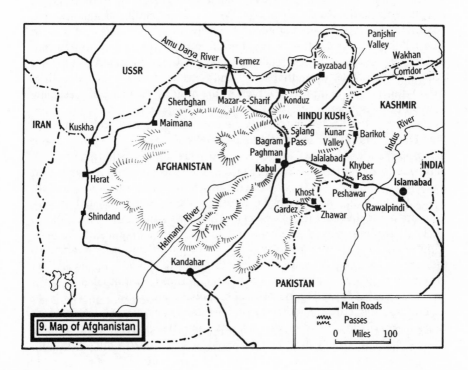

9. Map of Afghanistan

they continue on through Shindand and Herat to Kushka in the USSR. To the north the main cities are Konduz and Mazar-e-Sharif.

Some 480km (300 miles) from the sea and cut off from the Indian monsoon winds by the eastern mountains, Afghanistan has a dry and continental climate conditioned more by altitude than latitude. The seasons are well defined with cold air from the north bringing heavy snowfalls and very low temperatures in the Hindu Kush in winter; winds from the south-east and south-west produce hot and dry summers with high humidity and cloudless skies. Extremes of temperature affected both helicopter air and ground crew, while blowing sand caused damage, particularly to rotor blades and engines. Average rainfall in the south-west is about 7.5cm (3in), 35cm (14in) in Kabul and 140cm (55in) in the area of the Salang Pass.

The Initial Deployments

Throughout January and February 1980 Soviet ground forces poured into Afghanistan to garrison the major cities and some smaller towns. They were accompanied by no more than about 60 helicopters. The main helicopter base was Kabul International Airport while Bagram, Kandahar, Konduz, Jalalabad and Shindand were also host to helicopter units of varying size. From the very first day, helicopters were in action – on route reconnaissance and casualty evacuation – against Mujaheddin forces that were close to the Salang Highway or who threatened Kabul Airport. Helicopter traffic at Kabul was said to be so heavy that it interfered with normal airline operations and the Soviet air-bridge. With their unparalleled mobility and flexibility, helicopters quickly made themselves indispensable and it is no wonder that during 1980 their number more than quadrupled to approximately 250, to add to those already nominally with the Afghan Air Force. By now it had become clear that the 'Hind' was much more effective than fixed-wing aircraft in attacking targets in the mountains; many of these new helicopters were therefore 'Hinds'.

The principal Soviet helicopters were all Mil-designed and comprised the 'Hook' and 'Hip' for troop and freight lift and the 'Hind' attack helicopter; a few 'Hoplites' for general duties are also thought to have been deployed to Afghanistan. Since perhaps as many as 60 'Hind As' had been delivered to the Kabul regime before the invasion – of which most, if not all, were allegedly flown by Soviet pilots – the majority of helicopters accompanying the invading forces were 'Hips', with only a few 'Hind Ds'.

The 'Hoplites' played no significant role and they may well have been withdrawn quite early in the war due to their poor flying performance; or they may have been handed over to the Afghan Air Force. They have seats for eight passengers and can be armed. In addition to normal liaison tasks they were probably used for occasional reconnaissance.

By 1980 the 'Hook' had been in service for twenty years. It has a large cargo hold with rear-loading doors and a ramp which permits vehicles to drive directly into it. It can carry a payload of 12,000kg (26,455lb) internally or 8,000kg (17,637lb) as an underslung load. The 'Hook' has space for 65 lightly equipped troops or 41 stretchers and two medical attendants. Not only is it capable of heavy lift but it also has a creditable cruising speed of 250km/hr (155mph), helped, uniquely among transport helicopters, by having stub wings to offload the main rotor in forward flight. In accordance with Soviet philosophy even this huge helicopter is armed: a single-barrelled 12.7mm machine-gun is located in the nose. The number of 'Hooks' in Afghanistan remained more or less constant throughout the war at about 40.

At least three military versions of the 'Hip' probably entered Afghanistan with the invading forces, together with some Mi-8Ts in Aeroflot markings. The basic transport helicopter of the Soviet Air Force, the Mi-8T 'Hip C' can accommodate 24 troops or carry a load of 4,000kg (8,818lb). In operational service it is usually armed, typically with four pods containing sixteen 57mm unguided rockets each. The removable outriggers to which these pods are attached can also carry 250kg (550lb) bombs. Some of the helicopter units probably included a more heavily armed assault version of the 'Hip', the Mi-8TB 'Hip E'. This variant can carry 192 rockets in six pods; four AT-2 'Swatter' anti-tank guided missiles (ATGMs), two on either side, are mounted on top of the outriggers. These missiles have a maximum range of 4,000m and, like the French SS-11, are useful for firing into caves and at sangars. In the nose of the 'Hip E' is a traversable 12.7mm machine-gun. Even with all this armament and a full fuel load, the 'Hip E' can lift fourteen troops. The hot and high conditions to be found in Afghanistan, however, seriously degraded its performance, and also that of the 'Hip C'. After some months' experience with the 'Hip E' it may have been decided that this type had no specific role in Afghanistan, given the presence of the 'Hip' transports and 'Hind' attack helicopters. Futhermore, without armour plating and basically soft-skinned, the 'Hip' is vulnerable even to small arms fire. Thus the 'Hip E' was probably withdrawn before the end of 1980. In 1974 the 'Hip D', a converted C model, appeared in the USSR as an airborne command post helicopter, and it is quite likely that a few were brought into Afghanistan in the wake of the invasion.

The 'Hind' was a new breed of Soviet helicopter. Having observed the activities of American gunships in Vietnam, the Russians decided in the mid-1960s to develop their own gunship. They were not, however, convinced of the need for a dedicated two-seat attack helicopter in the mould of the Cheyenne and Cobra. What was wanted was a helicopter which could insert combat troops into a defended area using the helicopter's own weapons to suppress enemy fire. These requirements pointed to a fast and well-protected helicopter with integrated weapons, unlike the strap-on armaments of the 'Hip', and a cabin which could accommodate eight combat troops and to which there was quick and easy entry and exit.

Survivability became a major design factor after senior military officers had expressed doubts that an attack helicopter could compete in the sort of battle intensities anticipated for Central Europe during the last quarter of the century. Hand-in-hand with survivability went flying performance. Every effort was made to give the new helicopter a high speed and various measures were adopted to achieve this, including a retractable under-carriage and a small frontal area. In the event, cruising speed for the latest models of the 'Hind' is quoted as 280km/hr (174mph) and maximum speed as 335km/hr (208mph).

The 'Hind A' entered operational service in 1972. It had a large single cockpit housing both the pilot and the co-pilot/gunner. It was heavily armed with a 12.7mm machine-gun in the nose and on stub wings it carried four weapons pylons able to take 64 × 57mm unguided rockets in four pods, or four bombs; two 'Swatter' missiles were mounted on rails at each stub wing tip. At each of the eight windows in the cabin was a mounting which allowed the troops on board to fire their personal weapons while airborne. The 'Hind A's' performance as a combat helicopter exceeded Soviet expectations and it was decided to exploit it further. So in the mid-1970s more powerful engines were installed and significant other modifica-tions made; the new variant was designated 'Hind D' by NATO. This model has a completely redesigned front fuselage section with individual cockpits for the gunner in the front and the pilot above and behind him. The 12.7mm gun was replaced by a four-barrelled 12.7mm machine-gun in a turret under the nose. It has a rate of fire of some 4,000 rounds per minute. 32-shot 57mm rocket pods became an alternative to the 16-shot pods.

It is not known when the Mi-24V 'Hind E' first entered Afghanistan but it was probably during 1980. This variant is distinguished by having AT-6 'Spiral' ATGMs instead of 'Swatters'. The 'Spiral' has a longer range, is more lethal and much faster than its predecessor. Obviously the faster the missile and the greater its range, the less vulnerable the helicopter is when launching it.

Like the French in the early stages of their war in Algeria, the Russians soon discovered that they were ill-trained and improperly equipped for a guerrilla war against an elusive, hardy and brave enemy. Most of their attention had previously been focused on fighting a conventional war in Europe, which emphasized high-speed offensives with massed tanks and mechanized infantry combat vehicles. They had not been trained in counter-insurgency or mountain warfare and their traditional reliance on armoured fighting vehicles tied them to the roads and valley floors. It was difficult for ground vehicles to manoeuvre into positions to fire at the enemy, often above them, and their movement was sometimes constrained by mines. Measures to protect convoys from ambush had not been thought through and counter-ambush drills were often poorly executed. The absence of reconnaissance patrols and flank protection played into the hands of the more fleet-footed Mujaheddin.

The first offensives in March 1980, undertaken by large armoured formations, aimed to gain control of the key areas adjacent to the Pakistan border. A major incursion, preceded by a heavy artillery bombardment, was made into the Kunar Valley but no blocking troops were inserted by helicopter to prevent the Mujaheddin repeatedly ambushing the tanks before they escaped. As the Soviet force withdrew the Mujaheddin returned. Other similar operations quickly became bogged down in the mountainous terrain. Moreover, Soviet reaction to Mujaheddin attacks and their first attempts at cordon and search operations were slow, ponderous and largely unsuccessful. Such failures forced a change in tactics. As in Algeria and Vietnam, air power, fixed- and rotary-wing, was seen as being one way of redressing the balance. Another way was to employ smaller units and give them helicopter mobility which would allow greater flexibility and increase speed of reaction.

A major problem for the 40th Army was its lack of helicopters, a shortcoming that was never to be resolved fully; a second was the inadequate preparation of the pilots for their role in Afghanistan. While they were informed generally of their 'internationalist duty', little seems to have been done to tailor their flying training, while still in the Soviet Union, for the conditions in Afghanistan to which they were unaccustomed. Soviet Press reports indicated that mountain flying skills, so vital for the Hindu Kush, were generally at a low level. Flying in mountains requires practice and certain techniques to cope with the physiological effects of lack of oxygen (unless extra is specifically provided), the possibility of suffering from vertigo, and apprehension to a greater or lesser degree. Furthermore, there is no normal visual horizon when approaching to land on a pinnacle; weather conditions can change rapidly and the winds are often high and variable. It is not always easy to tell from which direction the wind is coming. To the usual problems associated with hot and high conditions then must be added severe turbulence and strong up- and downdraughts. Operations in these desolate and snow-covered mountains in winter posed problems of a different kind. For example, in poor visibility flying near slopes and assessing the radius of a turn in a narrowing valley demand great care.

Having arrived in the hover above the landing site, Soviet pilots frequently found that there was insufficient space to get all wheels on the ground. So sometimes they did not land at all, or they had to hold a hover with perhaps only one wheel touching. There were other times when they had to set a wheel down on a ledge with the rotor blades perilously close to a rock face. In any conditions on a pinnacle or ledge, this demands no ordinary skill, but when the hover has to be held for some minutes while loading or unloading is undertaken, and possibly with blowing snow or sand and when also under fire, strong nerves and courage are also needed. Soviet crews quickly found themselves visiting tiny platforms in the mountains at heights of 3,000m (9,850ft) and more. Stories of calamity and heroism in the mountains eventually found their way into the Soviet military press.

For the first year of the war or more Soviet helicopter crews seemed to have a rather low opinion of Mujaheddin fighting ability; indeed, Abdul

Haq, a Mujaheddin leader, confessed in an interview that at this stage combat helicopters were really feared. Moving so quickly, they gave little warning of their approach and therefore the Mujaheddin insufficient time to prepare to engage them or withdraw. The rebels did not know if the helicopters were about to attack them, land troops or were merely en route to somewhere else. Abdul Haq admitted that the Mujaheddin had no proper weapons to defend themselves. 'Hind' crews seemed to agree, believing that the aged 0.303in Lee-Enfield and Martini Henry rifles, Soviet 7.62mm AK-47 Kalashnikov rifles brought by Afghan Army deserters, and other small-calibre weapons with which the Mujaheddin were armed, were no match for their own heavier weapons, speed and armour protection. Thus these crews took few precautions to avoid Mujaheddin fire, sometimes almost hover-taxiing towards rebel positions or diving in full view of them from altitude and then closing to within range of rebel weapons. By 1981, however, after suffering losses and other damage to helicopters from these weapons and perhaps a few 12.7mm machine-guns as well, a more healthy regard for the Mujaheddin's military skills forced a change in tactics. Helicopters were ordered to transit at altitudes out of range of small arms and machine-gun fire before descending to as low a level as possible as they approached their targets. Fire was to be opened at greater ranges and other helicopters were to be used for reconnaissance and the acquisition of targets. Nevertheless, cases were reported of 'Hind' crews flying over known Mujaheddin air defence sites and failing to take evasive action when fired upon.

For the helicopter force 1980 had been a year of expansion, building up the support base with particular regard to holdings of spare parts, ammunition and fuel, abandoning preconceived tactical ideas and developing new tactics and techniques to suit enemy, terrain and climate, training in these new techniques and then putting them to the test in combat. By the end of the year open Western sources generally agree that Soviet helicopter units were deployed as follows:

- *Bagram*: 262 Helicopter Squadron
- *Fayzabad*: Helicopter squadron (detached from 181 Regiment at Konduz)
- *Jalalabad*: 335 Helicopter Regiment
- *Kabul*: Helicopter squadron
- *Kandahar*: 280 Helicopter Regiment
- *Konduz*: 181 Helicopter Regiment (less one squadron at Fayzabad)
- *Shindand*: Helicopter squadron.

Equipment Improvements

Apart from extra helicopters delivered to make good losses and perhaps a few to boost the holdings of understrength units, no helicopters were deployed to Afghanistan for the next two or three years. Steps were taken, however, to increase the effectiveness of the 'Hind' and 'Hip' and reduce their vulnerability to the growing number of Soviet-built shoulder-launched SA-7 SAMs getting into the hands of the Mujaheddin from 1982.

The Americans had pioneered protection devices for their helicopters and the Russians decided to follow their example. By 1983 'Hinds' and 'Hips' were to be seen ejecting decoy flares from dispensers strapped to the underside of the rear end of their tailbooms. Fired out to both sides of the fuselage, these flares were designed to decoy heat-seeking missiles away from the helicopter. The dispenser contained 128 flares and could be programmed to fire them singly, in pairs or in greater numbers. However, TV film of 'Hinds' and 'Hips' releasing flares seems to indicate that they were fired pre-emptively at intervals of about two to five seconds whenever the crew believed there was a threat, rather than automatically when integrated with a missile approach warner.

This was not the only measure taken. An infra-red (IR) jammer was mounted on a plinth on the top of the aft end of the cabin. Consisting of a cylindrical source emitting modulated IR energy much greater than that of the helicopter itself, the jammer seeks to confuse the missile's IR-seeker. The Americans had fitted scoops to the exhausts of some of their Hueys to deflect the exhaust gases upwards into the rotor downwash which then helped to cool and disperse them. The Russians fitted ribbed 'boxes' over the exhausts which also redirected the gases up into the downwash.

Experience had shown that when fired the SA-7 had a conspicuous white plume which revealed the position of launch which could then be attacked; furthermore, the missile's heat-seeking head was not very selective and tended to lock on to more or less anything hot. As a rule, however, it would not lock on to approaching targets and therefore could only be used against those that had already overflown the firer. The SA-7 was not an easy weapon to operate and considerable skill and training were necessary to ensure success. These weaknesses, together with the counter-measures, rendered the SA-7 largely useless and gave renewed confidence to the helicopter crews.

The standard rocket armament of both 'Hinds' and 'Hips' at this time was the 57mm unguided rocket. As respect for the Mujaheddin grew helicopter crews were less keen to get too close to them. Not only would a larger-calibre rocket offer greater lethality but also a longer range. Thus it was no surprise when 'Hinds' but not 'Hips' began to appear with 80mm rockets. Neither the 16-shot nor the 32-shot 57mm rocket pod was compatible with such a calibre, so a blunt-nosed pod to contain 20 rockets was produced; thus the 'Hind' could carry 80 × 80mm rockets.

In the same way that the 57mm rocket had inadequate range and destructive power, so the 'Hind's' 12.7mm Gatling gun was deemed insufficient as the sole means of machine-gun fire. Pylon-mounted pods for a 23mm cannon were a weapon option for 'Hinds' in Eastern Europe; such an option was needed even more urgently in Afghanistan.

Helicopter Roles

Despite the relatively small number of helicopters involved in Afghanistan (compared with Vietnam) it is no surprise that the conflict was dubbed by some commentators the 'Helicopter War'. In addition to the roles undertaken by helicopters in Algeria and Vietnam, Soviet helicopters were used regularly to provide protection for air bases and transport aircraft landing and taking off from them, to escort road convoys, to act as airborne radio relay stations in the mountains when communications were intermittent or impossible, to bomb and to lay mines. In the first couple of years helicopters were employed without much imagination or account being taken of the special circumstances obtaining in Afghanistan. Aircraft handling and tactical standards left something to be desired. Training in some techniques had not been given before leaving the USSR. But as experience was gained and pilots returned for second tours, tactics were refined and skill levels rose. Operations at night became less of a rarity, although no special night vision equipment seems to have been supplied.

Convoy Escort

The support for convoys absorbed a considerable flying effort. By the end of the first year, having suffered personnel and vehicle losses and much disruption to their road convoys, the Russians had learnt to picquet high ground overlooking convoy routes. Thereafter, no important or large convoy was without helicopter support. Troops were placed by a few 'Hips' in locations where they could dominate the route from both sides prior to the arrival of a convoy. As soon as it had passed, the helicopters returned to collect the troops and leapfrog them to another position. This tactic was itself hazardous if the Mujaheddin had got there first. Preparatory artillery and multiple rocket fire was thus put down on these and other likely rebel ambush positions, and followed up by fighter-bomber and helicopter gunship attacks. One or two pairs of 'Hinds' would usually reconnoitre a few kilometres ahead of the leading ground force elements, laying down suppressive fire. Others would escort the 'Hips' emplacing the flank protection parties on the crags overlooking the route and provide support for them, while yet others (if available) would remain overhead the convoy itself, ready to attack any targets that presented themselves or help if the convoy was ambushed.

As the convoy progressed, helicopters from one airfield would hand over their guard responsibilities to others at the next airfield down the route. All helicopters would be on the same communications net as the convoy itself, the traffic control and guard posts along the route and security forces on call. These escort tactics helped to reduce the chances of rebel ambush, but the Mujaheddin soon learnt to keep out of the way until the convoy was almost abreast of the ambush site before moving into position. Where appropriate the aim was often to destroy the leading couple of vehicles and the last two, thus trapping the remainder.

Close Air Support

As the principal means of close air support (CAS) the 'Hind' was allegedly the most feared weapon used by the Russians in Afghanistan. Able to manoeuvre in the steep-sided valleys, unlike fixed-wing fighters, the 'Hind' could bring its fire to bear on most targets. Flying more slowly, it was easier for the 'Hind' to acquire the target, usually a group of individuals with man-portable weapons, than it was for the much faster fighter-bombers which were better suited to the lower, wider valleys and desert plains. Further-more, the 'Hind' also had to substitute for tank and artillery fire since such weapon systems were often unable to manoeuvre in the difficult terrain and were too slow to react to Mujaheddin attacks.

The basic attack unit was a pair of 'Hinds' with the wingman flying between 100 and 500 metres behind and to one side of his leader. Because of the 'Hind's' poor hover and low-speed performance – and the lessons learnt during 1980 and 1981 – comparatively high-speed attacks were conducted with fire being opened at the maximum effective range of the selected weapon. Having made their final approach at low level, the 'Hinds' would, if necessary, climb quite steeply to allow the gunner to acquire the target and enable a shallow and stable dive towards it. As soon as possible they would turn away, possibly to re-position for another pass. While they did so another pair would usually go into the attack. To get the greatest weight of firepower onto the target in the shortest possible time, and thus prevent the Mujaheddin moving out of danger, more than two pairs were sometimes employed if enough 'Hinds' were available. The low-level tactics presented something of a problem: flying a helicopter weighing some 11,500kg (25,353lb) and with poor manoeuvrability close to the ground required skill, comprehensive training and constant practice.

The mountainous terrain often forced the attacking helicopters to use the same flight path to run in to the target, which allowed the rebels to scramble out of the way or realign their weapons. There were many occasions, however, when the helicopters could have run in from different directions but nevertheless still adhered to the same flight pattern, a hangover from unimaginative training routines; some pilots complained of the risk, sometimes to no avail. The terrain and such tactics combined to make it difficult for the 'Hind' formations to conceal themselves. The Mujaheddin quickly learnt to appreciate the most likely direction of approach and that to attack targets in the valleys helicopters had to descend below the hilltops. Positioned well above the valley floor, the rebels could then shoot down on them. This was particularly true of the Panjshir Valley where the mountains reach 3,000m (9,840ft) above the valley floor. To bomb and strafe the villages clustered along the River Panjshir, 'Hinds' and 'Hips' were thus vulnerable to guerrillas lying in wait above them with heavy machine-guns. With no protection on the upper surfaces, some helicopters were allegedly brought down. The Mujaheddin also learnt to let the formation leader pass and attack his wingman or the last aircraft in the formation.

According to the Mujaheddin, very few Soviet and Afghan ground operations went ahead without helicopter CAS, accompanied usually by a few fixed-wing aircraft such as the Su-17 'Fitter', Su-25 'Frogfoot' or MiG-21 'Fishbed'. As with convoy escort, it was standard practice to carry out a preparatory bombardment to pulverize the operational area, isolate it from reinforcements and cut off escape routes.

Bombing

A role for the 'Hind' and 'Hip' for which there seems to be little opening in the heavily air-defended territory of Europe is bombing. Both helicopter types can carry 250kg (550lb) or 500kg (1,100lb) bombs. But against lightly armed guerrillas and unarmed civilians the risk inherent in overflying the target was considered acceptable, particularly if delayed-action fuses were used. Thus both 'Hinds' and 'Hips' were used in this role to bomb Mujaheddin bases and storage depots, recalcitrant villages, water supplies, crops, defiles and any other targets which might contribute to the Mujaheddin's well-being and freedom of movement. The underlying scorched-earth policy appeared to be one of depopulating selected areas by denying the use of fertile land, thus forcing the inhabitants to flee to Pakistan and Iran and become refugees – and later often willing recruits to the rebel cause.

During the winter and early spring, when even some main roads through the mountains were closed, the majority of Mujaheddin bases could only be attacked by air – by heliborne forces or aircraft-delivered ordnance. Helicopter bombing was conducted on a regular basis and sometimes large numbers of helicopters were involved. For example, in October 1985 eighteen 'Hinds' bombed Paghman, west of Kabul, and in April 1986 a similar number bombed the area around Kandahar in retaliation for Mujaheddin attacks on convoys; twelve helicopters were said to have been shot down on this occasion.

US State Department reports claimed that helicopters also dropped chemical bombs and canisters of gas. The lethal, non-persistent 'yellow rain' was used to attack Mujaheddin strongholds and villages thought to be giving the rebels support. Another form of 'bombing' was leaflet-dropping. Helicopters sometimes scattered leaflets over towns and villages to spread information and propaganda and to deliver threats – all part of the psychological war.

Command and Control

The role of the 'Hip D' as an airborne command post has already been mentioned. Command and control from a helicopter was similar to that practised by the Americans in Vietnam but not brought to such a degree of refinement. Because of the mountainous terrain communications were often difficult, if not impossible, and helicopters and fixed-wing transport aircraft were then used as radio relay stations. The Mujaheddin reported seeing and hearing aircraft and helicopters flying race-track patterns out of harm's way during Soviet and Afghan operations. Such airborne posts were dubbed 'Flying Kremlins'.

The prevailing circumstances forced something of a relaxation of the normally tight ground control of air force operations as practised in Europe and gave added impetus and importance to FACs. These officers were usually pilots but, more often than not, ground-based with the unit requiring air support. In the early days, due to lack of experience and the extremely fluid battle situation, airborne FACs sometimes lost their bearings and directed fire onto their own troops. To prevent the possibility of such disasters recurring, aircrew learnt to ask the FAC, whether ground-based or airborne, to reveal his location by means of a smoke grenade and then give a heading and range to the target from this position. The formation leader might then make a pass to get his fire adjusted by the FAC before the formation's main attack.

Whereas NATO artillery forward observation officers would have been carried in helicopters to correct artillery and rocket fire from the air, the Russians set less store by this technique and it seems to have been undertaken only rarely. But such officers were often taken by helicopters to points on the ground from which they could observe the fall of shot and thus direct this fire.

Reconnaissance

Both the 'Hind' and the 'Hip' included reconnaissance among their roles. The 'Hip' used to carry ground commanders who wished to check routes and objectives. Generally, reconnaissance into a forthcoming area of operations was not conducted so as not to alert the Mujaheddin. Instead, a transit flight in a 'Hip' over the area had to suffice. Photographs might be taken and from these and maps a terrain mock-up would be constructed.

Before the American Stinger SAM reached the Mujaheddin in 1986 it was quite common for tactical 'Hind' sub-units to be accompanied by a single 'Hind', and occasionally 'Hip', acting as a reconnaissance and command and control aircraft. This helicopter would stay at altitude and try to locate the origin of fire directed at the attacking 'Hinds'. Another 'Hind' pair would then be directed to attack the rebels.

Although no evidence is to hand to show that Soviet helicopters carried out systematic surveillance of selected areas on a daily basis, as was done in both Algeria and Vietnam, it is probable that at least certain infiltration routes and choke points were kept under more or less constant observation by means of ground observation posts inserted by helicopter and by helicopter patrols. Actually seeing Mujaheddin foot patrols from the air against the background of rocks and bushes could not have been easy once the Mujaheddin learnt to stay still and not scatter when they heard helicopters approaching.

In interviews and articles Soviet helicopter pilots mentioned carrying out reconnaissance at night. Few details were given but it is more likely that what in fact was usually undertaken was surveillance of selected areas and routes, either to try to see what was happening or to deter movement. One way of achieving this would have been for fixed-wing aircraft to drop slow-burning illumination flares while the helicopters, at a much lower level, attempted to pick up any movement. Flying at night in mountainous terrain is extremely hazardous; while flares help in some respects, they also cast shadows and distort perspectives.

Troop Lift

In addition to the normal administrative carriage of personnel from one place to another, by the second half of 1981 helicopters were being used for troop lift in combat operations. Prior to a cordon, search and destroy mission by tanks and motor rifle troops, detachments, often of parachutists, were lifted into several blocking positions – the anvil to the hammer of the mechanized forces. The aim was to prevent reinforcements reaching the Mujaheddin and to stifle any endeavours at escaping the main attacking force. These heliborne troops were sometimes also able to attack the rebels from unexpected directions and, in co-ordination with other ground forces, to attempt encirclement.

Later in the war, according to the Mujaheddin, Spetsnaz groups of about 50 men were sometimes transported by helicopter to attack specific targets, such as storage depots. These raids lasted only a short time and the troops were then extracted again by helicopter. Spetsnaz were also infiltrated by helicopter into rebel-controlled areas – sometimes for as long as a week to ten days – to lay ambushes and mines. Occasionally they parachuted in from 'Hips' and 'Hooks'. These rear-area operations deeply worried the Mujaheddin.

Caravan Inspections

The infiltration over the borders of personnel, weapons, ammunition, non-lethal supplies, subversive literature and drugs was a serious worry and it was not long after the Soviet intervention that helicopters were used to search for caravans that might be carrying such goods. With information from local sympathizers and agents, it was sometimes possible to intercept them directly or to predict their routes and wait in ambush. Thus helicopters would patrol potential routes as a deterrent or land to stop and search caravans when found. For the inspection of vehicles or pack animals infantry were carried. The standard group being the pair, the patrol usually consisted of a couple of 'Hips' escorted by two 'Hinds' which orbitted the caravan while it was searched. Sometimes the caravan was shot up first and the troops were landed to survey the results.

Minelaying

Another way of disrupting the movement of Mujaheddin groups and the flow of supplies was by laying mines. The quickest and most flexible method was by helicopter. Both the 'Hind' and the 'Hip' were able to carry mine-dispensers on the wing pylons and outriggers respectively. The PFM-1 'Butterfly' anti-personnel mine was laid in huge numbers along caravan and other Mujaheddin routes. As well as causing many casualties, the discovery of such mines would bring the caravan to a halt, thus turning it into a stationary target for aircraft or artillery fire. Prior to some cordon and search operations, villages were isolated by mines laid by helicopter.

Temporary Soviet ambush sites, OPs and helicopter LZs, base airfields and long-term outposts were also protected by minefields. Helicopters would normally carry 144 PFM-1s in two dispensers, the airflow scattering the mines. Small exploding devices made to resemble toys were also spread widely, maiming innocent women and children in particular. To lay larger mines to destroy vehicles, the 'Hip' has a chute which protrudes from the rear of the cargo hold. The mines are simply rolled down the chute.

Casualty Evacuation

Casualty evacuation was an important role from the very first days of the war. Throughout the nine years of the conflict the Soviet military press was inundated with stirring articles about the rescue of the wounded. Given the Mujaheddin's merciless treatment of aircrew shot down and captured, every effort was made to find and rescue such unfortunates before the rebels arrived. Thus it was not long before 'Hips' and 'Hinds' were held on alert for such duties and it may even have been standard practice, as it was in Vietnam, for SAR helicopters to accompany heliborne assaults. The fundamental Soviet doctrine of using vehicles, ground and airborne, to take supplies forward and bring casualties back remained the standard procedure.

Soviet helicopters never fly alone and this is equally true of SAR helicopters. Thus two 'Hips' were probably earmarked for SAR, often with an escort of a couple of 'Hinds', whenever fixed-wing or helicopter operations were in progress. No details of how a search was conducted are known but aircrew ejecting or using a parachute had personal locator beacons onto which the helicopters could home. Once found, and largely following the American example in Vietnam, the 'Hinds', perhaps supported by fixed-wing aircraft in the vicinity or on call, provided suppressive fire to keep the Mujaheddin at bay while one of the 'Hips' went in to extract survivors. The other 'Hip' presumably acted as a reserve. In an emergency 'Hinds', with the benefit of a cabin, could be used to pick up survivors.

Apart from the obvious tactical advantages of attack and transport helicopters and aircraft flying in pairs, another benefit emerged. If one of the pair was shot down the other could watch events: Did the crew bale out? If so, how many did? Where did they land? What was the location of the crashed aircraft? Did there appear to be any obvious survivors among the passengers, if any? Were there any Mujaheddin close enough to capture the crew and passengers, and were they trying to do so? All this and more information was then passed to the SAR helicopter formation for immediate action while the crew of the unscathed aircraft orbitted the area giving what amounted to a running commentary on what was happening.

Resupply

Given the absence of a railway system, the inadequate road network and the Mujaheddin harassment of road convoys, it is no surprise that helicopters, principally the 'Hook' and 'Hip', were employed extensively to distribute food and water, ammunition, fuel, equipment and supplies over the shorter distances. This included the regular resupply of units to which all roads had been cut and the delivery of fuel, ammunition and a small stock of spare parts, such as batteries, to temporary helicopter operating bases. In addition, the changeover of personnel in remote outposts and their resupply every two weeks or so was effected by helicopter. These tasks absorbed many flying hours, not only by transport helicopters but also by attack helicopters escorting them. The demands made on helicopters for logistic tasks probably diminished the number of combat missions such as reconnaissance and CAS. Furthermore, the hot and high conditions reduced the load carried and necessitated more helicopters.

Underslung Loads

Despite the multitude of Soviet accounts of the fighting in Afghanistan, hardly a mention is made of underslinging any type of load: for example, artillery to set up temporary fire bases in otherwise inaccessible terrain, a technique so favoured by the Americans in South Vietnam. That it was done occasionally is probable, since exercises in the Caucasus mountains during the 1980s included the helicopter lift of artillery to mountain tops and ridges.

The airborne recovery of downed helicopters and aircraft also received remarkably little publicity and thus may have been infrequent.

Troop Control

Historically, the title Soviet Army includes the Ground Forces and the Air Forces. Being the highest level of command in Afghanistan, the 40th Army was given its own air force, which in turn commanded all Soviet Air Force units based in Afghanistan. These included so-called 'army aviation' units. These were helicopter units, manned and operated by Air Force personnel, which gave direct support to the ground forces. Some helicopter units were co-located with divisions and even though they may not have been an organic part of the division – as in Vietnam – the divisional commander probably had first call on them if they were not already earmarked for another operation by the 40th Army. The transport helicopter regiments were probably excluded from this arrangement and permanently under 40th Army control.

A small Air Force staff was located at each divisional command post. Usually air support for Soviet and Afghan ground operations was carefully pre-planned. Naturally, however, there were occasions when unplanned support was required. Requests for such support were then relayed up the normal ground forces chain of command to the divisional command post where the Air Force staff collated and co-ordinated them. They were then passed on up to the Air Force staff at 40th Army HQ, which assessed the need and allocated aircraft or helicopters as appropriate and if available. Divisional HQ was informed of the allocation at the same time as the airfield(s) concerned were notified of the task. It was a cumbersome procedure which was not well suited to the hit-and-run tactics of the Mujaheddin.

The use of FACs, deployed at regimental and battalion level, having the authority to call in helicopters orbiting in a holding zone or those on strip alert, was a good way of speeding things up. But to have helicopters at these readiness states was expensive in flying hours and crew fatigue.

Another shortcoming which was never wholly eradicated was the reliance on pre-planning and the consequent lack of desire among aircrews to use their initiative. This characteristic was a symptom of the Soviet communist system. Regimental and independent squadron commanders had built their careers in a system which insisted on centralized control and strict accountability. Commanders tended to restrict the exercise of initiative by subordinates for fear that any mistakes would reflect adversely on them. At the same time their subordinates did not care to take risks in case something went wrong and they invited the wrath of their commander.

When confronted with a situation that did not coincide with the plans made, the Mujaheddin noted that helicopter formation leaders appeared reluctant to take instant decisions, preferring to continue as planned or holding off while possibly checking with their commander at base. This reluctance inevitably inhibited taking advantage of the fleeting opportunities which so characterize guerrilla warfare, and sometimes resulted in needless casualties. Furthermore, their inherent inflexibility made it difficult for the Russians to respond rapidly to the sporadic, random and often unco-ordinated attacks of the Mujaheddin. Such problems were exacerbated by the difficulties in maintaining communications when flying low-level along valleys; radio relay aircraft often had then to be pressed into service.

Deployments

According to open sources, during the summer of 1982 Soviet helicopter units were deployed as follows:

- *Bagram*: 262 Helicopter Squadron; 103 Guards Airborne Division; 50 Composite Aviation Regiment (included two helicopter squadrons)
- *Fayzabad*: Detachment from 181 Transport Helicopter Regiment at Konduz; 860 Motor Rifle Regiment
- *Jalalabad*: 335 Helicopter Regiment; 66 Motor Rifle Brigade
- *Kabul*: No helicopter unit; 108 (previously 360) Motor Rifle Division
- *Kandahar*: 280 Transport Helicopter Regiment; 357 Motor Rifle Division and 70 Motor Rifle Brigade
- *Konduz*: 181 Transport Helicopter Regiment (less a detachment at Fayzabad); 254 Helicopter Squadron; 201 Motor Rifle Division
- *Shindand*: 302 Helicopter Squadron; 5 Guards Motor Rifle Division.

There had been no increase in the number of helicopters since 1980 – still some 250, of which about 40 were 'Hooks', 100 'Hinds' and 110 'Hips'.

In addition to these helicopter units there were probably others based in the Turkestan Military District which were operating regularly over northern Afghanistan. The strong Afghan 377th Helicopter Regiment was based in Kabul with other Afghan helicopter units located elsewhere.

If helicopters had been positioned only at these main operating bases, then it would have been difficult to provide immediate support to the ground troops and would have entailed much unproductive flying. Consequently temporary forward operating bases were established. These held supplies of fuel, ammunition and vital spare parts together with a few maintenance personnel, mainly officers. A team would be available to fly out to aircraft that had been forced down to repair and recover them. Repair on site was normal. If this could not be accomplished, then the helicopter might be brought back to base on the back of a truck or possibly underslung from another helicopter. If none of these measures was considered worthwhile, then the helicopter would be disabled and all weapons and other useful and sensitive items of equipment removed. If there was not time or it was too dangerous even to do this, the helicopter was destroyed.

Panjshir

Two of the biggest Soviet/Afghan offensives of the war took place during 1982. Both were in the 110km (68-mile)-long Panjshir Valley which harboured one of the strongest Mujaheddin groups in the country. It was also a redoubt from which Ahmad Shah Massoud and his resistance group could threaten the Salang Highway. The first of nine operations in the Valley, named 'Panjshir 1', had taken place in September 1980. Now, on 10 May 1982, 'Panjshir 5' started with the seizure of the entrance to the Valley. Once that had been achieved, a week of daylight bombing followed before a heliborne assault, possibly by a regiment of the 103rd Guards Airborne Division, was made into the area of Khenj. Simultaneously, a motor rifle regiment advanced up the Valley towards the parachutists.

Forewarned, the Mujaheddin had laid mines and prepared boulders to roll down onto the road. Air defences were thickened with the deployment of 12.7mm and 14.5mm machine-guns and a few 23mm ZU-23 anti-aircraft guns. As the ambushes brought the column to a halt and started causing casualties, 'Hinds' were called in by FACs to rocket supposed rebel positions; meanwhile 'Hips' evacuated those casualties that could be brought to them. Spasmodically maintained by helicopter resupply, the airborne regiment had to hold out against fierce attacks for three days while the mechanized convoy ground its way over the 40km (28 miles) separating them. The situation was relieved eventually by another column advancing down the Valley from the north-east and achieving link-up. A Pyrrhic victory: Massoud's men had withdrawn safely and remained intact as a fighting force, while the 15,000 Soviet and Afghan troops involved withdrew to either end of the Valley.

'Panjshir 6' began in August with a plan similar to that of 'Panjshir 5' but with the addition of attacks up the smaller valleys leading into the main one. Again heavy bombing was followed by a large heliborne assault into the area surrounding Khenj. This time the parachutists and reconnaissance troops were more aggressive, carrying out patrols in all directions and making positive attempts to link up with the ground column which included a tank regiment and two motor rifle regiments. Once this had been achieved the parachutists were lifted by helicopter into blocking positions in the smaller valleys. The attacks into these valleys forced the Mujaheddin further up into the mountains where they could provide no protection for the villagers whose houses and crops were then destroyed.

The Soviet decision to launch 'Panjshir 7' may have been as a result of Massoud's refusal to renew the Panjshir cease-fire which had lasted for most of 1983. This time even greater use was to be made of heliborne landings to cut off escape routes and to make raids on specific objectives. According to a Mujaheddin spokesman, Soviet and Afghan units between

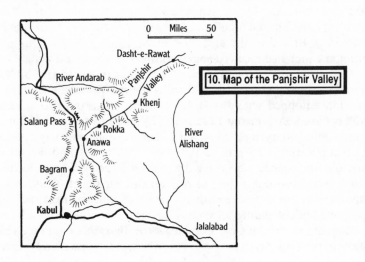

500 and 2,000 men strong were inserted by helicopters to surround villages; they were supported by attack helicopters and fixed-wing aircraft. Probably aware that an attack in strength was coming, Massoud decided to ride the blow, having mined key points in the Valley.

On 20 April 1984, as Massoud made a pre-emptive attack at the entrance to the Valley, the Soviet bombing started. A day later the ground forces rolled. The immediate objective was, as usual, Khenj which was reached three or four days later with the help of troops inserted ahead of the column by helicopter to act as cut-off parties. Snow prevented an advance beyond Khenj but an airborne battalion made a helicopter assault onto Dasht-e-Rawat further up the Valley.

These successes were followed in the first week of May by more air assaults of battalion size on the major passes out of the Panjshir. Heliborne forces were flown into the Andarab and Alishang valleys to the north and south. Meanwhile, the motor rifle troops in the main valley began to push into the smaller side valleys, now blocked, to trap Massoud's men. More heliborne troops were held in readiness to surround them as they attempted to escape.

'Panjshir 7' made more use of helicopters and was more successful than its predecessors. Nevertheless, the 10,000 Soviet and perhaps 5,000 Afghan troops failed to deal a mortal blow to the Mujaheddin in the Valley; nor were they rewarded with the capture of Massoud.

Air Assault

Although helicopters had been used to deploy troops during operations since the beginning of the war, it was not really before 1984 that the desire to exploit the potential of large heliborne assaults was translated into action. The Airborne Division based near Kabul often provided the troops for these assaults but it was not the only unit to do so. Possibly as early as 1981, the 56th Air Assault Brigade was deployed to Gardez. Additional assets included an independent air assault battalion in both the 66th and 70th Motor Rifle Brigades and some of the motor rifle divisions also had a battalion which had received some training in heliborne assault.

The 56th Air Assault Brigade, entirely air-transportable by 'Hip' and 'Hook', probably consisted of three 400-man parachute battalions, one battalion equipped with the BMD airborne infantry fighting vehicle, an artillery battalion of towed 122mm D-30 guns, a battery of 120mm mortars, an anti-tank battery, a reconnaissance company, an engineer company and other supporting elements. Unlike the 1st Cavalry and 101st Airborne Divisions in Vietnam, however, the Soviet brigade did not have its own helicopters. For these it had to rely on the Air Force. Thus, its speed of response did not compare with the American units and it was unable to match the understanding between American aircrews and assault troops.

Most of the 56th Brigade's, and airborne division's, operations had to be planned well in advance and the helicopters specifically earmarked.

Planning was conducted jointly by the airborne troops (known as desantniki) and the selected helicopter units, the same factors and options faced by the Americans in Vietnam being considered. Once the joint plan had been agreed, the helicopter commander would issue orders concerning his timings, type of formation, altitudes, speeds, escorting attack helicopters, supporting SAR helicopters and 'Flying Kremlins'.

With the comparatively few transport helicopters available the entire brigade could not be lifted in a single wave. It was more usual for only companies or battalions to be committed. A battalion operation often necessitated more than one wave. With support from the rest of the brigade as necessary, fixed- and rotary-wing aircraft and long-range artillery, such small units could operate for extended periods.

As in Vietnam, heliborne assaults were usually preceded by fixed-wing air strikes and artillery bombardment if sufficient guns were within range. Bad weather and low cloud sometimes prevented fixed-wing operations and 'Hinds' might then be tasked to undertake the preparatory softening-up process. Reconnaissance, if permitted, was discreet with one or two straightforward passes overhead, during which photographs were usually taken.

The Russians have always set great store by 'maskirovka' – a word used to describe a combination of concealment, deception and disinformation – to mislead the enemy as to Soviet capabilities and intentions with the aim of achieving surprise and increasing survivability. Some potential LZs in the area were thus 'prepared' even though they were not going to be used. Other 'maskirovka' measures included diversionary landings and dropping smoke-markers on all LZs, whether to be used or not. Given that the Russians knew that many Afghan units contained Mujaheddin sympathizers who informed the rebels of impending actions against them, it is quite probable that these units were sometimes passed false details of forthcoming operations with the intention that this information should be passed on to the Mujaheddin. Such disinformation could help to conceal the aim of the operation, timings, locations and scale.

Heliborne assaults in Afghanistan differed little in principle from those in Algeria and Vietnam. The difference between American and Soviet assaults was one of scale. The Russians simply did not have enough helicopters to match the huge assaults conducted by the Americans. From the available Soviet evidence it seems that usually no more than a company would be flown in on the first lift, perhaps because no more troops were needed, or the LZ was not big enough to accept any more than about eight helicopters at once, or because any more helicopters increased the risk of having some shot down. If more troops were needed, then a second wave could bring them into a secure LZ. 'Hinds' escorted the troop-carrying 'Hips' and Su-25 'Frogfoot' ground-attack aircraft provided top cover. A pair of 'Hips' went along for casualty evacuation and the rescue of aircrew shot down. 'Hooks' brought in the heavy equipment, more ammunition and sometimes a few BMDs and D-30 guns. An airborne command post, possibly a 'Hip', probably participated in the larger assaults. Even if it did not carry the overall commander of the operation, it is likely that it acted as a radio relay station between the ground troops and their higher authority.

Efforts were made to disguise the eventual destination by taking a slightly circuitous route and, when possible, making an approach from an unexpected direction. The 'Hips' averaged about 100–150m (330–500ft) above the ground en route at a speed which allowed the 'Hinds' to break off and attack ground targets and rejoin the formation – probably between about 130 and 180km/hr (80 and 110mph).

The threat posed by heliborne operations was of major concern to the Mujaheddin. Indeed, Abdul Haq believed them to be the most effective of all Soviet tactics. To prevent surprise and the risk of being outflanked, the Mujaheddin were forced to keep permanent picquets on certain hill-tops and be ready to move very fast into positions from which they could counter-attack heliborne landings. Where possible anti-tank mines were laid in likely helicopter LZs near Mujaheddin bases.

Many accounts of helicopter assaults appeared in the Soviet military press during the war. The following description by a 'Hip' squadron commander is typical:

'. . . I studied the proposed assault landing site from intelligence obtained through ground and air reconnaissance, as well as with mission planning photographic maps. I tried to determine the precise elevation above sea-level of the landing site and the deployment of the rebels' weapon positions. I then examined possible different approaches to and departure from the objective. That completed I ordered each aircrew to calculate their aircraft's maximum take-off weight and performance capability, given the forecast meteorological conditions.

'My officers worked carefully and enthusiastically. We decided on take-off sequence, en route formation and the co-ordinating signals with the escort. In preparing for the mission we made two operational plans for disembarking the troops: one was to land but, if the terrain did not permit this, the other was to drop them from the hover.

'The latter variation is more difficult, requiring a high degree of flying skill and self-control on the part of the aircrews. It is not child's play to hold a heavy helicopter at a height of two or three metres above the ground, at high altitude, and under hostile fire. In addition, troop delivery time should be minimal, since otherwise the helicopter becomes a sitting duck. It is not surprising that we devoted particular attention to preparation of the latter variation.

'At the designated time our helicopters appeared over the Hindu Kush. The snow-covered peaks rose practically to our flight altitude of 5,000m (16,400ft). Out in front I could see a number of helicopters – our escort. A similar element took up position behind us. I asked my navigator over the intercom: "How is our wingman doing?" Looking out of the side window, he gave me a thumbs-up sign – everything was fine.

'For some time we flew above a highway. At one point we saw a fuel tanker burning on the shoulder of the road; armoured personnel carriers had stopped by it. Yes, the roads of Afghanistan were not at all tranquil. Successfully completing our flight, we landed at the staging and troop pick-up point. The assault troops were ready and waiting. We went through a detailed mission briefing with the commander of the assault troops. We proceeded to load the troops on board. Prior to departure we once again went through the co-ordination procedures with the commander of the escort element. Not only the success of the mission but the lives of our comrades in arms depended on our mutual understanding.

'Take-off. My navigator fixed his attention on the force's movement. We were to reach the LZ at a precisely specified time. Late arrival, just as early arrival, was fraught with serious consequences. I heard the navigator's voice in my headset: "Approaching the landing area." We could see shellbursts ahead. The escort had engaged. Orbitting above the LZ, the attack helicopters were sweeping the area around it with fire. Completing the job, the escort leader radioed the landing conditions to us: wind direction, landing approach heading and the location of the rebels' anti-aircraft weapons.

'We began our descent – the most dangerous phase of the mission. The crew chief manned the machine-gun. Protection of the crew and assault troops was now in his hands. The escort was also positioned to protect the troop-lift helicopters. The LZ lay ahead. Now we had to devote our full attention to the landing. The crew chief reported height above ground. The navigator closely watched the main rotor rpm. Everyone was tense. Touchdown! The crew chief quickly emptied the helicopter of troops and returned to his place manning the machine-gun. We took off. Our wingman followed us in.

'Having disembarked their troops, the troop-lift helicopters joined up and headed home, again accompanied by the attack helicopter escort.'

It can be seen from this account that the standard 'Hip' crew was three, all officers: pilot; navigator, who also had a set of flying controls and therefore doubled as co-pilot; and crew chief, who was responsible for troop embarkation and disembarkation, tail rotor clearance close to the ground and, when installed, the manning of a traversable machine-gun mounted in one of the cabin windows. All three crewmen always carried their personal weapons, usually a Kalashnikov rifle, with them and as a matter of course wore a bullet-proof vest and parachute. These were not just to sit on; some were used in earnest.

Compared with the US Army 'Slicks' in Vietnam, the 'Hip' carried a smaller crew but usually a greater number of troops. Although able to accommodate up to 24 ready for combat, the 'Hip C's' performance was seriously affected by the prevailing hot and high conditions. Furthermore, with high importance being attached to keeping personnel losses to the minimum, particularly of élite troops from Spetsnaz, airborne and air assault units, the risk of carrying this number was apparently considered too great, both in the air and while embarking or disembarking under fire. If Soviet and Western news film is anything to go by, the 'Hip' rarely appeared to take more than about a dozen troops. One such film showed Spetsnaz troops being carried in a 'Hip'. It was something of a surprise to see two of the seven men sitting in style in armchairs, apparently without lap-straps – comfortable maybe, but not exactly safe!

New Aircraft

It was not many months into the war before the 'Hip C' began to reveal its shortcomings in earnest. In addition to its poor flying performance, it was inadequately armed with only forward-firing rockets and it was vulnerable to even the smallest calibre of fire. Fortunately for the Russians, the Mil Design Bureau had begun development of a derivative of the Mi-8 in the early 1970s, and in or about 1976 the new prototype made its maiden flight. The production military version was designated Mi-8MT ('Hip H' by NATO), while the civil and export military variants were designated Mi-17.

The most important new feature was the two more powerful engines, together offering an extra 400shp over the 'Hip C' and reduced fuel consumption. At maximum take-off weight, their extra output allowed an increase in cruising speed to 240km/hr (150mph), in range to 465km (290 miles), and served to double the hover ceiling and rate of climb. Equally significant was the ability to lift the full payload of 4,000kg (8,818lb) to altitude on a hot day, something the 'Hip C' could not do; 3,000kg (6,614lb) could be underslung. In the casualty evacuation role twelve stretchers could be accommodated. To protect the engine intakes from the ingestion of ice and various forms of debris, guards were fitted.

To provide better directional control, the tail rotor was moved from the starboard side of the fin to the port side. Further modifications included new avionics and various measures to simplify maintenance. Improvements in armaments and survivability were paramount objectives. Instead of the four weapons pylons of the 'Hip C', the 'H' model has six on which can be hung six 32-shot 57mm rocket pods, UPK-23 23mm podded cannon or bombs. In Afghanistan some 'Hip Hs' had a traversable single-barrelled 12.7mm machine-gun installed in the nose and a similar gun in the starboard clamshell rear-loading door. By firing tracer rounds the nose gun can be used for range-finding before rocket-firing. Unlike the 'Hip E', however, no anti-tank missiles are fitted. As with the 'Hind' exhaust gas scoops, an IR jammer and a decoy flare-dispenser were installed. To give some protection to the cockpit, armour plating was attached below both side windows.

The 'Hip H' was a major improvement on the 'Hip C' in every respect and was more of a combat helicopter than just a poorly armed transport helicopter. It is not known when the first arrived in Afghanistan but it was probably as early as 1981 or 1982, at which time the 'Hip Cs' began to be withdrawn.

Another variant of the 'Hip' which probably found its way into Afghanistan in the early 1980s was what the Russians designated the Mi-9 and NATO the 'Hip G'. It was a more sophisticated version of the airborne command post 'Hip D' with better avionics and without the rash of extra antennae on the tailboom which characterized its predecessor.

At much the same time a new variant of the 'Hind' was introduced. This was the Mi-24P 'Hind F'. The 'P' stands for 'Pushka' (gun, cannon) and denotes a 'Hind' with a twin-barrelled 30mm cannon fixed to the starboard side of the fuselage. This cannon replaced the four-barrelled 12.7mm Gatling machine-gun mounted in the turret under the nose. Because the new gun is fixed and forward-firing, the pilot has to turn the helicopter to face its target. Inevitably, this takes longer than traversing a flexible gun and may lead to steep, and possibly dangerous, diving angles. Furthermore, being larger, many fewer rounds can be stored and the rate of fire is probably not much more than half the 4,000 rounds per minute of the Gatling gun it replaced. On the other hand, the destructive power of a 30mm shell is much greater than that of a 12.7mm bullet and the range of the larger-calibre weapon is longer, perhaps as much as 2,000 metres. These attributes were becoming ever more necessary to reach into Mujaheddin caves and hideouts without getting into range of the rebels' own weapons. From just a handful of 12.7mm DShKM machine-guns as their largest-calibre weapon in the first couple of years of the war, the Mujaheddin had built up their stocks which soon included 14.5mm, 20mm and 23mm calibres.

The 'Hind F' quickly relieved any remaining 'Hind As' and 'Ds'. Film from Afghanistan showed that typical armament for the 'Hind E' and 'F' was two 80mm rocket pods, two 'Spiral' anti-tank missiles and their respective guns; often they also carried two auxiliary fuel tanks on two of their wing pylons.

Reports that the huge Mi-26 'Halo' was in service in Afghanistan have been unconfirmed. If 'Halos' had been based on one or more airfields, it is almost certain that they would have been seen, if not on the ground, then in the air. It is therefore reasonable to deduce that no 'Halos' were deployed permanently to Afghanistan. Some may have flown into the country to deliver heavy or bulky equipment to specific sites, a task too complex for any other means or which could not have been achieved otherwise. The 'Halo' can carry a 20,000kg (44,092lb) load over a distance of 800km (497 miles) at a cruising speed of 255km/hr (158mph) – a payload/range more than three times that of the 'Hook'. After the heavy-lift job was completed, the 'Halos' would have returned to their bases in the USSR. Any 'Halos' that did penetrate Afghan airspace may have been in Aeroflot markings.

Several reasons could be advanced to explain why the 'Halo' was not employed fully in Afghanistan. It did not enter production until about 1981 and may not have achieved operational status before 1983. The initial rate of production was slow, perhaps due to technical problems connected with the unique gearbox or main rotor system, or even both. This was perhaps not surprising as the design of the 'Halo' broke new ground: it was the first, and still is the only, helicopter in the world to have a single main rotor with eight blades. So, with comparatively few aircraft, dubious reliability and possibly a shortage of trained technical manpower and spare parts, the decision was taken not to commit the new helicopter to a hazardous and rugged environment before it was really ready. On the other hand, the war in Afghanistan was seen as a good opportunity to test new equipment and weapon systems under combat conditions, and from that point of view it is somewhat surprising that the 'Halo' did not play any significant role. In any event, the 'Hook' served in Afghanistan throughout the war. If more were needed they could have been sent.

1985

During 1984 the Russians had intensified their efforts to control the countryside, particularly the Panjshir Valley and the border areas. Soviet troops, principally a hard core of airborne and air assault, long-range reconnaissance and Spetsnaz, had become more daring in searching out the Mujaheddin in their various redoubts. The new determination found partial expression in the greater use of helicopters for genuine air assaults and to support Spetsnaz and other specialist operations. At the end of 1984, having seized and occupied more territory than in earlier years, the Russians were forced by the coming of the winter snows to withdraw to lower and safer positions.

Frequent night attacks on Kabul and the airport heralded the 1985 campaign. In February Soviet attention turned to the Panjshir Valley when heliborne troops were used in an effort to clear some of the side valleys and seal off the southern approaches. At much the same time an operation to relieve Barikot, close to the Pakistan border, was begun. More or less under siege since 1981, the garrison had had to rely largely on the bravery and skill of the helicopter crews ordered to sustain it. Now, with the support of more helicopters, Soviet mechanized troops edged their way up the Kunar Valley but were unable to reach Barikot. A second offensive in the Kunar Valley began in May with the aim of not only relieving Barikot but also opening the 170km (105-mile) stretch of road from there through to Jalalabad and establishing forward positions close to the border to disrupt the flow of supplies to the Mujaheddin.

For three weeks in May and June heavy fighting took place in the Valley. The bulk of the Soviet force was provided by two airborne regiments which were used in a heliborne assault role; making up the total of some 10,000 troops were Afghan units who comprised the ground column. Helicopters were in constant use to deploy flank protection parties, to deposit troops on crests overlooking the route, to insert forward detachments to assist the momentum of the advance and Spetsnaz troops into rear areas to harass the rebels, to evacuate casualties and units that had been cut off by the Mujaheddin, and finally to provide CAS. The rebels had no choice but to

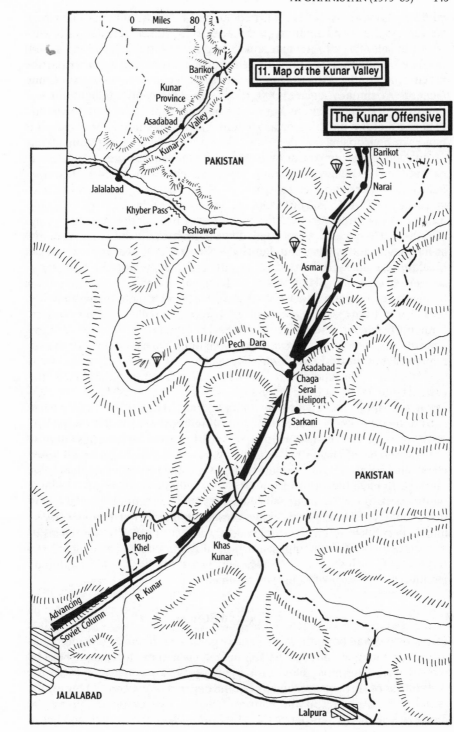

11. Map of the Kunar Valley

The Kunar Offensive

withdraw in the face of the overwhelming fire from tanks, artillery and aircraft. As the main column approached Barikot, helicopters lifted a Soviet airborne battalion into the garrison to lead the break-out. The success did not last long: within 24 hours the relieving force turned round and started moving down the Valley again towards Jalalabad. According to Army General Varennikov, over 11,000 troops were landed by helicopter during the Kunar Valley operations but not a single helicopter was shot down. He believed that the most important feature of these operations was the part played by helicopters.

In August a major operation in Paktia Province was begun to eliminate or neutralize Mujaheddin strongholds and infiltration routes near the Pakistan border, and subsequently to relieve the provincial capital and garrison town of Khost, just 24km (15 miles) from the border. Although quite a strong force occupied the town, it had been under siege for many months and had had to be resupplied by air. Prior to the operation as many as five Soviet and Afghan battalions were flown into Khost with the aim of breaking the rebel grip to north and south and to assist with the operations further north. Some 15,000 Soviet and Afghan troops were committed to this complex operation which involved simultaneous actions over a wide area. Several air assaults into nine LZs were conducted around Azra to form a cordon around Mujaheddin bases. Others were carried out to ambush rebel bands and caravans hurrying to help. The fighting continued for five days as the noose was gradually tightened.

Meanwhile, the Khost force attacked north towards Jaji and then south towards the large, and strongly fortified, rebel base at Zhawar. Its air defence weapons included three 40mm anti-aircraft guns, heavy machine-guns and some SA-7s. Appreciating the threat, the Mujaheddin rallied to resist the advance, finally bringing it to a halt only a few kilometres short of the town. The offensive was effectively over. The Russians could have classed it a success, though it was a meagre one and twelve helicopters were reported to have been shot down. The Mujaheddin, successful in keeping the Russians out of Zhawar, succumbed to the temptation to believe that they could defeat any large-scale onslaught and derived considerable morale benefits from this. The enjoyment was short-lived. Zhawar fell eight months later to a force composed mainly of Afghan units. Large quantities of weapons, including some SAMs and heavy weapons, were captured. Despite this, the siege of Khost was resumed.

Blowpipe and Stinger

Overall, 1985 had not been a particularly good year for the Mujaheddin but a mildy encouraging one for the Karmal regime and the Russians. The tide was to turn. The most significant event of 1986 was arguably not the withdrawal of six Soviet regiments but the delivery of Western SAMs to the Mujaheddin. As a result the nature of Soviet air support underwent a fundamental change. Hitherto, the Mujaheddin had had to rely largely on

12.7mm and 14.5mm machine-guns and a few recently acquired 20mm Oerlikon cannon. None of these was sufficiently mobile for the needs of the rebels; only the SA-7 was easily man-portable in the mountains, but it was regarded as ineffective.

During the spring of 1986 an unknown number of British-made Shorts Blowpipe shoulder-launched missile systems (perhaps about 300) reached the rebels. They were followed by a similar number of the basic version of the USA's General Dynamics Stinger, with a further 600 arriving the next year. The first known use of the Stinger in combat took place on 26 September when three 'Hinds' out of a group of four were shot down in quick succession near Jalalabad. The measures incorporated to counter the Soviet SA-7 were clearly ineffective against the new missiles.

Unlike the SA-7 the Blowpipe is not a heat-seeking missile and IR counter-measures are therefore irrelevant. The Blowpipe has to be guided to the target by the gunner who has a choice of two warhead fuses – proximity or impact. The missile is just supersonic and has minimum and maximum effective ranges of about 700m and 3,500m respectively; minimum and maximum altitudes are 10m and 2,500m respectively.

When the passive IR seeker of a Stinger missile has locked on to the target the gunner uncages the seeker and fires. As soon as the missile leaves its launch tube the gunner is free to turn his attention to other matters; he does not have to guide the missile as with the Blowpipe system. The Stinger must strike the target to destroy it. It flies roughly twice as fast as the Blowpipe and has minimum and maximum effective ranges of 200m and 4,000m respectively; minimum and maximum altitudes are more or less ground-level and 3,500m.

Despite the greater skill and time required of a Blowpipe gunner to achieve a hit compared with that of a Stinger gunner, Blowpipes were credited with the destruction of some Soviet and Afghan helicopters. However, while they were feared by aircrew because of the lack of available counter-measures, the Mujaheddin preferred to use the Stinger because of its comparative simplicity, less demanding training and the fact that it was in greater supply.

Against the Stinger missile the IR decoy flares ejected from the dispenser underneath a helicopter's tailboom were largely ineffective because they fell too far away behind and below the machine and thus provided minimal coverage. Both the Blowpipe and Stinger systems could attack from any angle and thus flares to decoy the Stinger missile needed to be fired into an appropriate position. This meant launching them diagonally forwards so that they remained closer to the helicopter – otherwise the missile seeker would ignore them – and slightly upwards so that they would stay in the air for as long as possible. To meet these requirements the flare-dispenser had to be moved. The new system comprised two triangular-shaped dispensers, each containing 96 flares, one mounted on either side of the helicopter's fuselage directly in line with the IR jammer.

With no missile approach or launch warning system the flares had to be fired pre-emptively. Given the limited number of flares carried, they were probably fired only when flying over areas known or suspected to be occupied by the Mujaheddin. As films have shown, flares were usually ejected simultaneously from both dispensers at intervals of between two and five seconds; on some occasions they were fired alternately to port and starboard at one-second intervals.

Technical counter-measures were not enough. Tactics were also reviewed. To avoid machine-gun fire, helicopters had often flown at altitude, but this put them into the SAM envelope. According to one squadron commander, 'It was better to come back with small holes from machine-guns than to get one big hole and not come back at all.' It therefore soon became standard practice to fly at low level, despite the difficulties, using the terrain to mask observation of the helicopters whenever possible. If a missile was seen to be approaching the helicopter, the immediate action was to turn towards it and descend if that were possible. Where appropriate, operations were conducted at night when it was more difficult for SAM operators to see the helicopters. Indeed, by this stage in the war it was not unusual for helicopters to provide close fire support and conduct bombing missions at night.

Great efforts were made to gather information on where Stingers and Blowpipes were located and considerable sums of money were offered for such information or, better still, the capture or acquisition of such missiles. Some heliborne Spetsnaz operations were directed specifically at SAM storage sites and into areas where they were known to be deployed. Caravans suspected of carrying them were ambushed. As a result several missiles were captured. Whenever a SAM was fired the location was noted and retaliatory action, either from the air or on the ground, was taken whenever possible. The combination of intelligence, technical counter-measures and new tactics took some months to implement, but once adopted helped to lessen the devastating impact made when the Stinger first appeared. Losses decreased as the opportunity to launch missiles declined. According to a Pakistani report, 100 Soviet and Afghan helicopters were lost to the Stinger during the first eighteen months of its operation.

Although the Blowpipe and Stinger did not drive Soviet and Afghan helicopters from the sky there is no doubt that they degraded their effectiveness. Furthermore, in trying to avoid the SAM envelope, helicopters fell prey to other weapons. With the threat uppermost in their minds, pilots may have flown too high, too low or too fast and made only a single pass to deliver their ordnance; weapon aiming and bombing accuracy suffered. The anticipated presence of SAMs probably curtailed some operations and may have led, at least temporarily, to some no-go areas. It became hazardous for helicopters to participate in attacks on Mujaheddin strongholds; even routine operations to patrol supply and infiltration routes and fly in supplies to besieged garrisons and outposts were inhibited.

Kabul and the airport had been attacked frequently throughout the war. The airport and the aircraft based there were important targets since they constituted a significant lifeline back to the Soviet Union. Large and small transport aircraft were particularly vulnerable as they made their approach to land or as they climbed away after take-off. By 1985 most military aircraft had been equipped with decoy flares, although civil transport aircraft had not been. With the more potent threat from the Stinger, such flares were ejected in a steady stream during both manoeuvres. A further protective measure was to deploy a detachment of 'Hinds' to patrol the security perimeter of the airport and escort all incoming and outgoing flights. The flares from the transport aircraft were only effective above a certain height, so one pair of 'Hinds' flew in formation to provide low-level flare protection while another pair searched the area below the flight paths for the presence of guerrillas.

While the morale of Soviet aircrews generally may have been robust enough to cope with the new threat, there is little doubt that they became more cautious and less inclined to press home their attacks; defecting Afghan pilots testified to the fact that it dented their morale seriously. Conversely, Mujaheddin morale soared, due both to the higher number of helicopters shot down and their own increased freedom to move, to concentrate forces, to distribute supplies and to fight, by day now as well as by night.

Inevitably, however, the Stinger's kill rate decreased as counter-measures were installed, the new tactics implemented, the sortie rate declined and the standard of training fell as Mujaheddin instructors took over from Pakistani instructors.

Khost

Because of its strategic location close to the Pakistan border, Khost had been the object of sporadic fighting and under siege for a number of years. With land communications severely disrupted, resupply had been largely by air. The introduction of the Stinger, however, had made this particularly hazardous and by October 1987 perhaps as many as 9,000 Mujaheddin under the command of Jalaludin Haqqani had been able to bring the air-bridge to a halt, dominate the road from Gardez and tighten the ring around the town. This had been achieved by constructing an intricate system of fortified, well-concealed and interconnecting strongpoints. As well as civilians Khost was occupied mainly by Afghan troops with more than a hundred Soviet advisers. Its fall to the Mujaheddin would be a political and military disaster.

The relief of Khost was to be the last major Afghan/Soviet operation. It was given the name 'Magistral' (Highway). Some 24,000 troops, predominantly Soviet, were concentrated for the onslaught which began on 18 November. In formulating the plan, according to Lieutenant General Boris Gromov, who had assumed command of the 40th Army in June 1987, the experience of conducting operations in the Caucasus and Carpathians during the Second World War was very carefully studied. Gromov was faced with numerous problems and if surprise could not be achieved the chances of success were not high. 'Maskirovka' this time would include a dummy parachute drop in the area of the Satu Kandau Pass, a critical choke point on the road some 20km (12.5 miles) from Gardez, to encourage the Mujaheddin to open fire and reveal their anti-aircraft and other weapon emplacements. As they fired at the dummy parachutists, Soviet and Afghan fighter-bombers and helicopters would sweep in to obliterate them. That is exactly what happened. The Pass was captured on 28 November.

The general plan was for Afghan units to drive down the main Gardez-Khost road, 120km (75 miles) long and heavily mined, with troops from the Soviet airborne division and 56 Air Assault Brigade protecting the flanks. For the next six weeks the combined force inched forward in the face of unrelenting Mujaheddin resistance. To capture Mirajan Bazaar, one of the towns en route, at least one airborne battalion was inserted by helicopter at low level at night in a classic, and highly professional, assault. In another airlift by night a Soviet airborne brigade was flown into Khost itself to help in a break-out towards Gardez.

Helicopters played a key role in providing reconnaissance, CAS, escort for the huge convoy of supply vehicles, command and control, casualty evacuation and the leapfrogging of troops to hold vital high ground overlooking the main advance. On at least one occasion a heliborne platoon was ambushed as it was moved too far forward and beyond mutual fire support.

The intense allied pressure, however, was bound to prevail in the end and on 30 December 1987 the first relieving troops entered the beleaguered

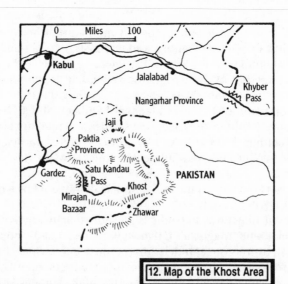

12. Map of the Khost Area

city. They were followed by an avalanche of lorries carrying supplies.

Operation 'Magistral' was portrayed in the Soviet media as a famous victory and it provided the right atmosphere for Mr Gorbachev to announce a month later that Soviet forces would be withdrawn from Afghanistan. The reality, however, was the resumption of the blockade as soon as Soviet and Afghan troops had left the area by the end of January 1988.

Hero of the Soviet Union

During the war in Afghanistan at least 80 officers and men, including General Gromov, received the Soviet Union's highest military honour – Hero of the Soviet Union. Of these, fifteen came from the airborne divisions and 56 Air Assault Brigade and another thirteen were helicopter pilots. One of these was Aleksandr Rutskoi, who in 1990 became the Vice-President of Russia. The first six awards were announced on 28 April 1980, one of them going to a helicopter unit commander.

The action which was to lead to Captain Valeriy Popkov becoming a Hero occurred just a few days before the final withdrawal. Flying a 'Hip' as wingman to Captain Ilgiz Sharipov on a reconnaissance mission, Popkov followed his leader through a solid layer of cloud and headed out over the mountains. Soviet helicopter pilots liked to fly above cloud because they were then safe from Mujaheddin missiles. Thirty minutes later the pair let down through the overcast, located the rebels after a while and radioed the information back to their command post.

Their duty done they headed up for home. A break in the cloud appeared and it was then, suddenly, that Popkov saw to his horror Sharipov's helicopter burst into flames, stall and then fall steeply. Suspecting that the 'Hip' had been hit by a missile, but disregarding the fact that his own helicopter might shortly become a victim, Popkov started a steep spiralling descent to keep Sharipov's 'Hip' in sight. He called his command post to report what was happening.

Popkov's crew saw three figures parachute from the burning helicopter but was unable to see where they landed. As Popkov headed on downwards, he suddenly noticed a bright orange canopy with a man standing by it. He also saw some Mujaheddin running towards the spot firing their weapons. Popkov turned his 'Hip' towards them and launched a few rockets while his crew chief fired a machine-gun through an open side window.

Landing near the parachute, and some 300 metres down slope from the burning 'Hip', Popkov could see that the survivor was Sharipov. Everybody was ordered out to get him aboard and find the remaining members of his crew. At that moment Popkov's helicopter was hit and a smell of fuel pervaded the 'Hip'. Nevertheless, Sharipov was bundled aboard as the crew chief and two others engaged the approaching Mujaheddin with their rifles. Instead of following Sharipov on board, the three of them dashed up the hillside to see if they could find Sharipov's colleagues. Popkov hover-taxied up after them to the summit. Again and again his helicopter was hit but escaped the rebels' heavier rocket-propelled grenades. By this time Sharipov had recovered sufficiently to start firing out of a side window. While Popkov manoeuvred the 'Hip' to avoid fire, a search of the downed helicopter and the surrounding area was undertaken. It revealed no sign of the missing crew. Disappointed, the search party clambered aboard their helicopter which promptly took off and returned to base.

The Soviet and Afghan Helicopter Fleets

By the time Mr Gorbachev announced in February 1988 that Soviet troops were to be withdrawn the fleet had grown to between 350 and 400 helicopters. They were backed up by perhaps another 100 operating out of bases just across the River Amu Darya in the USSR. More 'Hip Hs' and 'Hind Fs' had been introduced during the preceding two or three years, but the number of 'Hooks' is believed never to have exceeded 50. The extra helicopters allowed a greater territorial spread of deployments, which resulted in a reduction in unproductive flying time as helicopters carried out their missions.

While this study has been confined to Soviet helicopter operations, it would be incomplete without mentioning the contribution of Afghan Air Force helicopters. They represented a much higher percentage of the total helicopter force in Afghanistan than did South Vietnamese helicopters in South Vietnam. The 377th Hero of the Revolution Helicopter Regiment was based in Kabul and comprised perhaps as many as 60 to 80 'Hip Cs' and 'Hs' and 'Hind Ds' and 'Es'. An unknown number of other Afghan helicopter units were located alongside Soviet helicopter units possibly in Shindand, Kandahar and Jalalabad. One regiment, which included training helicopters, was based in the north at Mazar-e-Sharif. The Afghan Air Force may thus have possessed about 200 helicopters – or a third of all helicopters in Afghanistan. It is probable that it was regarded as an adjunct of the 40th Army's Air Force and did not carry out independent operations or participate in more than the occasional night operation.

Until 1982, by which time they had been destroyed or damaged beyond repair, some 'Hounds' and 'Hind As' were included in the Afghan inventory. Defecting Afghan pilots testified to significant losses being sustained, but they were made up by deliveries of more aircraft. At least one 'Hip' and seven 'Hinds' are thought to have been delivered by defecting aircrew to the Mujaheddin or flown to Pakistan.

Tasks undertaken by Afghan helicopter crews mirrored those of their Soviet colleagues, including CAS, bombing, casualty evacuation and resupply missions. Soviet tactics were used (many of the aircrew having been trained in the Soviet Union), with 'Hips' flying in pairs or fours and being escorted by 'Hinds'.

The Withdrawal

The Soviet withdrawal from Afghanistan took place in two phases. The Geneva Accords stipulated that 50 per cent of the LCSFA, variously reported by the Russians themselves as being as low as 100,300 men and as high as 120,000, would leave between 15 May and 15 August 1988 and the remainder by 15 February 1989. At the end of the first phase General Gromov announced that the Russians held two areas: Kabul and the road to Termez, and the area surrounding Shindand and Herat and the road to Kushka. Soviet troops were still deployed elsewhere but during the three-month period the smaller and more remote garrisons had been taken over by the Afghan Army or abandoned to the Mujaheddin. Offensive operations had by then virtually come to a standstill.

Helicopters played a major part in extracting Soviet troops and redeploying Afghan units. Where withdrawals had to be conducted by vehicle, heliborne detachments were used to secure routes in the time-honoured fashion while 'Hinds' escorted the convoys. Some helicopter sites were closed as helicopter units consolidated at the larger bases.

Inevitably withdrawal plans had to be modified in the light of sporadic Mujaheddin attacks, further defections by Afghan military personnel and alleged violations of the Geneva Accords. Attacks on withdrawing Soviet units and heavy fighting around Kandahar and Konduz also delayed preparations and necessitated the diversion of troops and aircraft to bring the local situation under control.

Afghan Air Force helicopters were left to take up the burden as Soviet helicopters redeployed from the southern half of the country to the north in preparation for the second phase of the withdrawal, which began in January 1989. TV film of the last days of the Soviet presence showed a constant stream of heavy transport aircraft coming into or leaving Kabul International Airport with 'Hind Fs' escorting them. An attack helicopter regiment was probably based at the airport for this purpose from January. As the last road convoy left the capital the regiment no doubt left with it, escorting it along the Salang Highway to Termez. General Gromov was reportedly the last Soviet soldier to leave Afghan territory as he crossed the Friendship Bridge at 11.55am on 15 February 1989, five minutes before the midday deadline set ten months earlier.

Epilogue

By blatantly disregarding military advice, a serious political misappreciation of the situation in Afghanistan was made in 1979. The victory over Nazi Germany and the successful intervention in Czechoslovakia in 1968 had led the Soviet leadership to believe that the Afghans would not resist but instead submit to overwhelming power. In ignoring British experience in three Afghan Wars (1839–42, 1879–80, 1919) to secure the north-west frontier of India, Brezhnev and his inner circle dangerously underestimated the nature of the country and the strength and tenacity of their opponents. Air power and advanced technology alone could not redress the balance. When the Russians departed over nine years later, they left a nation more divided than before they arrived, a devastated countryside, and suffering and poverty on a grand scale. Not for them the worry of killing innocent civilians or genuinely trying to win a hearts and minds campaign.

The war in Afghanistan was the first occasion that Soviet troops, in any substantial strength, had been engaged in battle since the end of the Second World War. While some of the experiences of that war were loosely relevant to most types of Soviet forces in Afghanistan, they were of little use in developing and refining helicopter tactics.

The disasters and defeats of the early months, and even years, were largely attributable to having organizations and equipment suited to a war in Europe and men trained in conventional tactics rather than those needed for a guerrilla war. It would seem that Western experiences of countering insurgencies since the Second World War had generated no more than passing interest and were considered more or less irrelevant. To begin with, only a comparatively small number of helicopters – but many more fighter-bombers – accompanied the invading forces. Worse still, many of the units introduced into Afghanistan at this time were poorly trained, unfit and not ready for combat.

It was soon realized that the balance of forces was wrong. Consequently some of the fixed-wing aircraft were withdrawn to be replaced by more helicopters, and extra infantry were substituted for air defence and other units. The 'Hind' quickly emerged as a pre-eminent weapon system, causing the Mujaheddin to say that, although they were not afraid of the Russians, they were afraid of their helicopters. It is therefore somewhat surprising that the Russians did not send more helicopters to Afghanistan, given their proven value. While the French had no more available for Algeria, the Russians could have deployed more helicopters had they so desired.

The Russians succumbed to the same temptation as the Americans did of using helicopters when perhaps they should have used infantry. The short-term results may have been beneficial and potential casualties thereby reduced, but long-lasting effects were usually minimal.

Nevertheless, Soviet military policy was to exploit their superior firepower and tactical mobility to overcome the advantages held by the Mujaheddin. With this mobility, provided by helicopters, they could concentrate their forces much more quickly than the Mujaheddin, who suffered severely from internal disputes, lack of co-ordination and in-adequate communications. Due to the nature of the terrain it was not possible for the Russians to rely, as in past wars, on massive ground-based firepower. Thus recourse was made to air power and, in particular, to helicopter close fire support. This worked well until the advent of the Stinger when the pendulum swung back towards the use of artillery and rocket fire.

On the occasion of the 60th Anniversary of the Soviet Airborne Forces, their commander, Colonel-General Achalov, declared that the co-ordination between parachute troops on the ground and army aviation helicopters was one of the most useful experiences gained during the war. However, the integration of air power with the land battle took some time to be implemented fully. Later it was rare for ground operations to take place without fixed- and rotary-wing support. Moreover, these aircraft mutually supported each other when attacking ground targets and 'Hips' accompanied them for SAR purposes. It was usual for pre-emptive strikes to be made to diminish the later need for fire support in the thick of battle.

One of the most significant differences from French and American policy was that the Russians attached less importance to surveillance by helicopter. The Russians did not have a specialist helicopter able to undertake covert surveillance and target acquisition. Little effort seems to have been applied to regular surveillance of selected areas and it was therefore harder to build up an intelligence picture. Aircrew did not get to know any area particularly well and so were less likely to detect any subtle changes. It was the air cavalry squadrons that triggered many actions in South Vietnam, helping the Americans in the struggle to attain the initiative and keep the Viet Cong off balance. On the other hand, a high priority was accorded by the Russians to the specific reconnaissance of routes and objectives. Additionally, reconnaissance helicopters, 'Hip' or 'Hind', accompanied attack helicopters when carrying out close fire support in an overwatch role to detect sources of enemy fire and acquire other targets.

It is probably true to say, however, that even if such techniques had been in force the 40th Army command structure, which relied on centralized control, would not have been able to take full advantage of the information gained. This was a guerrilla war that cried out for a system of command and control which was devolved to the tactical commanders in the field. But such a decentralized system was quite foreign to the Soviet Armed Forces and, despite over nine years' experience in Afghanistan, true decentralization was not practised.

The question of initiative at junior levels is closely connected and has already been mentioned. Its lack was recognized as a shortcoming and pilots were encouraged to be flexible and take tactical decisions when necessary. But it was hard for them to disregard a lifetime of unquestioning obedience. Their attitudes in this particular sphere were in stark contrast to their American colleagues in South Vietnam. A deputy commander for political affairs of a helicopter regiment and Hero of the Soviet Union, Lieutenant Colonel Nikolai Malyshev, who served two tours in Afghanistan, has since written that unconventional action and pilot initiative are the only ways to meet the requirements of modern warfare. Too few pilots, however, were prepared to take risks and accept responsibility for their actions. If attitudes do not change, then Soviet air power – whoever now inherits it – will not achieve its full potential. But to encourage junior officers and pilots to take decisions for themselves presupposes a radical change in society, with implications too uncertain at this stage to comment on.

Most helicopter crews served a year or so at a time – as the Americans did in South Vietnam. Such a policy did not capitalize fully on the experience gained by individuals and the general learning curve was thus a little shallow. On the other hand, the environment was very demanding for aircrew and a year was probably quite long enough. Furthermore, more pilots could be rotated through Afghanistan and benefit from the experience.

Where a good deal of initiative was shown was in devising and implementing technical modifications. The arrival of the more powerful 'Hip H' dramatically improved the ability to take troops and supplies into the mountains in high summer. More important still were the devices to counter heat-seeking missiles. While the air defence environment in Afghanistan was much less severe overall than in South Vietnam, the man-portable SAM threat was much greater. The speed of the technical response, although not fully effective, was nothing short of astonishing and probably owed much to individual initiative and a surprising absence of bureaucratic obstruction. Indeed, the reverse may have been true, with bureaucratic encouragement generated by a desire to minimize personnel and helicopter losses and the consequent drop in morale.

The psychological impact of the Stinger on both sides was significant and probably just as important, if not more so, than its physical impact. The combination of tactical and technical counter-measures against it were not completely successful. So, rather than lose a lot of helicopters, the Russians had little choice but to employ them more sparingly, and this reduction in support demoralized to some degree Soviet and Afghan ground troops. More care had to be taken in planning operations, choosing routes and arranging SAR and fighter cover. The previous reliance on helicopters had to be scaled down. Keeping control of the operational situation was thus made even more difficult. The realization that this was so may well have contributed to the decision to withdraw the LCSFA.

The calibre, range and effectiveness of weapons were enhanced during the course of the war. Not only were gun and rocket calibres enlarged and ranges extended, but new weapons were installed on helicopters: cannon in pods, grenade-launchers and anti-personnel mine-dispensers. Both the 'Hind' and the 'Hip' became very versatile weapons-carriers.

Heliborne assaults became more and more frequent as the war progressed, both in an offensive sense and because it was often too slow and risky to contemplate movement and attack by ground vehicles. Putting down large numbers of desantniki, particularly into mountainous areas where no helicopters had landed before and in the face of enemy fire, constituted a difficult challenge and one that required careful planning and consideration of LZs, fire and logistic support and the maintenance of communications. Nevertheless, such assaults and ambushes posed a serious threat to Mujaheddin supply columns and troop movements. The rebels soon came to realize that these troops, airborne, air assault and Spetsnaz, were better trained, better led, better motivated and more flexible than tank and motor rifle troops. But the Russians did not feel able, or did not wish, to copy the American example of having airmobile units with their own organic helicopters.

Unfortunately, but unsurprisingly, the Russians have published no statistics concerning flying hours or helicopter losses. Many estimates of losses sustained have appeared in the Western press but they rarely differentiate between Soviet and Afghan losses, giving the impression that all were suffered by the Russians. They appear to be based mainly on Mujaheddin claims, which are almost certainly exaggerated – understand-ably, for propaganda purposes and through wishful thinking. The highest figure quoted is about 1,000 helicopters lost from December 1979 until February 1989. Experience from previous wars might suggest that the true figure is no more than half this number or even less.

What is not in dispute is the manner in which these helicopters were lost. Small arms, machine-guns of 12.7mm and 14.5mm calibre, and 20mm and 23mm cannon all took their toll of low-flying helicopters. The Stinger was by far the most successful SAM, but the SA-7 and Blowpipe also achieved a few kills. Helicopters were destroyed on the ground at their own bases by Mujaheddin mortar fire and sabotage. A substantial proportion of the losses was probably due to operational accidents. Aircrew error, due partly to lapses of judgment, fatigue, insufficient skill or inadequate briefing, led to mid-air collisions, flying into high ground in poor visibility, crashes when landing on difficult terrain and other types of accident. Inevitably, some accidents must have been caused by technical malfunctions and mistakes by servicing and maintenance crews.

On 17 August 1989 the Soviet authorities announced that 13,833 military personnel had been killed or died from wounds, disease or accidents during the war; 311 were still missing.

As in all such guerrilla wars, the conflict in Afghanistan proved to be an excellent training centre and a good testing ground for new weapons, equipment, organizations and tactics. Many aircrew had not flown in mountainous terrain before under hot and high or snow and white-out conditions. Very few had come under fire or been called to think for themselves. The realization dawned that aircrew could not be posted into combat direct from a unit stationed in some far-off place in the USSR or Eastern Europe; basic theatre training in the adjacent Turkestan Military District, followed by operational familiarization training, was necessary first. Soviet analysis of aircrew performance resulted in calls for higher quality and more realistic peacetime training, new tactics and the relaxation of control to permit more initiative at lower command levels – i.e., flight leaders and even individual pilots. For aircrew, it was suggested that more realistic training could be achieved only by slackening the grip of flight safety regulations. While flight safety remains vitally important, it ought not to paralyse the desire to be innovative in planning and execution. Not flying in bad weather for safety reasons in peacetime is poor preparation for war. It can lead to accidents, which might have been avoided had more constructive training been conducted, or failure to complete, or even begin, missions.

Some of the lessons learnt have been embodied in the designs of the next generation of attack helicopters, Afghan veterans having been canvassed for their views. For instance, the Kamov 'Hokum' and Mi-28 'Havoc' are true, dedicated attack helicopters with no passenger cabin. However, the 'Havoc's' avionics bay in the fuselage is large enough to accommodate two people (in some discomfort) – the crew of another crashed 'Havoc' for example. As much attention was paid to crew protection and survivability as to flying performance, which has been enhanced to give both helicopters a much better low speed and hover manoeuvre capability than the 'Hind'. Another high-priority requirement was for a really good gun – traversable, long-range, lethal and reliable. The choice fell on the 30mm cannon of the ubiquitous BMP 2 mechanized infantry combat vehicle, adapted for airborne use.

It is estimated that half a million Soviet troops served in Afghanistan, of whom more than 80,000 were officers. A former Chief of the General Staff, Marshal Sergei Akhromeyev, described these officers as 'the golden fund of the Army . . . we must treat them with care, train them conscientiously and promote them'. How many of them continue to serve in any centralized armed forces or in Republican Armies or National Guards, and are encouraged to apply the lessons learnt, not least a creative and independent approach to problem solving, remains to be seen. Certainly the 'Afghantsy' (Afghan veterans) have much experience in guerrilla warfare to offer, experience that was called upon as ethnic conflict in parts of the former Soviet Union grew after the war was over. It will remain relevant if clashes of interests between and within republics continue and internecine warfare results.

General War
(1950–2000)

For centuries the overall speed of movement to and over the battlefield was restricted to the pace of the infantryman; animals were used largely for reconnaissance and logistic purposes. The introduction of the self-powered vehicle led to the demise of animals but, constrained largely to prepared surfaces and in insufficient numbers, did nothing to speed the pace of actual battle.

The cross-country mobility of tracked vehicles was seen as a means of raising the tempo of preparation and assembly for battle and the battle itself. But there were flaws in this idea too. Movement across country is slower than on roads; more fuel is needed and general wear and tear is much greater; historically, funding has always been insufficient to make all supply vehicles tracked and they must generally stick to the roads, thus confining flexibility. So, while the pace of battle quickened, tracks did not provide the leap forward in mobility that many envisaged in the 1920s and 1930s. However, the German blitzkrieg in the West in 1940 and against the Soviet Union in 1941 gave a taste of what might be possible.

As aviation prospered, use of the third dimension seemed a possible way out of this logjam. Airmobility had been born during the Korean War and Major General Gavin and other luminaries had ensured that the momentum gained during the 1950s, although faltering at times, was not allowed to grind to a halt. It was not until the 1960s, however, that helicopters of moderate capability and in any really significant numbers became available.

In September 1961 Robert McNamara, the US Secretary of State of Defence, reviewed Army Aviation plans and subsequently instituted a two-month study of them. In April 1962, having seen the results of this study, he expressed the opinion that the Army's programme was 'dangerously conservative'. It fell short of meeting procurement requirements, had not explored the opportunities offered by emerging technology and lacked imagination concerning the cost-effectiveness of aircraft. A bold re-examination of land warfare mobility was indicated and McNamara emphasized that he would be 'disappointed if the Army's re-examination [of airmobility] merely produces logistics-oriented recommendations to procure more of the same, rather than a plan for implementing fresh and perhaps unorthodox concepts which will give us a significant increase in mobility'.

Under the chairmanship of Lieutenant General Hamilton H. Howze, a Board was established to conduct an examination of the roles of Army Aviation, particularly the organizational and operational concepts of airmobility, and aircraft requirements. In August 1962 the Board submitted its final report. The value of airmobility was resoundingly endorsed. The Board recommended the replacement of some conventional forces by airmobile forces, specifically the creation of five air assault divisions, three air cavalry combat brigades and five air transport brigades over a period of six years; reorganization of another eleven conventional divisions was also proposed. The air assault division was to have two-thirds fewer ground vehicles than a standard division but have 459 aircraft which would be able to lift a third of its assault elements simultaneously. The air cavalry combat brigade would have 316 aircraft, of which 144 would be attack helicopters, for reconnaissance purposes and to fight rearguard actions to delay an enemy advance. The air transport brigade, with a mix of D.H. Canada Caribou fixed-wing transports and Chinook helicopters, would be structured for logistic support. The Board further recommended that a programme of field trials should be conducted to test the proposed force structure. Five months later the 11th Air Assault Division (Test) and the 10th Air Transport Brigade were activated for this purpose.

During the trials in 1963 and 1964 it became apparent that airmobility had enormous potential to influence the conduct of the land battle. Air assault forces, in the view of General Kinnard, could be held as a highly mobile reserve or act as a screen force capable of operating over long distances. Under the threat of nuclear weapons they could disperse widely and concentrate quickly.

Although the Howze Board had been concerned with airmobility in high-intensity operations in Europe, and trials to that end had taken place, it had become clear by early 1965 that European considerations would have to take second place to the needs of the war in Vietnam. The concept of airmobility had been validated and the sensible thing to do now was to retain the expertise gained over the previous two years and put it to the test of actual combat. Easier said than done: the adoption of any new military concept requires feasibility, the will and adequate funding.

For many reasons, not least the Vietnam War, few of the Howze Board's recommendations were actually implemented. Nevertheless, the US Army has today, and has had for many years, an air assault division (the 101st Airborne Division (Air Assault)) and an air cavalry combat brigade (the 6th Cavalry Brigade Air Combat).

Army Aviation

A brief explanation of the term 'army aviation' should be interjected here. Russian helicopters operating in support of the ground forces are termed 'army aviation' because operational control of them is vested in the commanders of certain ground armies; Military District commanders in peacetime and front commanders in war also have helicopter units operationally subordinated to them. The principal reason for establishing Soviet Army Aviation in the late 1970s was to respond to mounting criticism of the time taken by helicopter units in the Tactical Air Armies to react to calls for support and their poor co-ordination with the ground forces. These army aviation helicopters, however, belong to the Air Force which remains responsible for manning them, air and groundcrew training, equipment procurement, maintenance, logistic support and flight safety. Ground forces HQ and command posts include Air Force staffs who are responsible for arranging and co-ordinating fixed-wing aircraft and helicopter support. Nevertheless, army aviation became a formal branch of the Ground Forces in 1990 and its Air Force Commander is subordinate to the Commander-in-Chief of the Ground Forces. Further steps towards the creation of a Russian Army Aviation Corps, belonging to and funded by the Army, may not be far off.

In the West, where battlefield helicopters are usually owned and operated by the Army (for example, the British Army Air Corps, French ALAT, German Heeresflieger and US Army Aviation), the term clearly has a different meaning. In the view of most NATO armies it is a mistake to have vehicles that are intimately involved with the land battle operated by another Service. It is generally believed that Air Force understanding of the needs of the ground troops is inevitably not as good as that of soldiers trained subsequently as aircrew. NATO helicopters are regarded as akin to ground vehicles using the third dimension. Given their tactics and modes of operation close to the ground, this is a sound view. The Russians, on the other hand, with helicopters lacking a good hover performance, are unable to conduct the sort of stealth techniques practised by their NATO counterparts; they are therefore regarded, not as a vertical extension of the battlefield, but as the low-speed end of air operations. How this view may change when the new Russian attack helicopters, the Mi-28 'Havoc' and the Ka-? 'Hokum', enter service remains to be seen. The British continue with a unique arrangement whereby light combat helicopters are owned and operated by the Army and battlefield transport helicopters by the RAF.

The Threat to Combat Helicopters

Before examining some of the roles that helicopters did not undertake in the three campaigns studied (except anti-tank briefly in Vietnam) – but which will be of paramount importance in any future general war – it would be wise to examine the threats combat helicopters might face when they are within range of enemy fire. These threats can be degraded by a combination of technical counter-measures, firepower, helicopter tactics and close co-operation with ground forces.

Ever since aircraft arrived to add a new dimension to the battlefield, it has been largely the responsibility of the air forces and ground-based air defence to remove them from it. The crews of fixed-wing aircraft, unable to fly as low or as slowly or turn as sharply as a helicopter, have never found it easy to acquire and engage a helicopter whose pilot is aware of their presence. Nevertheless, most modern fighters have a look-down, shoot-down capability which could be targeted against helicopters if necessary. However, unless a comparatively slow or low-flying aircraft is specifically designed for such a role, the threat from fixed-wing aircraft is probably not high since they are likely to have more important targets which other weapon systems have difficulty in engaging. The threat from enemy helicopters is a different matter and is discussed later.

There is no army that can deploy enough air defence weapons to counter the highly mobile threat posed by helicopters. Nevertheless, there are many tactical systems for the attack of low-flying aircraft and helicopters. They range from self-propelled or towed gun and missile systems to man-portable shoulder or tripod-launched weapons. Within the next few years some of these may be replaced by hyper-velocity missiles (HVMs) travelling at speeds of about Mach 4. All these systems have their limitations. But those systems that constitute the greatest worry for helicopter crews are probably: man-portable missiles, because their presence is difficult to detect and because they are becoming increasingly able to engage targets at very low level without succumbing to background clutter; rapid-firing gun systems; and HVM, because of their speed.

The response time for field artillery is inadequate to match the mobility of the helicopter but it can put shells into possible helicopter ambush or loiter positions, although not for long since actual targets are more worthy of the limited supply of ammunition; the same goes for multiple rocket fire. The accuracy of tank main guns is a threat indeed, but not to helicopters standing off outside their range and using their own missiles or to helicopters flying at speed. Tanks like the Soviet T-64B and T-80, which have main guns capable of firing ATGMs as well as shells, pose a serious threat to hovering or slow-moving helicopters. Tanks, infantry fighting vehicles and armoured personnel carriers (APCs), armed reconnaissance vehicles and dismounted infantry are all equipped with a variety of machine-guns and cannon with calibres ranging from 5.45mm to 73mm. While NATO armoured fighting vehicles (AFVs) are generally not overly concerned with the engagement of enemy aircraft or helicopters at low level, Soviet tanks mount a 14.5mm machine-gun on the turret specifically for this purpose. The use of laser rangefinders significantly increases the probability of the first burst of fire hitting the target.

Apart from their well-known roles as rangefinders and target designators, low-energy lasers constitute a direct threat to human eyes and sensors. Canopies can be yellowed and crazed by laser damage weapons. When flying NOE even momentary blindness could prove fatal. Sensors such as thermal imagers are vulnerable and their failure may prevent the mission being completed. Technical counter-measures are under development and these include protective visors for crew helmets, filters for sensors, special coatings resistant to laser energy and so on. Some of these passive counter-measures are coupled with warning receivers to detect and identify hostile lasers. The threat these pose is already serious and is likely to grow.

A new anti-helicopter weapon now under development is a mine with an acoustic sensor. It exploits the fact that each type of helicopter has its own acoustic signature derived from the rotation of the rotor blades. Extra measures will have to be taken if adversaries operate the same type of helicopter. The mine is designed to detect and classify helicopters flying within about 5km (3 miles) and at no more than about 60m (200ft) and then be fired upwards at hostile targets flying within a lethal radius of about 100m. In addition to taking a toll of helicopters, these mines will also, in theory, force them to fly higher where they will become vulnerable to other weapons. They could be laid to keep enemy helicopters away from certain areas such as vital ground and undefended flanks, or channel them into 'killing zones' or protect specific high-value targets.

Despite these various weapons all available evidence from operational analysis, field exercises and actual combat shows that helicopters are no more vulnerable on the battlefield than any other vehicle.

Anti-Tank Warfare

In his book *Military Strategy* published in 1962, Soviet Marshal Sokolovsky wrote: 'An offensive should be mounted primarily using tanks and armoured troop carriers. Dismounted attack will be a rare phenomenon. Mechanized firepower and manoeuvres of troops in vehicles will now reign on the battlefield.' The most obvious difference between the campaigns in Algeria, Vietnam and Afghanistan, and indeed all other so-called low-intensity operations elsewhere, and general war is the presence of large numbers of AFVs and, in particular, tanks.

The effectiveness of tank-killing aircraft was proved during the Second World War. They were all, however, fixed-wing aircraft but this role has now been usurped to a large extent by anti-tank/attack helicopters. Fixed-wing aircraft are forced to fly higher than helicopters because of weapon delivery dive angles and their greater speed leaves much less time to avoid ground obstacles and to identify their targets. Thus the likelihood of hitting friendly AFVs, as tragically occurred during the Gulf War, is higher with fast jets than with helicopters. Unable to use cover like a helicopter, they more easily attract the attention of the enemy with their ever-increasingly sophisticated air defence weapon systems. Some of the theories surrounding the employment of helicopters in the armoured battle have been put to the test in combat in Operation 'Peace for Galilee' in 1982 between Israeli Cobras and 500MD Defenders and Syrian and PLO tanks, during the Iran–Iraq War and the Gulf War. The tank-killing capability of suitably armed helicopters has been proved to the satisfaction of many countries, now in the process of upgrading them or procuring them for the first time.

The preponderance and menace of Soviet tanks facing the newly established NATO in the early 1950s demanded counter-measures if they were to be deterred from rolling westwards. Matching them numerically was out of the question; tactics and technology, therefore, would have to provide answers. One such was the ATGM which would help to close the substantial gap between the range at which tank targets could be acquired and the lesser range at which the high-velocity gun of a defending tank could hope to achieve a first-round hit. By exploiting a missile's high first-round probability of a kill and its longer range the mismatch could be reduced and attrition could start earlier. Furthermore, tank guns usually fired kinetic energy rounds to defeat tank armour while missiles used chemical energy in the shape of hollow (or shaped) charge high-explosive anti-tank warheads. This type of warhead was the most effective given the need to keep missile weight as low as possible. Employing a chemical energy warhead offered another advantage: future tanks would have to incorporate more complex armour protection against both kinetic and chemical energy warheads. Because helicopters had the mobility to fire from different angles and thus extend the three-dimensional arc of attack, the distribution of this protection would have to be rearranged.

The high first-round kill probability depended on the warhead's lethality, system reliability and accuracy in hitting the target. The latter in turn depended on the guidance system and the ease with which the missile could be controlled in flight. Unlike gun systems, missile accuracy does not decrease with range, but it does depend on the gunner's target tracking ability.

It did not take long for those engaged in studies on the tactical uses of helicopters to hit upon the idea of mounting missiles on them. By doing so another significant advantage would be gained: the ability to move across all types of terrain and minefields at high speeds would allow a much quicker response to sudden and unwelcome changes in the tactical situation. At a comparatively low cost a great number of ATGMs could be concentrated rapidly to engage enemy tanks.

The French were the first into the new era. The SS-10 (Sol-Sol, ground-ground) with a range of only 1,600m and a leisurely speed of 80 metres per second (288km/hr; 179mph) entered service in 1955. A year later it was followed by a bigger, 3,000m-range version, the SS-11/AS-11. The AS-11 was first tested on a helicopter in 1958. It was attached to an Alouette II and, as has been noted, was used in Algeria against targets other than tanks.

Since then much research and development has been devoted to all aspects of ATGMs, including those adapted or specifically designed for use on helicopters: propulsion, guidance, missile control, the airframe, warheads, fuses and so on. Ideally, to enhance their survivability, helicopters should have a 'fire and forget' missile which is fast (supersonic), agile, lethal and long range. If it is not fire-and-forget, then it should have as short a time of flight as possible and the system should allow the pilot to carry out evasive manoeuvres between missile launch and impact.

Many second-generation systems, such as the TOW and HOT, both developed from man-portable systems, are still in service although they have benefited from upgrading. They use semi-automatic command to line-of-sight (SACLOS) guidance whereby all the gunner has to do is keep the missile sight's cross-hairs on the target for the missile to strike it. This requires less gunner skill than the earlier MACLOS guidance. These second-generation ATGMs are subsonic and usually take seventeen seconds or more to reach their maximum range of between 3,750 and 4,000m. The Soviet AT-6 'Spiral' is a case apart, having been designed specifically as a heliborne missile. Also SACLOS, it has a range of at least 5,000m which it can reach in about ten seconds.

The end of American involvement in Vietnam in 1973, followed a few months later by the Arab-Israeli Yom Kippur War, encouraged renewed attention to a potential European battlefield which, given the plethora of modern weapons on both sides, could be expected to outstrip even the Yom Kippur War in intensity. Strapping weapons, particularly missiles, onto utility helicopters and then calling them anti-tank helicopters was all that most countries could afford but it was far from ideal. What was needed was a purpose-designed anti-tank helicopter or, better still, attack helicopter. The fundamental difference between the two is that an anti-tank helicopter is a comparatively simple platform to carry missiles and the necessary sensors to the point where they are needed. Such helicopters are being superseded now by attack helicopters which have a wider and more offensive role and are armed with both missiles and other weapons able to attack a variety of targets. The Cobra attack helicopter was already in service and it was now a short step to modify it for the carriage of eight TOW missiles; trials began in 1973. In the same year the Soviet 'Hind A' with four AT-2 'Swatter' missiles and other weapons entered service.

Faced with this new missile threat, tank designers had to think again about armour protection and as they improved it so the missile designers had to think of new ways to defeat it. Some tanks now carry explosive reactive armour (ERA) in vulnerable areas. This has the effect of increasing the thickness of the armour. To defeat tanks with ERA, for example, the TOW 2A and HOT 3 ATGMs have tandem warheads, the first to trigger the explosives in the reactive armour and the second to penetrate the protective armour. The TOW 2 and HOT 2, both with larger warheads, were in action during the Gulf War. Other variants of the TOW, the 2B and the British FITOW (Further Improvements to TOW), aim to attack tanks, not from the front or side, but from above – overhead top attack – where the armour protection is thinner.

The quest for a fire-and-forget capability continues. With the current generation of missiles helicopters have to unmask to fire and remain in view of the enemy until missile impact, although they can manoeuvre to a certain extent. Naturally, every effort is made to minimize exposure. The first version of the American Hellfire missile, which entered service in 1985, could be fired and forgotten in certain circumstances. With a direct fire range of 7,000–8,000m, it was chosen as the primary point target weapon for the Apache and development proceeded in parallel. This missile has a semi-active laser homing head which seeks a laser spot put on the target by a laser designator. If the target is marked by the designator on board the same helicopter, then the missile is not fire-and-forget since the spot has to be held on the target until missile impact. If, however, the spot is held on the target by a ground-based designator or by another helicopter, then the Hellfire can be said to be fire-and-forget; in fact, the launching helicopter need never see the target if the lock-on after launch option is used. The Hellfire was widely used during the Gulf War and proved highly successful.

Better still, of course, is a true fire-and-forget capability at all times. It is planned that the Hellfire should obtain such a capability in 1997 with the help of a millimetre-wave fire-control radar mounted on the Apache's mast above the main rotor system. Target data will be processed and then handed down to a new active radar seeker in the missile. The complete system is known as Longbow. Various attack options will be available but the preferred one might be to raise the Apache to a height where a radio-frequency interferometer mounted just below the radar can search passively for, and identify, hostile weapon systems whose radar is operating before the active Longbow radar acquires the necessary target data. The helicopter would then descend behind cover and the missile would be launched under inertial guidance to lock on to its target when en route. Clearly, the Apache's time of exposure to the enemy will be much less than when firing a missile which has to be guided all the way to the target. Longbow Hellfire will, it is hoped, be effective in rain, snow, fog, smoke and battlefield obscurants, day and night.

First production deliveries of the Franco-German Tiger anti-tank helicopter – designated the Panzerabwehrhubschrauber 2 (PAH-2) in Germany – are scheduled for 1998 and a little later it is to be equipped with the fire-and-forget 4.5km-range TRIGAT ATGM, a co-operative venture between Britain, France and Germany. TRIGAT has a passive infra-red imaging seeker and tandem warhead. The gunner will be able to track four targets simultaneously. Target data is passed to the missiles and as soon as their IR seekers have locked on all four missiles can be launched in a salvo. The Tiger will also have a sight mounted above the main rotor. The 'Spiral' entered service in 1976 and the new Russian attack helicopter, the 'Hokum', possibly to enter service in 1993, will be equipped with a new laser-guided ATGM. The 'Havoc', if it enters operational service, will probably be similarly equipped. Both helicopters, however, have their missile sights located under the nose, necessitating almost complete exposure of the helicopter at least during target acquisition.

Anti-tank and attack helicopters are assets that are normally too precious to be allowed to find the targets they are to engage themselves; this is something for armed reconnaissance helicopters which are usually part of the attack team, the ratio depending on the tactical situation. In defence the primary task for reconnaissance helicopters is to ascertain the main and subsidiary axes of the enemy's advance. Deployed forward to monitor enemy movement and pass back information, they can also acquire, recognize and designate targets for helicopters, artillery and close-support aircraft. Using their height advantage and target acquisition devices, their ability to 'see' further than ground troops is crucial. By exploiting this capability and the long range of ATGMs, helicopters can begin the destruction of enemy armour at a range beyond all ground-based weapons save artillery. This long-range anti-tank fire from helicopters may also force the enemy to deploy off the line of march earlier than anticipated, which will slow down the speed of the advance and buy time for the ground commander to make any necessary changes to his defences. In an advance reconnaissance helicopters search out and designate targets, choose the route forward and provide a protective escort for the anti-tank/attack helicopters.

The Bell OH-58D Kiowa Warrior, an almost unrecognizable derivative of the OH-58 Kiowa which saw service in Vietnam, has set a new benchmark in reconnaissance capability and proved its worth in the Gulf War. Mounted on its rotor mast is a large 'ball' which contains a TV sensor, a thermal imager, a laser rangefinder and designator and an optical boresight system. The line-of-sight is 81cm (32in) above the rotor, thus allowing the gunner to observe while the rest of the helicopter remains behind cover. Most other reconnaissance helicopters have their sights mounted in the cockpit roof. With plenty of power, the Kiowa Warrior can be armed with a mix of weapons including Hellfire, Stinger, Hydra 70 rockets and guns.

NATO anti-tank and attack helicopters usually try to acquire and engage their allotted targets from concealed ambush positions while in the hover, the aim being to achieve surprise and concerted attack from different directions. As targets, tanks are less of a priority than any weapon system posing an immediate threat, air defence systems, command vehicles, bridging equipment and possibly mine ploughs. Radars, artillery and rocket systems, and command and mortar bunkers were all targets for helicopters during the Gulf War. While this target engagement phase is in progress, the reconnaisance helicopters keep track of the developing battle situation, watch out for any enemy weapon systems that might threaten the anti-tank/attack helicopters and if necessary draw their attention to them, and control any artillery or CAS aircraft allocated.

A key feature of the next-generation US reconnaissance/attack helicopter, the RAH-66 Comanche which, if approved for production, will not enter service before 2000 due to budget cuts, will be its electronic systems. Advantage will be taken of new technology to provide enhanced night piloting and targeting systems to broaden operations at night and in adverse weather to increase the range at which targets can be detected and recognized, and to reduce the time the Comanche is exposed to the enemy. Included will be a night vision pilotage system and an aided target detection/classification (ATD/C) system integrated with the Comanche's electro-optic target acquisition and designation system. Instead of popping up to acquire and engage targets as most current helicopters do, the

Comanche may rise above cover, briefly scan the terrain and record the picture on video, and then descend. The processors (and gunner) will examine the pictures to determine what kinds of targets have been detected, even if they are well camouflaged or partially obscured: perhaps a tank or light armoured vehicle, wheeled or tracked air defence system, self-propelled artillery or truck. Assessing also ranges and speeds, the ATD/C will put into priority targets to be engaged, annotating them on the helmet-mounted and cockpit displays. The targets may then be attacked in order or, since the Comanche's primary role will be armed reconnaissance, handed over to other helicopters. The likelihood of different helicopters firing at the same target, thereby delaying destruction of the enemy and wasting ordnance, should be diminished.

A number of factors conspire to make Russian attack procedures quite different from those practised by NATO helicopters. In their inventory the Russians have no helicopter capable of conducting sustained covert reconnaissance and surveillance, and none that matches the sophistication of modern Western reconnaissance helicopters. The 'Hind', with its missile sight underneath the front cockpit, and sometimes the 'Hip', are used for armed reconnaissance. Until the emphasis switched to a defensive posture, a covert reconnaissance capability was not really necessary, given the offensive doctrine of Soviet forces; formerly, it was envisaged that 'Hinds' would be supporting advancing ground forces rather than waiting for the enemy to come to them. The 'Hind's' low speed and hover performance is poor and the aircraft is not very stable in this regime. The strong rotor downwash kicks up considerable debris, such as dust and leaves, which might reveal the helicopter's position and obscure visibility through the sight. Finally, the 'Hind' is slow to accelerate away from the hover and is thus more vulnerable to enemy fire. For these reasons, when carrying out ground-attack missions, 'Hinds' usually fly forward at about 30m (100ft) above obstacles at an average speed of 250km/hr (155mph). They then ascend steeply to perhaps 50–150m (165–500ft) above ground-level to allow the gunners to find their targets, before beginning a shallow dive, firing the selected weapons at the maximum effective range. Such an attack profile makes them very vulnerable unless their attacks are co-ordinated with artillery and other fire.

Considerable attention has been paid to survivability and the integration of weapons to cater for most targets in the design of the 'Hokum' and 'Havoc'. With a much improved hover performance, their crews will have the option of carrying out high-speed diving attacks like the 'Hind' or NATO-style ambush attacks. The latter are more suited to defensive operations and will reduce vulnerability to modern air defence weapons such as HVMs. But in open and flat areas where there are relatively few places for helicopters to hide, speed may still have to be used instead of stealth.

The Gulf War presented an environment quite unlike that of Europe and different techniques were therefore appropriate; fortunately there was time to develop and practise them. Hovering or moving slowly over sand is likely to cause loose particles to be whipped up to form a cloud which may be visible from a long way off. Furthermore, visibility from the aircraft can be severely restricted. It is usually inappropriate to fire missiles in such conditions and so missile launch may take place in forward flight; exposure to the enemy will therefore probably be longer than when using standard NATO tactics. During the Gulf War, ATGMs were sometimes fired from a helicopter on the ground or when moving forward at about 30km/hr (18mph) at heights between 3 and 15m (10–50ft). Another factor to be taken into account in the desert is the heat haze which builds up during the day. It plays optical tricks and bedevils observation and target acquisition and engagement. Sand-covered terrain can be featureless, presenting problems of perception (judgment of range, thus necessitating a laser rangefinder, and height above ground when using night vision goggles, or when the sun is directly overhead and thus creating no shadows), navigation and concealment, both for loitering helicopters and forward arming and refuelling points (FARPs). Added to which, blowing sand, in particular, finds its way into every nook and cranny, clogging filters and causing damage to optics, canopies, rotor blades, engines, missile seeker heads and other assemblies and components. Maintenance takes longer and this adversely affects the number of helicopters available for immediate operations. Sandstorms, which can persist for days, can simply prohibit flying.

Close Air Support

The anti-tank, or anti-armour, role can be extended to embrace CAS, traditionally undertaken by fixed-wing fighter aircraft. The 'Hind' is classed as a CAS aircraft, mainly for the attack of mobile ground targets, and assumes most of this burden for the Russian ground forces; the 'Hokum' is likely to follow suit. The Apache in Israeli service performs some of the CAS missions that the cancelled Lavi fighter was designed to undertake. Western forces, in contrast, still rely on fixed-wing aircraft although their capability in this role is gradually being diminished through an inability to meet the required shorter response times, advances in air defence and a change in priorities. The number of fighters earmarked for CAS might be expected to dwindle in the coming years because of relatively poor cost-effectiveness and the perceived greater need for aircraft to win the air battle and to interdict enemy forces following up, or held in counter-attack positions, behind the forward troops.

The attack of targets on or just beyond the forward edge of the battle area (FEBA) by combat helicopters frees expensive fixed-wing aircraft to exploit their ability to penetrate enemy defences and attack forces in depth, out of range of helicopters. It is not speed that matters at the FEBA but the ability to loiter safely and engage a number of consecutive and selected targets, both by day and night, in fair weather and foul. A mix of weapons is necessary to cater for the different types of target and modern attack helicopters meet this requirement. They can also respond more quickly to a local crisis or opportunity because they are positioned much closer to the forward troops and they can operate in much lower cloud cover than fixed-wing aircraft. Furthermore, the ground commander's flexibility is enhanced by having such helicopter forces under his command or operational control and readily available. It is also easier to keep the crews briefed on the current positions of their own friendly forces and this should help to avoid instances of fratricide. On the other hand, helicopters cannot carry the same weight of ordnance as fixed-wing aircraft, lack speed and combat radius to operate far from their bases, and their FARPs and ambush positions are vulnerable to long-range artillery, missile and rocket fire. Fixed-wing CAS is controlled at the highest level and can be concentrated at a selected point within a large area to produce a shock effect against a mass of individual targets.

Both fixed- and rotary-wing types have their strengths and weaknesses in the CAS role and they are therefore complementary. Each can contribute to the other's survival and effectiveness, as was demonstrated by USAF A-10s and US Army Apaches working together in the Gulf War. Helicopters can attack enemy anti-aircraft weapon systems to open safe corridors through enemy defences. They can blunt an enemy advance, slowing its momentum and forcing vehicles to bunch, thus providing an attractive target for fixed-wing fighters and bombers. Or they can fly alongside their own advancing troops to strike targets beyond tank main gun range or provide instantaneous and intimate fire support. In the Gulf War Allied control of the skies and the lack of Iraqi resistance facilitated their CAS, but it is rare for one side to enjoy such advantages.

Modern warfare is joint warfare. Any Service is naturally reluctant to give up a traditional role, but it is not inconceivable that at some time in the future Western Armed Forces may follow the Soviet lead and let attack helicopters assume the responsibility for CAS while air interdiction receives greater emphasis for the Air Force.

Helicopter Air Combat

It is hard to envisage any future major conflict without helicopters: unarmed or lightly armed transport helicopters at one end of the scale, and sophisticated and heavily armed attack helicopters, even air combat helicopters, at the other. Unlike the Iraqis, countries with armed helicopters would be expected to use them in the event of war. Inevitably opposing helicopters will meet, particularly if operating in enemy territory, and when they do it is unlikely that they will ignore each other – although the lightly armed might prefer otherwise!

On the yet-to-be proved premise that an armed helicopter is the best weapon system to fight another helicopter, combat between the two, besides being inevitable, is also actually desirable. It could be argued that only helicopters share the combination of speed range, manoeuvrability and agility, firepower and operating environment. If this is so, dedicated air combat helicopters are needed and those countries which integrate them into the combined arms battle will give themselves greater flexibility and freedom of action in the air/land battle, not only by day but also by night.

Helicopter air combat is not like fixed-wing air combat for two main reasons. Any combat helicopter mission is inextricably tied to events on the ground and ground-based weapon systems will probably intervene whenever possible; secondly, the threat from these weapons and from fixed-wing aircraft will inhibit any desire to manoeuvre in the vertical plane. Hugging the ground gives protection but proximity to ground obstacles will add another major hazard. Thus fixed-wing tactics are not relevant and should not be emulated, although it would be foolish to ignore them completely.

There are perhaps four levels of helicopter air combat. The lowest is purely defensive where a helicopter is armed with only a self-defence weapon, probably a gun, to be used only when attacked. This would be suitable for transport helicopters – as was the case in the Gulf War. The second level embraces attack/anti-tank and reconnaissance helicopters which use their air-to-ground weapons to engage other helicopters, either defensively or, in a secondary role, offensively; they can also be armed with air-to-air missiles (AAM) of some sort to qualify for the third level. For example, some Kiowa Warriors are equipped with the Stinger and some French Gazelles are to have four shoulder-launched Mistrals adapted for helicopter-launch from 1993, in addition to a 20mm cannon; in fact, four Gazelles carried this missile during the Gulf War. Air combat was a factor in the design of the Comanche and attention was paid to making it difficult to detect, capable of good agility at low level, equipping it with appropriate weapons and associated equipment, and giving the crew good situational awareness.

The fourth level is to design, equip and deploy helicopters with air combat as their primary role. Such a level may not be considered cost-effective, at least not in the foreseeable future. So far, no nation has gone beyond the third level but the inevitability of helicopter combat may lead to this fourth level some day. The challenge will then be on to develop the optimum airframe/engine/flying controls package, survivability features, weapons and sensors, and integrate them all with a single pilot. The problems associated with air combat at night present an even greater challenge. Whatever night vision sensors are installed, the necessary information will have to be presented to the crew heads-up and looking out.

In the meantime, the helicopter coming nearest to the fourth level is the French Gerfaut, a combat support variant of the Tiger, to protect it, armoured and mechanized forces. Fast, manoeuvrable and agile, it will be armed with Mistral AAMs and a 30mm cannon. It is due in service in 1998.

What has held back the development of helicopter air combat has been a certain lack of will and the consequent absence of an agreed doctrine and tactics. In 1977 the US Army and Air Force undertook a series of field trials on how to counter the growing threat from large numbers of enemy helicopters but came to no agreement. A year later the USMC began to train its helicopter aircrews in air combat. Nevertheless, progress in formulating doctrine and the development of role equipment has been slow. In the American view, at least, helicopter air combat is seen as a natural extension of the ground battle and Army Aviation's contribution to low-level air defence in the forward area. Flying trials have shown that helicopters armed with AAMs can shoot down fixed-wing aircraft flying low-level at well over 750km/hr (465mph). As the USMC and US Army move somewhat hesitantly forwards, others are following, not least the Russians.

From the late 1970s articles on the subject have appeared in the Soviet military press, some openly advocating a response to Western developments. Currently, the 'Hind' is the helicopter most likely to indulge in air combat but, given its poor manoeuvrability, handling qualities and cockpit visibility, the results might not be entirely satisfactory; good speed and excellent weapons help to mitigate these shortcomings. But this is a role which 'Hind' crews may have to undertake and therefore they must be prepared for it. There is little doubt, particularly since the flight of the young German, Matthias Rust, into Moscow's Red Square in May 1987, that 'Hind' crews do train to intercept, track, identify and force or shoot down slow and low-flying intruders into CIS airspace. This is air interception but it is a useful preliminary stage; it probably leads onto training in battlefield air combat.

The Russians fully appreciate the shortcomings of the 'Hind' in this role, about which probably little can be done. Both the 'Hokum' and 'Havoc', with their improved manoeuvrability and agility, will be better. No Kamov military helicopter has ever operated permanently in support of the Soviet or Russian ground forces, all having been delivered to the Navy. However, with its co-axial contra-rotating rotor system and retractable undercarriage, the 'Hokum' is expected to have a high top speed and good manoeuvrability and agility. Like the Comanche, it will have the capability to range between the second and third levels as required.

In the meantime, until the case for an air combat helicopter is accepted by all the combat arms (and those responsible for funding such projects), attack and escort helicopters may be given the task of driving off enemy helicopters if they are interfering too successfully in the battle; this might be near the local FEBA or when they are penetrating friendly rear areas. In the former case it may be difficult to get close to the attacking helicopters if they do not cross the FEBA to carry out their attacks. If possible, long-range ambush engagements are to be preferred since the defenders will have the major advantages of initial detection and when to open fire. From a design point of view, such helicopters require a good hover and low-speed manoeuvre performance, but at the same time quick acceleration and deceleration to permit rapid movement from one area of concealment to another.

To counter a penetration, success will depend on good intelligence as to probable objectives, quick decision-making, speed of reaction and flying speed. Obviously, the faster the defending helicopters can fly, the more likely they are to be able to intercept the attacking force en route or, if a helicopter assault, while it is on the ground disembarking troops and equipment. The requirement for high speed, however, conflicts to some degree with the one stated above for good low-speed manoeuvre and agility. Ultimately, in the lethal environment near the FEBA, NOE altitude is the key to surviving to fight another day – and this is not compatible with high speed. So the flight performance design characteristics of attack helicopters, unlike any future air combat helicopters, must incorporate the best compromise between speed, range/endurance and manoeuvrability. Combat may degenerate into single helicopter versus helicopter but only as part of a larger battle between helicopter formations, large or small. For one helicopter to concentrate on another enemy helicopter alone may well invite retribution from a wingman. Most engagements will be fleeting. Constant lookout will be essential and cockpits must be designed to facilitate this.

Most important will be command and control and the degree of initiative allowed to the aircrew. Appreciation of, and obedience to, the rules of engagement will be vital. Enthusiastic indulgence in countering enemy helicopters at the expense of the anti-tank task could lead to disaster. This is not a failing from which the Russians are likely to suffer. Despite the Afghan experience and exhortations from senior officers to their subordinates, the traditional Soviet tendency towards strict control may persist in the armed forces of the CIS. But to stand any chance of success, helicopter air combat demands great flexibility on the part of those involved and Russian crews should be encouraged to exercise their own judgment more and be prepared to seize any opportunities that arise.

The next generation of combat helicopters, the Comanche, Gerfaut, Tiger, 'Hokum' and 'Havoc', will incorporate an air combat capability. None is designed as a dedicated air combat helicopter but all will be able to undertake this role while carrying out their primary missions.

A more positive attitude than is currently fashionable may be to task some attack helicopters more or less permanently in the air combat role. A certain proportion of such helicopters in a unit – the number depending on the circumstances – might be given the duty of escorting other attack, reconnaissance or transport helicopters – rather like the Gerfaut. These crews might have received some specialist training. Better still would be a flight within a squadron or regiment dedicated to the role with the appropriate weapons and training. Such sub-units would have air combat as their primary role and could be tasked to go out offensively and search for enemy helicopters, in addition to being available in a defensive escort role. In so doing, they would be contributing to the overall army air defence effort; indeed, in undertaking this particular task, they could be given the responsibility for covering areas that ground-based systems could not reach due to impassable terrain or line-of-sight problems. However, the possession of such sub-units does not preclude the need for all helicopters to be able to defend themselves with either passive and/or active countermeasures.

A vital element in air combat is target acquisition and it is generally accepted that the crews who see their opponents first have a distinct advantage. Passive and active sensors on-board the helicopter and information from ground units will play a part. At NOE levels, terrain features and built-up areas will be used to provide ambush positions, whether in defence or attack. These are likely to be more available in Europe than in the Middle East or other desert areas where there is less natural cover and where blowing sand and glint caused by the sun may reveal ambush positions. In a sophisticated environment the use of passive sensors such as thermal imaging, radio-frequency interferometer (as found on the Longbow Apache) and laser and radar warning receivers are preferable to using active systems such as millimetric-wave radar. These sensors must then cue the helicopter's weapon systems for rapid target acquisition and engagement. A quick and easy method of alerting all other helicopters in the formation to the approaching enemy is needed.

Short- and long-range engagements must be catered for, but there is no single weapon which can meet this requirement. A gun is necessary for manoeuvring targets out to about 1,200m. It should be traversable so that it may be fired at targets off the line of flight, particularly those encountered suddenly and at short range, a likely outcome when in an ambush position. The minimum effective calibre today is probably 12.7mm. This will not be good enough in the future when nothing less than 20mm will do. This is the calibre chosen for the Comanche's gun. The Apache's 30mm Chain Gun is inadequate with its 625 rounds per minute, and the 'Hokum's' and 'Havoc's' 30mm cannon is not much better at its high rate of 800–900. The Comanche's triple-barrelled cannon will have two rates of fire: 750 rounds per minute for the attack of ground targets and 1,500 rounds per minute for air targets. The Gerfaut will have a 30mm cannon mounted in a nose turret but its rate of fire will be nominally 750 rounds per minute. Whereas the Apache can carry up to 1,200 rounds, the Comanche and 'Hokum' will have just 500, the Tiger 450 and the 'Havoc' only about 300 – about 20 seconds' worth of fire. All helicopter gun systems currently in service are area weapons and optimized for the air-to-ground role. Programmes are now in hand to improve the accuracy of helicopter cannon in the air-to-air mode and the Comanche will benefit from this.

Maximum gun and minimum missile ranges should overlap. ATGMs, particularly those that are both fast and manoeuvrable, have an air-to-air capability. But, except for Longbow Hellfire and TRIGAT, all have to be guided to the target whereas fire-and-forget is what is really needed. But if the situation permits or the priority is high enough then purpose-designed AAMs are to be preferred. The heat-seeking, and thus fire-and-forget, missiles now being mounted on helicopters, such as the Stinger and the

Mistral, suffer from certain disadvantages: it is sometimes difficult for them to lock on, and maintain lock-on, to targets whose IR signature has been suppressed to some degree and which are at low level where ground obstacles get in the way; they are susceptible to decoy flares; they have a minimum range, usually not less than 500m, below which they cannot manoeuvre; and a few seconds are required to activate and launch them. Missile launch constraints reduce the manoeuvre envelope of the helicopter during the search, lock-on and firing sequence.

A better bet in the future could be HVMs. A modified air-to-air variant – Helstreak – of the British Starstreak, a laser beam-riding HVM system which travels at about 1km/sec to its maximum effective battlefield range, might be a contender. Damage to the target is done by the combined kinetic and chemical energy of its three darts. Helstreak should have a better capability in ground clutter than IR missiles and of course will be very difficult to evade because of its speed. HVMs will probably offer an added bonus: the ability to take on light armoured vehicles. However, Helstreak has to be pointed more or less at the target and it has yet to demonstrate its effectiveness in the air-to-air role. At this stage HVMs appear to offer a cost-effective means of attacking enemy helicopters out to a visual range of about 4km (2.5 miles) which are exposed for only a very short time. All weapons for air combat ideally require fire-control systems optimized for air-to-air engagements, allowing rapid and accurate aiming and firing.

Other Roles

In addition to those already described in this and previous sections, combat helicopters undertake other less common roles.

Electronic warfare (EW) capabilities continue to make dramatic progress and the efforts devoted to further developments tend to confirm the general belief that the initiative in battle will be held by the side that commands the electro-magnetic spectrum, a belief reinforced by the Gulf War. EW embraces defensive electronic counter-measures (ECM), which every combat helicopter needs to a greater or lesser degree, and electronic support measures (ESM). ESM includes the interception, location and jamming of enemy transmitters and the collection of electronic information.

Another aspect of EW is radar surveillance of the enemy. In any kind of confrontation or conflict the collection of information about the enemy is essential to success. As the battlefield becomes more complex and sophisticated and the intensity of 24-hour operations increases, it becomes ever more important that timely and accurate information on enemy movements and deployments is gathered without pause to avoid the possibility of being surprised. The Gulf War afforded a good example of this. The Allies' intelligence on Iraqi dispositions was comprehensive, whereas information on Allied movements was negligible once the Iraqis had conceded their own airspace. They were thus susceptible to deceptive measures and were duly surprised. Satellites, fixed-wing aircraft such as the airborne warning and control system (AWACS), the joint surveillance and target attack radar system (JSTARS) and other reconnaissance types, remotely piloted vehicles and drones, all have a part to play. But there is no reason why a helicopter with a radar and secure data links to the appropriate ground stations cannot also help to meet this requirement for continuous surveillance at the tactical and operational levels.

The advantages offered by a helicopter rather than a fixed-wing aircraft in this role include the ability to loiter safely close to the operational area before being directed to observe a target, a quick reaction to this order, NOE transit from one location to another, no requirememnt for a runway susceptible to attack and thus greater flexibility in the choice of operational bases and forward sites, together with greater security when on the ground because of these dispersed sites, and more rapid climbs and descents to reduce vulnerability to enemy fire. Finally, in Armies with no light fixed-wing aircraft there is an advantage in having a few organic Army helicopters equipped for this role and under command, or at least operational control, rather than having to rely on the good offices of the Air Force. In range/endurance, however, the helicopter is inferior to an equivalent fixed-wing aircraft.

The speedy passage of the information collected is crucial. A battle is quite likely to proceed more quickly than the information about it can be relayed to higher HQ. It then has to be collated and evaluated, by which time plans may be made on outdated intelligence.

At one time the French Army had planned to form two units each with ten AS.532 Cougar (previously Super Puma) helicopters and three ground stations in 1997. The Cougars were to be equipped with the Orchidée (Observatoire Radar Cohérent Héliporté d'Investigation des Eléments Ennemis) battlefield surveillance radar. To refine the raw data provided by Orchidée, drones would be used for the precise acquisition and identification of targets, mainly armoured vehicles in convoy and combat helicopters. The French requirement was for the radar to be able to detect, measure the speed if moving and classify such vehicles as wheeled, tracked or airborne at ranges up to 150km (93 miles) in all weathers; also to find targets for Hades, a mobile tactical missile.

Despite counter-measure devices, to remain invulnerable to enemy SAMs radar surveillance helicopters would have to be deployed some tens of kilometres behind their own FEBA and, for the radar to achieve the desired range, they would have to fly at heights of up to 3,050m (10,000ft). The basic principle of operation might be to have several helicopters deployed in pairs simultaneously. On the direction of a ground station one of a pair would ascend rapidly to its observation altitude, switch on its radar for no more than a minute and then descend again. Meanwhile the other helicopter positions itself for its climb. Survivability would thus be enhanced by using short and intermittent radar bursts from two separate helicopters.

In the French case the data gathered was not to be processed on-board but transmitted direct via an ECM-resistant data link to ground stations which were to analyze, correlate and distribute them as necessary. The Orchidée project, however, was cancelled in mid-1990 after only one Puma-based technology demonstrator had been built, the decision being based on the fact that the radar was designed principally for war in Central Europe, which was now considered to be remote. Nevertheless, the demonstrator, renamed Horizon, with a less capable EW suite than that planned for production, took part in the Gulf War and was used by day and night to search for mobile Scud-launchers and any movement of possible Iraqi reinforcements, to track retreating vehicle convoys and to locate targets for attack helicopters including Apaches. Because of its success, the cheaper and lighter Horizon, possibly without the advanced ECM systems planned for Orchidée and with simplified on-board data processing, may be developed for the French Army and for export.

By using aircraft considerable increases in range for communications interception, direction-finding and different types of offensive jamming can be achieved. Helicopters have undertaken these roles for some years, notably the American EH-1H Quick Fix 1 equipped with the AN/ALQ-151 battlefield radio jammer and the Soviet Mi-8 'Hip J' and 'K' used to noise-jam surveillance, target-tracking and fire-control radars and some ground-based communications systems from stand-off positions well behind their own FEBA. Such jamming might play a significant part in disrupting enemy command, control and target-acquisition systems, and therefore hinder battle planning and its execution. Naturally, strenuous efforts are being made to obviate the effects of jamming.

Modern combat helicopters usually have their own self-protection jammers: IR jammers are commonplace and some helicopters have radar jammers as well. Helicopters are sensitive to the weight, size and electrical power requirements of such jammers, all of which serve to limit their capabilities. On the other hand, these jammers only have to counter comparatively short-range weapon systems. They must however be readily adaptable to meet new and better systems.

Heliborne offensive jammers offer much the same advantages as heliborne surveillance radars, particularly line-of-sight to the target which is more difficult for ground-based jammers. They must keep fairly well to the rear to ensure their safety, but that gives them freedom to go higher to extend their effective jamming range.

The US Army operates a modified version of the standard Black Hawk assault helicopter, the EH-60C with the Quick Fix 2B equipment to intercept, locate, monitor and jam enemy battlefield communications. Some were in operation during the Gulf War. In the Russian Air Force it is to be expected that the more powerful and newer 'Hip H', operated by many Armed Forces around the world, will be converted to assume the roles currently undertaken by the 'Hip J' and 'K'. The Russians already have a few and the Hungarian Air Force modified at least two 'Hip Hs' in 1990 for the communications jamming role. It is possible that the Russians might convert a few 'Halos' for the same purpose.

While the likelihood of nuclear war, at least in Europe, is receding, the possibility of chemical warfare, particularly in the Middle East, seems to be increasing as more and more countries develop or procure chemical weapons. Helicopters can be equipped to monitor radiation levels and chemical contamination. For example, the Mi-24R 'Hind G' carries a device on each wing tip, in place of the usual missiles; the helicopter having landed, one device is pivoted towards the ground so that it can scoop up a sample of soil. The procedure is repeated in a second location and then samples are delivered to a ground station for analysis. Ideally, cockpits and cabins should be pressurized to protect the helicopter crew when flying in a nuclear or chemically contaminated environment. If helicopters are not so designed, then the crews will have to wear protective equipment including respirators, which inevitably tires them more quickly and degrades their performance. The evacuation of chemically contaminated casualties presents a major problem and special measures are needed to prevent any contamination of helicopter cabins.

How Helicopters Contribute to the Land Battle

The concept of an air/land battle was originally conceived in the USA as a means of overcoming numerically superior Warsaw Pact forces by exploiting high-technology weapons and equipment. It was believed that smaller NATO forces could prevail against a larger enemy by moving more rapidly and striking synchronously in different places, both close in and deep. Air and ground power are thus fused into one force, the epitome of combined arms action, to keep the enemy off balance. In a process of constant development since the 1950s the concept of airmobility has expanded and evolved into combat aviation. No longer does it merely contribute to fire support and mobility. It has become one of the main components of the air/land battle along with armoured, infantry, artillery and other units of the ground forces. Airmobility is now just a part of combat aviation – the carriage of troops into battle by helicopter. Combat aviation embraces the whole gamut of helicopter operations from attack and armed reconnaissance to battle-casualty evacuation and logistic support in all phases of war at tactical and operational levels of command. The helicopter's unique mobility is exploited to override the limitations of time, distance and terrain; its flexibility to match or change the tempo of battle and to respond to opportunities or crises.

In the air/land battle combat aviation ranges far and wide: from friendly rear areas where it is concerned with security to the main battle area to cross-FLOT missions. In fact, the edges are blurred between them all and the notion of a 'front line', FEBA or FLOT, is becoming difficult to sustain, given the inevitable gaps and open flanks in the defence and both antagonists' desire to take advantage of them to seize the initiative; a local

FEBA will apply when opposing forces clash in what might be called an area, or pocket, of combat.

To exploit the benefits of aerial manoeuvre, different countries have established a wide variety of specialist airmobile/air assault units and formations. Infantry units trained to move by helicopters supplied by the air force, like some Russian motor rifle battalions, probably represent the least sophisticated level. Much more capable is the British 24th Airmobile Brigade, with its two airmobile battalions, a wheeled APC battalion, 28 organic AAC Lynx anti-tank and light transport helicopters, a few Gazelle reconnaissance helicopters and some RAF Chinook and Puma medium transport helicopters on call. However, it has too few helicopters and the RAF ones are not under command – a frustrating arrangement for the brigade commander who is unable always to make plans in the knowledge that he will get the helicopters he wants. How fortunate was the commander of the 1st Cavalry Division in Vietnam in this respect and its successor, the 101st Airborne Division (Air Assault) with some 400 organic helicopters. The Germans group an anti-tank, a light and a medium helicopter transport regiment into an aviation brigade at corps level, and are also planning to contribute an airborne brigade to NATO's airmobile division. The Russian Armed Forces include a number of so-called independent airborne brigades and battalions. Not all the personnel are parachute-trained and the units do not have their own dedicated helicopters, for which they must rely on the Air Force. They are therefore neither truly independent nor airborne, but rather airmobile.

The French 4th Airmobile Division, a key element of the Force d'Action Rapide (Rapid Deployment Force), was formed in July 1985. It has a particularly high ratio of helicopters to troops. With a strength of 6,500 men and 244 helicopters, the division is structured to fight at helicopter speed, perhaps eight to ten times faster than conventional tank warfare. The French, therefore, are the first in Europe to achieve such a revolutionary goal. The division can operate independently and consists of three combat helicopter regiments, a command and transport helicopter regiment, an airmobile combat regiment of ground troops to support the combat helicopters, and an airmobile support regiment. The 160 Gazelles are used in the anti-tank, reconnaissance, fire support, escort, and command and control roles; the 84 Pumas and Cougars undertake troop and logistic transport and airborne command post duties. What is currently lacking is a heavy-lift capability, equivalent to that of a Chinook or Sea Stallion, and a modern attack helicopter. The American equivalent of this division is the 6th Cavalry Brigade (Air Combat) with, when reinforced in time of war, six attack helicopter battalions, two or three battalions of assault helicopters and two medium helicopter battalions – a very hard-hitting force of over 400 helicopters. It is not however expected to fight independently but in support of other larger formations.

To match the changed political and military situation in Europe a new NATO operational concept is being developed. Dispensing with comparatively static forward defences, NATO forces are being structured at three readiness levels: rapid reaction forces (a strengthened version of SACEUR's present ACE Mobile Forces, to be called the Immediate Reaction Force, a multi-national ground corps of seven divisions and a Rapid Reaction Force (Air)), so-called main defence forces and augmentation forces (reinforcements). Units of the rapid reaction forces could possibly be made available for operations beyond NATO territory if agreement to such a concept were forthcoming. Mobility will be the key, the quantity of forces being smaller than today and the area larger than previously with the inclusion of what was East Germany. The rapid reaction corps will include a multi-national airmobile division composed of brigades from Belgium, Britain, Germany and the Netherlands. Operating different types of equipment in accordance with varying tactics and procedures, non-standard training and possible language difficulties will present considerable problems, at least until a degree of interoperability and standardization can be worked up.

In addition to the airmobile/air assault formations mentioned, these countries and others have various types of helicopter units consisting of attack, reconnaissance, assault and medium-lift helicopters to support their ground forces in all phases of war.

It is likely that for defensive operations in Europe or elsewhere helicopters will be employed in a screen or covering force for surveillance and target acquisition. Enemy forces are unlikely to have much difficulty in infiltrating between defensive strongpoints and helicopters are well suited to finding them, imposing losses and slowing their progress. Once the covering force has been driven back by the enemy, any surviving elements can re-group to take part in the subsequent battles.

The number of anti-tank/attack and reconnaissance helicopters available for these battles will dictate how they are used. They will have an important role, engaging tanks, other vehicles and helicopters and resisting attempts at outflanking manoeuvres. If a breakthrough occurs, helicopters can then act in a counter-penetration role to try to prevent any momentum building up. It is normal for anti-tank helicopters to operate behind their own FLOT, although in the even more fluid battle now anticipated, inadvertent crossing of what purports to be this line is to be expected; there may be occasions when it would be advantageous to do so. Even when over nominally friendly territory crews may expect to carry out attacks above unfamiliar terrain which may also be insecure. In principle, sufficient helicopters should be employed to achieve a shock impact since a few small teams nibbling away at the enemy are unlikely to produce decisive results. On the other hand, there may well be times when just a few helicopters, rapidly deployed at a critical moment, can nip an enemy action in the bud. Given ever-improving surveillance devices, a large number of helicopters are susceptible to detection before they can open fire, are more difficult to control and, if trying to remain concealed, a vast amount of terrain may be needed to provide sufficient cover. It is the terrain which dictates the availability of concealed fire positions and engagement areas. It is highly improbable that every one of a large group of helicopters, if in concealed positions, will have a line-of-sight to their targets at the same time. These positions should not normally be compromised merely to try to achieve a simultaneous missile launch.

Helicopters cannot sustain an action for long before having to rearm and possibly refuel. So, to maintain constant pressure on the enemy, the force may have to split into three groups: one engaging the enemy, one in position a few kilometres behind the FEBA, ready and waiting to enter the battle, and the third refuelling and rearming. To augment this heliborne firepower, infantry with portable ATGMs can be rapidly deployed by assault helicopter and airborne observers can direct artillery and rocket fire.

It cannot be emphasized too strongly that, to give full value in the air/land battle, helicopter units must be employed as an integral part of ground formations. Co-operation between helicopter and ground-based units should be as close as that between tanks and mechanized infantry. This is no easy matter, given the widely differing characteristics of their equipment. Nevertheless, to derive full benefit from combat aviation, helicopter units should be treated just like other ground manoeuvre units, not as Air Force units or as detached sub-units. Ideally, they should be tactically and logistically independent so that they can be grouped when necessary at division, corps or army level. There is no reason why a helicopter brigade, regiment or battalion commander cannot take tank, mechanized infantry and artillery units under command and be given missions like any other tactical commander. A helicopter unit commander should not just be a distributor of helicopter assets.

Defensive operations may prevent defeat but they will not lead to the downfall of the enemy; for that, offence is necessary. A key part of the air/land battle, so successfully planned and carried out in the Gulf War, involves the use of helicopters for attack and assault combined with powerful and rapid armoured thrusts under the cover of massive artillery and air bombardment. The new generation of attack helicopters, 'Havoc', 'Hokum', Longbow Apache, Tiger and Comanche with their advanced flying performance, weapons and survivability, will play their part, reaching out across the FLOT to attack enemy reserves and important targets deep in the enemy rear, perhaps 100km (62 miles) or more, that for one reason or another air interdiction aircraft cannot attack. Such attacks might take place almost on the spur of the moment to take advantage of the discovery of an open flank or gap, or they might be pre-planned. They could be part of a larger deception plan. Heliborne assault troops may also carry out cross-FLOT attacks: either in the manner of a raid, when they return to friendly territory as soon as the mission is completed, or when attacking an objective with the intention of staying there until linking up with advancing ground forces. Small tactical assaults would probably remain within range of organic divisional artillery, say 20km (12.5 miles). The 101st Division's establishment of the 'Cobra' base in the Gulf War so far ahead of the ground troops was only possible because of Allied air supremacy and because the area was sparsely defended by a demoralized enemy.

The possession of sophisticated night vision sensors and navigation aids will encourage commanders to order these operations at night to reduce the risk of enemy interference and to take advantage of the poor capability of optical air defence weapons. Successful night operations can have a devastating impact on the enemy, but the undoubted risks must be weighed against the potential gains. There is much that can go wrong, particularly over unknown territory in poor weather, and a supreme level of training, and some luck probably, will be necessary. The greater the number of helicopters taking part, the greater will be the need for tight command and control, close co-ordination with escorting helicopters, slick communications (particularly when things start to go wrong), pinpoint navigation, faultless formation-keeping, accurate supporting fire, deceptive measures and rigid discipline. Good quality intelligence will be vital. Nevertheless, the initiative lies with the attacker and with good security and well-trained troops surprise should be achieved.

Attack helicopters would play an essential role in any heliborne assault to seize important ground to help in a counter-attack or, more offensively, into enemy rear areas whether on a raid or a holding operation. In enemy rear areas such a force might be tasked with attacking nuclear weapon sites, command posts and communication centres, capturing airfields, bridges or good river crossing sites, or disrupting the movement of enemy forces or logistic arrangements. The effect on the morale of enemy units attacked in areas they considered to be safe, or simply threatened from both front and rear, should not be overlooked; in any case, precautions will have to be taken against such a threat. Many factors would have to be considered by the assault force, such as the distance between the target and leading friendly forces, how long the force will have to stay on its objective before relief and also how to extract it; artillery and CAS; the strength of the defending forces and therefore what support weapons the assault force will need; whether to go by day or night; the availability of helicopters (two or more lifts may be necessary); the points at which the FEBA, however tenuous, should be crossed; the selection of LZs and routes to them; the resupply of fuel and ammunition, casualty evacuation and many others.

The heliborne assault is unlikely to deviate much in terms of technique from assaults carried out in Vietnam and Afghanistan. The air defence environment, however, will be much more dangerous and every measure to reduce helicopter vulnerability will be essential: deception, low-level flying, unexpected routes, suppression of enemy defences, speed, protection by attack helicopters on all sides of the assault helicopter formation, the jamming of enemy radars and communications, and so on.

Operations on the FEBA or beyond the FLOT cannot be sustained if friendly rear areas, logistic and C3 centres, are not secure. Because helicopter bases are also quite attractive targets for artillery and rocket fire, they are usually located well to the rear. Forward arming and refuelling points and personnel pick-up points are established as necessary. Enemy parachute and heliborne assault forces, special forces and forward detachments all pose threats which, if they materialize, need to be thwarted as quickly as possible. It is not always easy to anticipate where such forces may strike but a survey of attractive targets and vulnerable areas can certainly be made. As usual, any intelligence as to enemy actions and intentions will help and may allow the interception of these forces, even while still airborne, before they can reach their objectives. Rapid reaction is vital to prevent their consolidation. Thus some kind of combat aviation force should be included in the reserve for this task. It should be included in the defenders' counter-penetration and counter-attack plans and it should prepare its own plans for independent operations on the flanks and to counter enemy forces preparing to attack, or actually attacking, selected targets.

While reconnaissance and attack helicopters are suitable for discovering the strength and location of the enemy force and can start to contain it, armoured units and/or mechanized infantry are probably better able to destroy it. Problems lie in the likelihood that rear-area assets are required as reserves to reinforce forward units and that they will be numerically insufficient to cover all eventualities. The risk will grow as the number of possible rear-area targets grows. The commander will have to decide the priorities: whether to strengthen rear-area security at the expense of main battle area and possible cross-FLOT operations, or try to win or maintain the initiative forward at the risk of diminishing protection in the rear.

The Future

On 1 July 1991 the Warsaw Pact was dissolved. Nevertheless, the Armed Forces of the CIS remain the most powerful in Europe, despite the Conventional Armed Forces in Europe (CFE) Treaty, signed on 19 November 1990, and the new Soviet military doctrine, proclaimed in May 1987, which incorporated the principle of 'reasonable sufficiency' and the concept of non-offensive defence. The aim of this new doctrine was to prevent war rather than prepare for it. The combination of a defensive doctrine with reasonable sufficiency did not necessarily confirm, however, that the predominance of offensive action had been rejected – particularly since the belief that this is the only way to achieve victory had been encouraged over many decades. Indeed, Soviet military leaders stressed that an aggressor cannot be defeated by defensive measures alone; the Iraqi conduct of the Gulf War merely served to confirm the truth of this.

Certainly by 1991 it was realized that, given the dissolution of the Warsaw Pact, the assumptions on which the 1987 defensive military doctrine was based had become invalid. For one thing, the Soviet Union no longer had any Warsaw Pact allies and for another, with troop withdrawals from Eastern Europe, her defence would henceforth start on her western borders instead of the frontier between East and West Germany. The ability to deliver an 'adequate response' to aggression was considered to be essential and this would inevitably include counter-offensives and outright offence; in fact, the distinction between offence and defence would be blurred.

The repercussions of the failed coup in August 1991 continue to reverberate, but the new military leadership quickly declared that there would be no change in doctrine. Although the likelihood of precipitating a war in Europe, particularly one that could escalate to a catastrophic nuclear exchange, is currently remote, intentions, unlike capabilities, can change overnight; and, given the instability in the former Soviet Union, the possibility of internal conflict spilling over international borders remains. The risk of conflict in Europe stems from ethnic and territorial disputes exacerbated by economic, political and social problems.

While the likelihood of general war in Europe has receded, it has not done so in other parts of the world. A number of countries, particularly in the Middle East, North Africa and the Far East, possess large forces and huge quantities of modern weapons and could indulge in general war. It might be difficult to control the spread of a conflict which could then suck in forces from further afield. The shifting nature of international relations will not change and the likelihood will remain that a country or countries will resort to military action if it or they believe this to be profitable. The unprovoked invasion of Kuwait on 2 August 1990 demonstrates that peace and stability should not be taken for granted. The Gulf War – more a triumphal procession for the Allies than a ground battle, in the wake of a devastating onslaught from the air – should not be taken as a model for a future general war, given the five and a half months available to prepare the Allied forces and its subsequent one-sided nature.

As the run-down of forces in Europe proceeds, new defensive plans will have to be devised by both NATO and the CIS. One factor to be taken into account will be less reliance on resort to nuclear weapons. Another will be the less dense deployment of ground forces, the greater gaps within and between units and formations, and therefore the greater distances to be covered by firepower and the movement of men and supplies. How to counter wide outflanking movements or attacks deep into friendly territory with heavy air support will be a major concern. Reliance on fewer and more dispersed troops will necessitate a more active defence in depth and will result in greater dependence on mobile firepower and stronger and more mobile reserves. Static and linear defences, as the Iraqis discovered, are largely worthless. At the same time, advances in technology will allow commanders to fight the battle at longer ranges, both in defence and attack, with highly accurate indirect-fire weapon systems, and at a much faster pace; the only way to survive the effects of precision weapons may be by frequent movement.

Surveillance will become even more important, particularly of enemy spearheads, follow-on forces, the gaps and all flanks – features also significant in desert warfare. At divisional and corps level more reliance is likely to be placed on remotely piloted vehicles. Since it will sometimes be possible to deceive electronic systems, some of the results of these flights may have to be confirmed by reconnaissance helicopters. Surveillance and target-acquisition systems will become more capable in worse visibility by day and night and will make it increasingly difficult for large armoured forces to achieve anything more than local tactical surprise. When employed as reserves to counter enemy spearheads, armoured forces may have to be widely dispersed in depth and then move quickly once the decision to commit them has been taken. But this may be difficult due to enemy interference, awkward terrain, obstacles and an insufficient number of routes.

Because of the problems, the decision to order these forces into action will be a difficult one and may have to be taken before the full extent of the enemy's axis of advance is known, thus increasing the possibility of the decision being overtaken by events; even then these reserves may be unable to match the speed of the leading enemy troops or air assault forces. Yet to be effective reserves must have greater flexibility, speed and mobility than the attacker. Unless recourse to the third dimension is made, this will be difficult to achieve. A significant part of a reserve force should, ideally, comprise combat aviation with airmobile elements; although warned for action, the decision to commit it can be delayed for longer because of its speed of movement.

In the same way, any screen or covering force, aimed at determining the enemy's composition and strength, axis of advance and possible intentions, will have to be backed up by long-range weapon systems and quick-reaction forces able to delay the enemy advance for long enough to allow the main defensive force to deploy as necessary to stop it and create the conditions required for a counter-attack. The aim generally will be to destroy enemy forces, not fight for ground. As well as airborne surveillance and reconnaissance, EW, command and control, troop mobility and mobile firepower, particularly direct fire at long range, will become essential – a package of requirements that can best be met by combat helicopters which can concentrate quickly from dispersed sites and reach the point of action in a matter of minutes. This facility becomes even more valuable under a chemical or nuclear threat, or when such weapons are actually being used. Indeed, it is probably only the helicopter with its speed and flexibility that can get inside the enemy's decision-making process – speeded now by a high degree of automation – and render less effective the enemy's high-precision weapons. The helicopter's ability to cover gaps and operate to, and even across, corps boundaries gives it an operational dimension in addition to its more confined tactical roles; its excellent communications facilities enable transfer from one corps or army to another and even from one national command to another.

The combat helicopters that are to enter service in Europe and elsewhere before the year 2000 are now in various stages of development and some are already flying. They include the American Comanche and

Longbow Apache, the Franco-German Tiger and Gerfaut, the Russian 'Havoc' and 'Hokum' and a tactical transport version of the NATO Helicopter 90 (NH 90), due to become operational in 1998; the Anglo-Italian EH-101 may be procured as a tactical transport helicopter in addition to its naval roles. These helicopters will join the Apache, the Cobra, the Italian Mangusta and the 'Hind', all of which are expected to remain in service until 2000, and other armed helicopters such as the Kiowa Warrior, Lynx, Gazelle, BO 105 and others.

Less clear are the weapons with which the new helicopters will be armed and the mission avionics that they will have, to take advantage of developing technology. All that may be assumed is that they will be able to operate round the clock in fair and foul weather, will have much improved target-acquisition and recognition systems and will possess a better probability of first-round hit and kill against all manner of targets. Cockpits are being designed, not to lower crew workload as such, but to enable higher productivity. The longer weapon ranges and the greater expanse of the battlefield will necessitate an increase in the range and endurance characteristics of future helicopters: so that they can be based well to the rear but still reach across corps boundaries and into enemy rear areas and, for those that need to, remain on station for extended periods.

By the turn of the century the Gerfaut will be operating in the air combat role and other types may well have taken over, almost completely, the CAS role. Operations will be as, if not more, common by night as by day. Helicopter power will have entered a new era. There is a danger, however, that conservatism and an attachment to tradition, and a lack of imagination and creative thinking, will result in a failure to match these technical and tactical developments in terms of new organizational structures and arrangements for command and control; in other words, to exploit the ever-increasing potential of the combat helicopter. There are not a few instances in military history of failure to capitalize on new equipment; a perfect example was the general feeling in the British Army during the 1920s and 1930s that tanks should be deployed in support of the infantry rather than concentrated to operate at tank speed and achieve shock action. Although that lesson has been well learnt, armoured formations still suffer from certain shortcomings which are becoming more grave in the face of emerging technology: a lack of strategic mobility, susceptibility to terrain-imposed limitations such as mountains, forests and man-made obstacles, comparatively slow tactical movement, the need to concentrate and therefore inevitably to present an attractive target, real difficulty in training in peacetime because of restricted training areas, and a heavy demand for skilled manpower, including a crew of three or four men for each vehicle. There is a case therefore for reducing reliance on heavy armour and shifting it to combat systems that have greater strategic and tactical mobility, longer range and more lethal weapons, and which require less manpower.

Any plans for the reorganization of combat aviation units will have to take account of the CFE Treaty. As far as helicopters are concerned, it only limits the number of guided missile-armed helicopters stationed between the Atlantic Ocean and the Ural Mountains in Russia; neither NATO nor the countries that once formed the Warsaw Pact may have more than 2,000, with no one country having more than 1,500. The remaining combat helicopters may be armed with any other weapons. The only NATO countries allowed more than 150 guided missile-armed helicopters are Britain with 360, France with 450, Germany with 420 and US forces in Europe with 475. Very few of the NATO member countries possess now, or have on order, the number of such helicopters they are permitted. Of the members of the defunct Warsaw Pact (including the now independent Baltic States), only the states of the former Soviet Union together are close to their limit of 1,500. The only constraint may be to inhibit the number of helicopters that might have been armed with AAMs.

Of ground forces' combat vehicles the helicopter is the only one that has a degree of strategic mobility – a capability that is growing in importance. A few types already can refuel in flight and the Comanche, with two ferry tanks, will have an unrefuelled range of 2,335km (1,450 miles); some US Army Chinooks flew from their bases in Germany to Saudi Arabia to participate in the Gulf War. The ability to self-deploy over strategic distances, or be easily air-transportable (eight Comanches can be carried in a C-5 Galaxy) may help to deter, or stop, an attack while heavy ground forces are brought in. While warning times in Europe may be lengthening they may be getting shorter elsewhere. As bases overseas are closed and troops withdrawn to their home countries, the ability to deploy them to the scene of trouble quickly and support them there must be enhanced. This is addressed in Air-Land Operations, a successor to Air/Land Battle, a new doctrine for the 21st century in which US combat forces may anticipate facing a multi-dimensional threat anywhere in the world with fewer forces and reduced resources. The helicopter is also the only ground forces' combat vehicle that can lie up 100km (62 miles) or more behind the battle area in comparative safety, move forward at speed in small groups over different and unpredictable routes, and then concentrate at a given moment to fight and then disperse quickly.

The development of battlefield firepower has progressed since the Second World War to a level undreamt of in 1945; mobility, on the other hand, has moved forward only from walking pace to about 25km/hr (15mph), the average speed of armoured and mechanized infantry as they fight their way forwards. This can be raised substantially by using helicopters to move airmobile infantry but, once dropped, they revert to walking pace and, furthermore, are much less well protected. The Russians, for example, tried to solve this problem of 'secondary' mobility by equipping some air assault units with the BMD tracked infantry fighting vehicle, which carries both a gun and ATGMs and can accommodate a crew of two and five infantrymen. But airlifting a sufficient number exacted an enormous bill in helicopter lift: the 'Hip' cannot carry a BMD and so the 'Hook', which can take one, and the 'Halo', which can take two, had to undertake this task. Even the Russians simply did, and do, not have enough large transport helicopters to make the concept work and the BMD was later withdrawn from these units. The Germans use the wheeled Kraka and tracked Wiesel for infantry support weapons, particularly ATGMs, but neither carries troops. But if, for some special reason, vehicles and helicopters were made available for an operation, they would widen the tactical options and allow LZs to be chosen in safer areas clear of the objective.

To match the superlative firepower now available a new form of fighting mobility is needed: 'air mechanization' was the term coined nearly ten years ago by General Dr von Senger und Etterlin, a former Commander-in-Chief Allied Forces Central Europe. His 'flying tank' he called a Main Battle Air Vehicle (MBAV), although in reality it was an advanced attack helicopter. Air mechanization, he proposed, should be embodied in a tactically and logistically autonomous air-mechanized brigade; not a brigade that supported conventional ground forces to improve their combat effectiveness, but one that operated independently in an expanded arena. It should be composed of two attack battalions with 28 MBAVs each and single reconnaissance, air defence and anti-helicopter companies. The brigade should be capable of taking on ground-based and other air-mechanized forces. Supporting infantry, well equipped with long-range anti-tank weapons, might be needed and such units could be grouped into an airmobile brigade with an air transport brigade, capable of lifting one of its battalions in a single lift, in support. Von Senger suggested that single air-mechanized, airmobile and air transport brigades should be grouped into an autonomous air-mechanized division. A few divisions in NATO's Central Region could, he believed, form a powerful airmobile reserve of corps strength.

Von Senger mentioned the problems of vulnerability and logistic support. He did not envisage the MBAVs crossing into enemy-held territory and concluded that if they used ground cover and operated within the protection of their own air defence systems, they would have a good chance of survival. Now, such a view would be thought unduly cautious and lacking in vigour and aggression. The logistic penalty, he believed, could be accepted, given the increase in combat effectiveness.

Interest in von Senger's proposals was expressed but NATO as an organization did little until the recent moves to establish an airmobile division. The Americans and French in particular continued with the praiseworthy development of their own combat aviation and air assault forces and the British converted a brigade in West Germany to undertake airmobile trials; with these complete, it reverted to its original role and 24 Brigade in the UK became an airmobile brigade. But adherence to the 'mystique' of the tank and excessive emphasis on the perceived limitations of the helicopter ensured that NATO rotary-wing aviation in general would continue to suffer from a certain lack of vision and wholesale support. It is essential to preserve 'balance', essentially a mix of weapon systems to cater for any eventuality, but it is equally important to ensure that the components that contribute to it embody modern concepts and technology. For the foreseeable future some tasks are likely to remain best suited to AFVs and others to helicopters; both have their strengths and weaknesses. What is required is the most cost- and combat-effective mix of weapon systems.

Helicopters and their associated logistic support are expensive and funds for defence in practically every country are, and no doubt will remain, scarce. If they can demonstrate their cost-effectiveness, there will be a strong case for strengthening the combat aviation capability at the expense of more traditional close-quarter battle units. A smaller manpower pool, diminished budget and higher costs would probably lead to fewer units overall, but this reduction would be offset by a substantial enhancement in combat-effectiveness.

Air forces around the world have adopted, by and large, the principle of centralizing their power at the highest levels; those Armies with their own aviation assets, on the other hand, have tended to delegate operational control to as low a level as possible commensurate with the ability to use them positively and keep them flying. Experience seems to show that, while decentralization of control allows almost immediate and intimate support, that support lacks much of an impact and the full potential of all helicopter assets used together is not realized.

There are three fundamental options. First, to spread all helicopters around in penny packets in support of a large number of ground-based units. Second, to group some of them into a few purely helicopter units and delegate the rest to ground units. And finally, to consolidate virtually all helicopters into autonomous manoeuvre units. There is no country rich enough to possess and operate all the helicopters it wants, so a choice has to be made. Consolidation allows a battle tempo at helicopter speed and enables advantage to be taken of the helicopter's radius of action, ability to concentrate a large force quickly and its flexibility. Such attributes offer the potential to achieve surprise.

The ever-increasing capabilities of combat helicopters, which permit them to assume some of the roles presently undertaken by AFVs and fixed-wing aircraft, and the tactical and operational lessons of the past, mainly derived from armoured and mechanized warfare, encourage the consolidation of helicopters into autonomous formations; helicopter brigades should be formed to fight as manoeuvre brigades, not as supporting units. There might be two kinds: an attack helicopter brigade as one of the two or three manoeuvre brigades in an armoured or tank division (as suggested by General Sir Martin Farndale, a former Commander-in-Chief of NATO's Northern Army Group) and a combat helicopter brigade at corps. It is arguable that two or more attack helicopter brigades, together with some additional divisional troops, should form instead a helicopter division. Such a division would only be within reach of a very few countries, some of which might have to have one brigade at cadre status to be brought up to strength by reserves when required. Given the non-linear battlefield of the future, however, divisional commanders will certainly wish to have the ability to carry out long-range reconnaissance, if only to verify the results of electronic surveillance by other means, and to strike deep. Attack helicopter brigades might consist of two attack helicopter battalions and an air assault battalion as their main attack units, or they could have three battalions of mixed attack and assault helicopters.

A corps combat helicopter brigade should be stronger and more capable; a possible organization is shown in Fig. 13. Its operational combat effectiveness would be of a high order and would be equivalent to an armoured division in combat power. Given its day/night capability, a major problem may well be one of fatigue; it may be necessary to earmark one battalion, or perhaps one attack company per battalion, solely for operations at night over a specific period. To overcome the problem facing infantry when they finally dismount, assault helicopters would be used in much the same way as infantry fighting vehicles are now. Non-heliportable vehicles and systems should be kept to the minimum so as not to detract from the brigade's mobility. Theory is all very well but to get combat-worthy and affordable solutions, these must be subjected to detailed operational analysis and rigorous field testing.

A combat helicopter brigade, not confined to corps boundaries even though at corps level, which could operate independently as a self-contained manoeuvre formation, would be able to take advantage of fleeting opportunities both in defence and attack by exploiting the helicopter's flexibility, speed and short reaction time. Although well able to operate independently, the brigade would normally fight alongside other manoeuvre divisions and brigades. It should be able to conduct sustained action against the enemy's main armoured forces and, although not tailored to hold ground against them, should be able to dominate selected areas for a given time; in this event it might need infantry anti-tank and artillery support, and freedom to manoeuvre.

The advent of yet heavier, more accurate and longer-range firepower will tend to hold in check any significant increases in the pace of armoured and mechanized warfare emanating from a less dense battlefield. Only higher speeds of manoeuvre can erode the effects of this firepower, and these higher speeds can only be achieved by combat aviation. It can move some ten times faster than its armoured and mechanized counterparts. Future concepts and organizations must be tailored to take advantage of this: helicopter brigades can raise the tempo of battle and vastly expand time available or distance covered or both. The next generation of helicopters will be able to exploit darkness and bad weather and their radius of action will permit attacks deep in the enemy rear. Not only will they be able to outmanoeuvre armoured forces, but they will also be able to provide a highly mobile contribution to the ground forces' air defence capability by attacking enemy helicopters and their forward bases and even fixed-wing CAS aircraft.

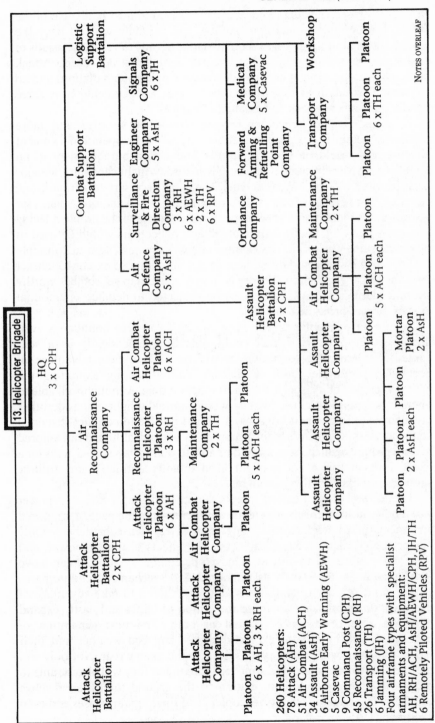

13. Helicopter Brigade

HQ
3 x CPH

Attack Helicopter Battalion
2 x CPH

Air Reconnaissance Company

Assault Helicopter Battalion
2 x CPH

Combat Support Battalion

Logistic Support Battalion

Attack Helicopter Battalion

Attack Helicopter Company

Platoon Platoon Platoon
6 x AH, 3 x RH each

Attack Helicopter Platoon
6 x AH

Air Combat Helicopter Company

Maintenance Company
2 x TH

Platoon Platoon Platoon
5 x ACH each

Reconnaissance Helicopter Platoon
3 x RH

Air Combat Helicopter Platoon
6 x ACH

Assault Helicopter Company

Assault Helicopter Company

Assault Helicopter Company

Platoon Platoon Platoon
2 x AsH each

Mortar Platoon
2 x AsH

Platoon Platoon Platoon
5 x ACH each

Air Combat Helicopter Company

Maintenance Company
2 x TH

Air Defence Company
5 x AsH

Surveillance & Fire Direction Company
3 x RH
6 x AEWH
2 x TH
6 x RPV

Engineer Company
5 x AsH

Signals Company
6 x JH

Ordnance Company

Forward Arming & Refuelling Point Company

Medical Company
5 x Casevac

Transport Company

Workshop

Platoon Platoon Platoon
6 x TH each

260 Helicopters:
78 Attack (AH)
51 Air Combat (ACH)
34 Assault (AsH)
6 Airborne Early Warning (AEWH)
5 Casevac
9 Command Post (CPH)
45 Reconnaissance (RH)
26 Transport (TH)
6 Jamming (JH)
Four airframe types with specialist
armaments and equipment:
AH, RH/ACH, AsH/AEWH/CPH, JH/TH
6 Remotely Piloted Vehicles (RPV)

NOTES OVERLEAF

Notes:

Unit	Roles	Weapons/Equipment	Remarks
Brigade	1. Independent manoeuvre tasks 2. Mobile reserve 3. Operations in enemy territory 4. Rear-area security 5. Operate with divisions in specific offensive and defensive actions	174 missile-armed helicopters	Brigade could act as a covering force
Attack Helicopter Battalion	1. Anti-armour 2. Anti-helicopter 3. Suppression of air defences 4. Operations in enemy territory 5. Protect flanks 6. Escort ground units, assault and transport helicopters 7. Channel enemy advances 8. Counter parachute and heliborne assaults	Attack helicopter: ATGM, rockets, cannon Reconnaissance helicopter: AAM, rockets, cannon, day/night mast-mounted sight Air combat helicopter: AAM, cannon	In the ATTU Zone it may not be possible to arm all reconnaissance helicopters with AAMs because of the terms of the CFE Treaty. Air combat helicopters will have priority for these weapons in this Zone
Air Reconnaissance Company	1. Armed reconnaissance 2. Target acquisition identification and designation 3. Visual confirmation of selected data gathered by other sensors 4. Covering force surveillance 5. Surveillance of flanks and gaps between units 6. Direction of gun and rocket fire 7. Anti-helicopter 8. Rear-area surveillance 9. Radio relay 10. Route reconnaissance (air and ground) 11. Battle damage assessment 12. NBC radiation monitoring	As helicopters in attack helicopter battalion	e.g., satellites, AWACS
Surveillance and Fire Direction Company	1. Target acquisition at long range 2. Surveillance of friendly and enemy movements and deployments 3. Liaison with and direction of all supporting artillery 4. Provision of forward air controllers	Transport helicopter: unarmed, rear ramp, sling-load facility AEW helicopter: unarmed, airborne surveillance radar Remotely piloted vehicle: real-time data transmission Airportable artillery an optional extra	Two ground-based fire direction centres RPVs capable of very long duration (12 + hours) surveillance and detection of targets for attack helicopters
Air Defence Company	1. Provision of ground-based air defence for FARPs, LZs if necessary, air assault	Assault helicopter: self-defence gun, 12 shoulder-launched/pedestal-	

Unit	Roles	Weapons/Equipment	Remarks
	objectives, helicopter operating bases	mounted SAM systems	
Engineer Company	1. Preparation of defences including aerial minelaying	Assault helicopter: self-defence gun, aerial mine-laying equipment	
	2. Channel enemy advances 3. Mine clearance, demolitions and explosives disposal		
Signals Company	1. Conventional signals support 2. Jamming of enemy air defence and battlefield radars, communications and radio relay systems	Jamming helicopter: unarmed	
Assault Helicopter Battalion	1. Air assault in offensive and defensive operations 2. Counter-penetration	Assault and air combat helicopter: as above Ground mobility for support weapons provided by light cross-country vehicles	This battalion includes air assault infantry-men strongly equipped with anti-tank and air defence weapons
	3. Assaults behind enemy lines and raids 4. Rapid reinforcement of units under pressure	Assault helicopter should be able to lift every type of crew-served weapon in the battalion with its associated vehicle, crew, ammunition or 20 armed troops or 4,000kg (8,818lb)	At 80 per cent availability of the 24 troop-carrying helicopters, 380 troops including three mortar
	5. Strengthening anti-tank defences by inserting infantry anti-tank teams 6. Seal gaps and protect flanks 7. Fighting in built-up areas 8. Rear-area security 9. Counter parachute and heliborne assaults 10. Ground defence of FARPs 11. Assist in logistic support and casualty evacuation	Mortar platoon has 120mm mortars with top attack munitions	platoons can be lifted simultaneously
Logistic Support Battalion	1. Provide logistic support to the brigade 2. Limited casualty evacuation 3. Establish FARPs	Transport helicopter: unarmed, Chinook capability	Helicopters will attempt to stay out of aimed enemy fire The brigade has heavy logistic requirements, particularly of fuel and ammu-nition, and will depend to some degree on cargo vehicles in the main base area

List of Abbreviations

AAC — Army Air Corps (British)
AAM — Air-to-Air Missile
ACE — Allied Command Europe
Aéro-navale — Aéronautique Navale (French Naval Air Arm)
AFV — Armoured Fighting Vehicle
ALAT — Aviation Légère de l'Armée de Terre (French Army Aviation)
ALN — Armée de Libération Nationale (Algerian)
AM — Amplitude Modulation
APC — Armoured Personnel Carrier
ARA — Aerial Rocket Artillery
ARVN — Army of the Republic of Vietnam (South Vietnam)
ASW — Anti-Submarine Warfare
ATGM — Anti-Tank Guided Missile

BMD — Boevaya Mashina Desantnaya – Airborne combat vehicle (Russian)
BMP — Boevaya Mashina Pekhoty – Infantry combat vehicle (Russian)

C3 — Command, Control and Communications
CAS — Close Air Support
CFE — Conventional Armed Forces in Europe (Treaty)
CIS — Commonwealth of Independent States
CP — Command Post

DH — de Havilland
DIH — Détachment d'Intervention Héliportée (French)

ECM — Electronic Counter-Measures
ESM — Electronic Support Measures
EW — Electronic Warfare

FAC — Forward Air Controller
FARP — Forward Arming and Refuelling Point
FEBA — Forward Edge of the Battle Area
FLN — Front de Libération Nationale (Algerian)
FLOT — Forward Line of Own Troops. No troops are ahead of this line while a few, for example reconnaissance and screen forces, will be between the FLOT and the FEBA
FM — Frequency Modulation
ft — Feet

GATAC — Groupement Aérien Tactique – Tactical Air Command (French)
GHAN — Groupe d'Hélicoptères de l'Aéronautique Navale (French)
GMT — Greenwich Mean Time

HE	High-Explosive	km	Kilometres
HF	High Frequency	km/hr	Kilometres per hour
HOGE	Hover out of Ground Effect. The downwash of air from the main rotor is reflected back upwards from the ground to produce a 'cushion' of air beneath the helicopter. The depth of the cushion is approximately equivalent to the length of the helicopter's main rotor blade. The effect of hovering within the cushion is that less power is required, but more when outside it	Laser	Light Amplification by Stimulated Emission of Radiation
		LCSFA	Limited Contingent of Soviet Forces in Afghanistan
		LOAL	Lock-on after Launch
		LOH	Light Observation Helicopter
		LZ	Landing Zone
HOT	Haut subsonique Optiquement téléguidé (tiré d'un Tube)	m	Metres
		MACLOS	Manual Command to Line-of-Sight
hp	Horsepower	MACV	Military Assistance Command Vietnam
HQ	Headquarters	MAF	Museum of Army Flying (British)
HVM	Hyper-Velocity Missile; a missile that has a velocity greater than 1,500 metres per second (4,920ft/sec)	MASH	Mobile Army Surgical Hospital (US)
		MBAV	Main Battle Aerial Vehicle
		MBB	Messerschmitt-Bölkow-Blohm
		MCHC	Marine Corps Historical Center (US)
in	Inches	mm	Millimetres
INFANT	Iroquois Night Fighter and Night Tracker	mph	Miles per hour
IOC	Initial Operating Capability. The date when the first item of a new piece of equipment arrives in an operational unit together with trained air and ground crew and all supporting documentation (US)	MVD	Ministerstvo Vnutrennikh Del – Ministry of Internal Affairs (Russian)
		NATO	North Atlantic Treaty Organization
		NBC	Nuclear, Biological, Chemical
IR	Infra-red (radiation)	NOE	Nap of the Earth. Very low-level tactical flying using natural terrain cover and contours
JOC	Joint Operations Centre	NVA	North Vietnamese Army
KGB	Komitet Gosudarstvennoi Bezopasnosti – Committee of State Security (Russian); now defunct	OAS	Organisation Armée Secrète (French)
		OP	Observation Post

PDPA   People's Democratic Party of Afghanistan

PLO   Palestine Liberation Organization

RAF   Royal Air Force

rpm   Revolutions per minute

RV   Rendezvous

SACEUR   Supreme Allied Commander Europe

SACLOS   Semi-Automatic Command to Line-of-Sight

SAM   Surface-to-Air Missile

SAR   Search and Rescue

shp   Shaft horsepower

SNCASE   Société Nationale de Constructions Aéronautiques de Sud-Est (French aircraft manufacturer)

SNCASO   Société Nationale de Constructions Aéronautiques de Sud-Ouest (French aircraft manufacturer)

Spetsnaz   Spetsialnoe Naznachenie – Special Purpose Forces (Russian)

TAS   Target Acquisition Sub-system

TOW   Tube-launched, Optically tracked, Wire-guided

TRIGAT   A third-generation anti-tank missile

UHF   Ultra High Frequency

UIH   Unité d'Intervention Héli-portée (French)

USAF   United States Air Force

USAAM   United States Army Aviation Museum

USMC   United States Marine Corps

UTTHCO   Utility Tactical Transport Helicopter Company

VHF   Very High Frequency

Glossary

Agility	The rate at which a helicopter can accelerate and decelerate in any direction
Air assault	The delivery by helicopter of specially trained troops directly into battle on their own territory or the enemy's. Air assault units have their own dedicated helicopters which are the primary means of manoeuvre, firepower, reconnaissance and logistic support
Airborne	An airborne unit is one that is taken to the area of operations by air, personnel and equipment then being dropped by parachute. Some air assault units are entitled airborne for historical reasons, viz. 101st Airborne Division (Air Assault)
Air combat	Combat between helicopters
Airmobile unit	A unit that is organized, equipped and trained to move by air as a cohesive tactical force. It is rarely delivered directly into battle but to positions from which it can later fight. The bulk of the helicopters used to move it are provided from other sources
Air transportability	The transport of troops, equipment and supplies in non-tactical loads to areas short of their battle positions
Anti-tank helicopter	A helicopter, equipped with ATGMs and the necessary sighting system, whose primary role is to attack tanks and other AFVs
Assault helicopter	A helicopter, usually but not necessarily armed, which carries assault troops into action as well as undertaking many other combat support tasks within range of enemy fire
Attack helicopter	A helicopter which is designed, in terms of flying performance, multiple integrated weapons systems and survivability features, to engage a variety of targets
Autogiro	A rotorcraft driven by a propeller and lifted by a rotor which turns freely in flight under the single influence of the air flowing through the blades
Battlefield helicopter	Any helicopter used on the battlefield

CFE Treaty	This Treaty limits the numbers of selected types of equipment to be held between the Atlantic Ocean and the Ural Mountains. NATO and the erstwhile members of the Warsaw Pact may have up to 2,000 missile-armed helicopters each with no single country allowed to have more than 1,500
Combat aviation	The complete spectrum of helicopter operations: attack, reconnaissance, command and control, direction of fire, casualty evacuation, minelaying, logistic support, etc
Combat helicopter	Any helicopter involved in combat – e.g., anti-tank/attack, assault, reconnaissance, air combat, special operations
Desant	Russian term for the landing of forces on enemy territory. Desantniki are the specially trained troops who carry out such landings
Dust Off	Radio call-sign for American casualty evacuation helicopter units in South Vietnam
Fauj	ALN section
Fellagha	Algerian guerrilla
Ferka	ALN platoon
Fidayine	Algerian terrorist
Fire and forget	A missile which locks onto its target either before or after launch and which requires no further external input to hit the target. Immediately after launch the helicopter crew can turn their attention elsewhere
'Frog'	American UH-1B/C with the M-5 armaments system
General War	A major unrestricted war with or without the use of nuclear, biological or chemical weapons
'Heavy Hog'	UH-1B/C with the XM-3 and M-5 armaments systems
'Hog'	UH-1B/C with the XM-3 armament system
Hot and High	The adverse combination of high altitude and high ambient temperatures
Katiba	ALN company
Limited War	A war limited in the objectives chosen, the means used to wage it or the geographical area
Manoeuvre	The movement of forces on the battlefield in combination with firepower to obtain a position of advantage over the enemy
Manoeuvrability	The ability of a helicopter to change speed and direction
Maskirovka	Russian term to describe a combination of concealment,

	camouflage, deception and disinformation to conceal the activities and deployments of friendly troops and to mislead the enemy as to their groupings and intentions
Moussabiline	ALN auxiliary
Mujaheddin	A freedom fighter in Algeria and Afghanistan
Operational level	The link between military strategy and the tactical employment of forces on the battlefield. The level at which military resources are used to achieve strategic objectives
Payload	The weight of passengers, freight or armaments
Quadrillage	The French pattern of garrisoning cities, towns, villages and farms in Algeria
Reasonable Sufficiency	A rather imprecise Russian term to describe a military-political strategy and meaning roughly: The possession of as many armed forces as necessary for a successful defence against external aggression but not enough to initiate or wage large-scale and deep offensive operations
Sangar	A small protective fortification built of rocks and stones, usually constructed in mountainous terrain where it is not possible to dig a trench or foxhole
'Slick'	The nickname given to American Huey assault helicopters in Vietnam
Tempo	The rate of battlefield activity by day and night in all types of weather
Useful Load	Usable fuel and payload
Viet Cong	South Vietnamese Communists
Viet Minh	The title given to those Vietnamese, both nationalists and Communists, who fought the French between 1946 and 1954. A contraction for the 'League for the Independence of Vietnam'
Vietnamization	A gradual handover of responsibility for the prosecution of the war from the US Armed Forces to those of South Vietnam
War Zones	ARVN terms to describe major Viet Cong guerrilla areas north of Saigon. War Zone C bordered Cambodia while Zone D was to its east
Wilaya	ALN military districts

Bibliography

A History of Marine Medium Helicopter Squadron 161, History and Museums Division, HQ US Marine Corps, Washington, D.C., 1978

Airmobility 1961–1971, Vietnam Studies, Department of the Army, Washington, D.C., 1973

Bail, René, *Hélicoptères et Commandos-Marine en Algérie*, Charles Lavauzelle, Paris-Limoges, 1983

Chenoweth, Bob, *Army Gunships in Vietnam*, Pall Mall Press, London, 1963

Collins, Joseph, *The Soviet Invasion of Afghanistan*, Lexington Books, 1986

Croizat, Lt-Col Victor J., *Report of French Military Operations in Algeria*, 1957

Dorland, Peter and Nanney, James, *Dust Off: Army Aeromedical Evacuation in Vietnam*, Center of Military History, US Army, Washington, D.C., 1982

Dunstan, Simon, *Vietnam Choppers: Helicopters in Battle 1950–1975*, Osprey, London, 1988

Everett-Heath, John, *Soviet Helicopters*, Jane's Information Group, 1988

Fall, Bernard, *The Two Vietnams*, Pall Mall Press, London, 1963

Flament, Marc, . . . *et le Baroud vint du Ciel* (. . . and Combat Power came out of the Sky), Jacques Grancher, Paris, 1984

Francillon, René, *Vietnam Air Wars*, Temple Press, 1987

Gillespie, Joan, *Algeria, Rebellion and Revolution*, Ernest Benn, London, 1960

Guerrilla Warfare and Air Power in Algeria 1954–60, Aerospace Studies Institute, Air University, Maxwell Air Force Base, Alabama, 1965

Hyman, Anthony, *Afghanistan under Soviet Domination 1964-81*, Macmillan, 1982

Isby, David, *War in a Distant Country*, Arms and Armour Press, London, 1989

Jureidini, Paul, *Case Studies in Insurgency and Revolutionary Warfare: Algeria 1954-62*, Special Operations Research Office, The American University, Washington, D.C., 1963

Leulliette, Pierre, *Saint Michel et le Dragon*, Les Editions de Minuit 1961, Heinemann, London, 1964

Littauer, Raphael and Uphoff, Norman (editors), *The Air War in Indo-*

China, Air War Study Group, Cornell University, Beacon Press, Boston, 1972

Marines and Helicopters 1946–1962 and *1962–1973*, History and Museums Division, HQ US Marine Corps, Washington, D.C., 1976 and 1978

Mason, Robert, *Chickenhawk*, Corgi Books, London, 1984

Montross, Lynn, *Cavalry of the Sky*, Harper and Brothers, New York, 1954

Newell, Nancy Peabody and Richard S., *The Struggle for Afghanistan*, Cornell University Press, Ithaca and London, 1981

O'Ballance, Edgar, *The Algerian Insurrection 1954–62*, Faber and Faber, London, 1967

Sharpening the Combat Edge, Vietnam Studies, Department of the Army, Washington, D.C., 1974

Sheehan, Neil, *A Bright Shining Lie*, Jonathan Cape, London, 1989

South Vietnam: US-Communist Confrontation in South-East Asia, Facts on File Inc., New York, 1973

Stanton, Shelby L., *Vietnam Order of Battle*, Galahad Books, New York, 1987

Strategic Surveys (various), International Institute for Strategic Studies, London

Summers, Harry G., *Vietnam Almanac*, Facts on File Publications, New York, 1985

Towle, Philip Anthony, *Pilots and Rebels: The Use of Aircraft in Unconventional Warfare 1919–1988*, Brassey's, UK, 1989

Urban, Mark, *War in Afghanistan*, Macmillan, 1988

Wheeler, Howard A., *Attack Helicopters*, Greenhill Books, London, 1987

Appendix 1. Helicopters in Algeria

	Bell 47G (H-13)	Sikorsky H-19	Vertol H-21	Sikorsky H-34/HSS-1	SNCASO Djinn	SNCASE Alouette II
Engine type	Piston 200hp	Piston 700hp	Piston 1,425hp	Piston 1,525hp	Turbo-generator 240shp	Turbine 360shp
Rotor diameter	10.71m (35ft 1½in)	16.15m (53ft)	2 × 13.41m (44ft)	17.07m (56ft)	11m (36ft 1in)	10.2m (33ft 5in)
Fuselage length	9.62m (31ft 7in)	12.85m (42ft 2in)	16m (52ft 6in)	14.25m (46ft 9in)	5.3m (17ft 4in)	9.7m (31ft 10in)
Height	2.84m (9ft 3½in)	4.06m (13ft 4in)	4.7m (15ft 5in)	4.86m (15ft 11in)	2.6m (8ft 5in)	2.75m (9ft)
Weight empty	710kg (1,565lb)	2,245kg (4,950lb)	3,629kg (8,000lb)	3,583kg (7,900lb)	360kg (794lb)	890kg (1,962lb)
Max. gross weight	1,066kg (2,350lb)	3,266kg (7,200lb)	6,804kg (15,000lb)	6,040kg (13,316lb)	800kg (1,764lb)	1,650kg (3,638lb)
Useful load	272kg (600lb)	700kg (1,543lb)	2,270kg (5,004lb)	1,935kg (4,265lb)	220kg (485lb)	600kg (1,323lb)
Passenger seats	2[1]	10	20	15	1	4[2]
Cruising speed	130km/hr (81mph)	137km/hr (85mph)	163km/hr (101mph)	160km/hr (99mph)	105km/hr (65mph)	165km/hr (103mph)
First flight	8 December 1945	10 November 1949	11 April 1952	8 March 1954	2 January 1953	12 March 1955

[1] Two external litters for casualties could be carried instead.   [2] Or two stretchers and a medical attendant.

Appendix 2. Helicopters in Vietnam

	Hughes OH-6A	Bell OH-58A	Bell UH-1B	Bell UH-1C	Bell UH-1D	Bell UH-1H	Bell AH-1G
Engine type	Turbine 252shp	Turbine 317shp	Turbine 960/1,100shp	Turbine 1,100shp	Turbine 1,100shp	Turbine 1,400shp	Turbine 1,100shp
Rotor diameter	8.03m (26ft 4in)	10.77m (35ft 4in)	13.4m (44ft)	13.4m (44ft)	14.63m (48ft)	14.63m (48ft)	13.41m (44ft)
Fuselage length	6.48m (21ft 3in)	9.84 (32ft 3½in)	12.98m (42ft 7in)	12.98m (42ft 7in)	12.8m (42ft)	12.77m (41ft 10in)	13.54m (44ft 5in)
Height	2.48m (8ft 1½in)	2.91m (9ft 6½in)	3.87m (12ft 8in)	3.87m (12ft 8in)	4.42m (14ft 6in)	4.42m (14ft 6in)	4.09m (13ft 5in)
Weight empty	557kg (1,228lb)	718kg (1,583lb)	2,050kg (4,519lb)	2,155kg (4,750lb)	2,240kg (4,939lb)	2,255kg (4,973lb)	2,754kg (6,071lb)
Max. gross weight	1,225kg (2,700lb)	1,361kg (3,000lb)	3,856kg (8,500lb)	4,309kg (9,500lb)	4,309kg (9,500lb)	4,309kg (9,500lb)	4,309kg (9,500lb)
Useful load	561kg (1,237lb)	590kg (1,300lb)	1,769kg (3,900lb)	2,118kg (4,670lb)	2,069kg (4,561lb)	1,860kg (4,100lb)	497kg (1,096lb)
Passenger seats	2	2	8[1]	None[2]	11[3]	14[4]	–
Cruising speed	216km/hr (134mph)	188km/hr (117mph)	167km/hr (104mph)	177km/hr (110mph)	185km/hr (115mph)	204km/hr (127mph)	241km/hr (150mph)
First flight	27 February 1963	10 January 1966	27 April 1960	?	16 August 1961	?	7 September 1965

[1] Also used as a gunship.   [2] Only a gunship.   [3] Or six stretchers and a medical attendant.   [4] Or six stretchers and a medical attendant.

	Sikorsky CH-37	Boeing CH-46D	Boeing CH-47A	Boeing CH-47C	Sikorsky HH-3E	Sikorsky HH-53B[9]	Sikorsky CH-54A
Engine type	2 × Piston 2 × 2,100hp	2 × Turbine 2 × 1,400shp	2 × Turbine 2 × 2,650shp	2 × Turbine 2 × 3,750shp	2 × Turbine 2 × 1,500shp	2 × Turbine 2 × 3,080shp	2 × Turbine 2 × 4,500shp
Rotor diameter	21.95m (72ft)	2 × 15.24m (50ft)	2 × 18.02m (59ft 1in)	2 × 18.29m (60ft)	18.9m (62ft)	22.02m (72ft 3in)	21.95m (72ft)
Fuselage length	19.58m (64ft 3in)	13.66m (44ft 10in)	15.54m (51ft)	15.54m (51ft)	19.05m (62ft 6in)	20.47m (67ft 2in)	21.41m (70ft 3in)
Height	5.08m (16ft 8in)	5.09m (16ft 8in)	5.67m (18ft 7in)	5.67m (18ft 7in)	5.51m (18ft 1in)	7.6m (24ft 11in)	7.75m (25ft 5in)
Weight empty	9,753kg (21,502lb)	5,927kg (13,067lb)	8,216kg (18,112lb)	9,320kg (20,547lb)	5,295kg (11,673lb)	10,490kg (23,125lb)	8,732kg (19,250lb)
Max. gross weight	14,062kg (31,000lb)	10,443kg (23,000lb)	14,969kg (33,000lb)	20,866kg (46,000lb)	10,002kg (22,050lb)	19,050kg (42,000lb)	19,050kg (42,000lb)
Useful load	5,000kg (11,023lb)	4,535kg (10,000lb)	4,590kg (10,120lb)	10,424kg (22,981lb)	2,268kg (5,000lb)	9,072kg (20,000lb)	9,072kg (20,000lb)
Passenger seats	26[5]	26	33	33–44[7]	30[8]	38[10]	45[11]
Cruising speed	185km/hr (115mph)	248km/hr (154mph)	212km/hr (132mph)	254km/hr (158mph)	232km/hr (144mph)	278km/hr (173mph)	175km/hr (109mph)
First flight	18 December 1953	27 August 1959[6]	21 September 1961	14 October 1967	17 June 1963	15 March 1967	9 May 1962

[5] Or 24 stretchers and four medical attendants.   [6] Of CH-46A.   [7] Depends on seating arrangement; or 24 stretchers.   [8] Or 15 stretchers.
[9] CH-53A similar but with 2 × 2,850shp engines.   [10] Or 24 stretchers and four medical attendants.   [11] In a pod; or 24 stretchers.

Appendix 3. Helicopter Weapon Systems Used in Vietnam

Designation	Guns	Rockets	Grenades	Missiles	Mounting	Helicopter Type
XM-1	2 × 0.30in M37C MG				Side	OH-13, OH-23
M-2	2 × M60C 7.62mm MG				Side, door	OH-13, UH-1H
GAU-2B/A	6-barrelled 7.62mm MG					
XM-3		48 × 70mm			2 pods (24 rockets each)	UH-1B/C
M-5			M-75 40mm grenade-launcher with 150 or 315 grenades		Nose turret	UH-1B/C, A/ACH-47A
M-6	4 × M60C MG				2 guns per side	UH-1B/C
XM-8			40mm grenade-launcher with 156 grenades		Port side	OH-6
XM-14	2 × 0.50in MG				1 podded gun per side	UH-1B (limited use)
XM-16	4 × M60C MG	2 × XM-158			2 guns, 1 pod per side	UH-1B/C
XM-18	M-134 7.62mm minigun				Pod	UH-1B, AH-1G, A/ACH-47A
M-21	2 × M-134	2 × XM-158			1 gun, 1 pod per side	UH-1B/C

Designation	Guns	Rockets	Grenades	Missiles	Mounting	Helicopter Type
M-22				6 × AGM-22B anti-tank (French SS-11)	3 per side on outriggers	UH-1B/C
M-23	2 × M60D MG				Door	UH-1D/H
M-24	2 × M60D MG				Door	CH-47
M-24A1	20mm cannon				Side	A/ACH-47A
XM-26				6 × TOW anti-tank	2 pods	UH-1B/C
XM-27	GAU-2B/A				Port side	OH-6, OH-58
XM-28	2 × GAU-2B/A or or 1 GAU-2B/A	and	2 × M-75 with 600 grenades 1 × M-75			UH-1B, AH-1G
XM-29	M60D				Chin turret	UH-1B/C
XM-31	2 × M-24A1				1 per side (sometimes in pod)	UH-1B/C, A/ACH-47A
XM-32	4 × 0.50in AN-M2 or 4 × M60D				2 per side	A/ACH-47A
XM-33	AN-M2 or M60D				Rear ramp	A/ACH-47A
XM-34	2 × M-24A1				1 per side	A/ACH-47A
XM-35	XM-195				Pylon	AH-1G

M-37C	0.30in MG	Side	UH-1A/B
M60C	7.62mm MG	Side	CH-21, UH-1B
M60D	7.62mm MG	Door	
M61A1	6-barrelled 20mm Vulcan cannon		
M-73	7.62mm MG		
M-75		40mm grenade-launcher	
XM-93	M-134	Door	UH-1N
TAT-101	2 × M60C	Chin turret	UH-1E
TAT-102	GAU-2B/A	Chin turret	AH-1G
XM-129		40mm grenade-launcher (re-designed M-75)	Chin turret	AH-1G
M-134	6-barrelled 7.62mm MG (same as GAU-2B/A)	Door, side	UH-1B/C, AH-1G
XM-153	4 × M-73	2 per side	CH-21
XM-154	4 × M-73	2 per side	UH-34
XM-155	4 × M-73		
XM-156		Multi-purpose armaments mount	

Designation	Guns	Rockets	Grenades	Missiles	Mounting	Helicopter Type
XM-157		7 × 70mm			Pod	UH-1B/C
XM-158		7 × 70mm			Pod	UH-1B/C
XM-159		19 × 70mm			Pod	UH-1B/C, AH-1G, A/ACH-47A
XM-195	6-barrelled 20mm cannon				Pylon	AH-1G
M-1919	0.30in MG				Door	CH-21
MADS	81mm Mortar Air Delivery System			UH-1C/D/H		
Bombs: Napalm CS gas						UH-1H, A/ACH-47A UH-1B/D/H, A/ACH-47A UH-1 CH-54
45kg (100lb) HE 4,536kg (10,000lb) Daisy Cutter						
Smoke-dischargers						UH-1B/D/H

Appendix 4. Helicopters in Afghanistan

	Mi-6 'Hook'	Mi-8T 'Hip C'	Mi-8MT 'Hip H'	Mi-24 'Hind E/F'
Engine type	2 × Turbine 2 × 5,500shp	2 × Turbine 2 × 1,700shp	2 × Turbine 2 × 1,900shp	2 × Turbine 2 × 2,200shp
Rotor diameter	35m (114ft 10in)	21.29m (69ft 10½in)	21.29m (69ft 10½in)	17.3m (56ft 9in)
Fuselage length	33.18m (108ft 10½in)	18.17m (59ft 7½in)	18.42m (60ft 5½in)	17.5m (57ft 5in)
Height	6.71m (22ft)	4.7m (15ft 5in)	4.75m (15ft 7¼in)	3.97m (13ft 3in)
Weight empty	27,240kg (60,055lb)	7,260kg (16,007lb)	7,100kg (15,653lb)	8,200kg (18,078lb)
Max. gross weight	42,500kg (93,700lb)	12,000kg (26,455lb)	13,000kg (28,660lb)	12,000kg (26,455lb)
Useful load	12,000kg (26,455lb)[1]	4,000kg (8,818lb)[3]	4,000kg (8,818lb)[3]	1,500kg (3,307lb)[4]
Passenger seats	65[2]	24	24	8
Cruising speed	250km/hr (155mph)	225km/hr (140mph)	240km/hr (150mph)	280km/hr (174mph)
First flight	September 1967	1961	1977?	1976/1980?

[1]8,000kg (17,637lb) maximum underslung load. [2]Or 41 stretchers. [3]3,000kg (6,614lb) maximum underslung load or 12 stretchers.
[4]External weapons load.

Appendix 5. Russian Helicopter Weapons

Helicopter	Guns	Rockets	Missiles	Bombs	Others
'Hip C'	–	64 or 128 × 57mm	–	4 × 250kg or 2 × 500kg	2 × mine-dispensers Mine chute
'Hip E'	12.7mm	192 × 57mm	4 × 'Swatter'	6 × 250kg or 2 × 500kg	4 × mine-dispensers
'Hip H'	12.7mm (nose) 12.7mm (clamshell door) 4 × 23mm (outrigger gun pods)	192 × 57mm or 80 × 80mm	–	As 'Hip E'	As 'Hip E'
'Hind D'	12.7mm (nose) 4 × 23mm (wing gun pods)	128 × 57mm or 80 × 80mm	4 × 'Swatter'	4 × 250kg or 2 × 500kg	
'Hind E'	As 'Hind D'	As 'Hind D'	4 × 'Spiral'	As 'Hind D'	2 × mine-dispensers
'Hind F'	30mm 4 × 23mm (wing gun pods)	As 'Hind D'	As 'Hind E'	As 'Hind D'	As 'Hind E'
'Hook'	12.7mm	–	–	–	–

The 'Hip C', 'Hind D', 'E' and 'F' each have four weapons pylons on outriggers or wings; 'Hip E' and 'H' have six pylons. These pylons can carry a selection of weapons: e.g., on a 'Hind E', two 80mm rocket pods for 40 rockets and two bombs or two 23mm gun pods or two auxiliary fuel tanks. 'Hinds' were all equipped with attachments for two anti-tank missiles at each wing tip in addition to the weapons pylons.

Appendix 6. Modern Helicopters

	McDonnell Douglas AH-64 Apache	Agusta A-129 Mangusta	Mil Mi-28 'Havoc'	Kamov Ka-? 'Hokum'[2]	Bell OH-58D Kiowa Warrior
Engine type	2 × T700-GE-701 2 × 1,690shp	2 × Gem 2 2 × 825shp	2 × TV3-117 2 × 2,200shp	2 × TV3-117VK 2 × 2,225shp	250-C30R 650shp
Rotor diameter	14.63m (48ft)	11.9m (39ft 1/2in)	17.2m (56ft 5in)	2 × 14.5m (47ft 7in)	10.67m (35ft)
Fuselage length	14.93m (49ft)	12.275m (40ft 3 1/4in)	16.85m (55ft 3 1/2in)	13.5m (44ft 3 1/2in)	10.31m (33ft 10in)
Height	4.66m (15ft 3 1/2in)	3.35m (11ft)	4.81m (15ft 9in)	5.4m (17ft 8in)	3.9m (12ft 9 1/2in)[3]
Weight empty	4,881kg (10,760lb)	2,529kg (5,575lb)	7,017kg (15,470lb)	5,500kg (12,125lb)	1,281kg (2,825lb)
Max. gross weight	9,525kg (21,000lb)	4,070kg (8,973lb)	11,400kg (25,132lb)	9,750kg (21,495lb)	2,041kg (4,500lb)
Standard armaments load	8 Hellfire ATGM 38 × 70mm rockets 320 × 30mm rounds	8 TOW 2 ATGM 14 × 70mm rockets	16 laser-guided ATGM 40 × 80mm rockets 250 × 30mm rounds	16 laser-guided ATGM 40 × 80mm rockets 500 × 30mm rounds	[4]
Passenger seats	–	–	–[1]	–	–
Cruising speed	296km/hr (184mph)	259km/hr (161mph)	265km/hr (165mph)	320km/hr (199mph)	222km/hr (138mph)
First flight	30 September 1975	11 September 1983	10 November 1982	27 July 1982	October 1983

[1] Room for 2 or 3 people in avionics bay in emergency. [2] Estimated. [3] To top of mast-mounted sight. [4] Choice of guns, Hydra 70 rockets, Hellfire ATGM and Stinger AAM.

	Eurocopter Tiger	Boeing/Sikorsky RAH-66 Comanche	Mil Mi-26 'Halo'	Boeing Vertol CH-47D Chinook	NH Industries TTH-90[10]
Engine type	2 × MTR-390 2 × 1,285shp	2 × T800-LHT-801 2 × 1,344shp	2 × D-136 2 × 11,400shp	2 × T55-L-712 2 × 4,500shp	2 × RTM-322 (2 × 2,100shp) or 2 × CT7-6 (2 × 2,020shp)
Rotor diameter	13m (42ft 7½in)	11.9m (39ft ½in)	32m (105ft)	2 × 18.29m (60ft)	16m (52ft 6in)
Fuselage length	14m (45ft 11¼in)	13.22m (43ft 4½in)	33.73m (110ft 8in)	15.54m (51ft)	16.1m (52ft 10in)
Height	3.81m (12ft 6in)	3.39m (11ft 1in)	8.145m (26ft 9in)	5.68m (18ft 7½in)	4.05m (13ft 3½in)
Weight empty	3,300kg (7,275lb)	3,605kg (7,950lb)	28,200kg (62,170lb)	10,500kg (23,149lb)	5,000kg (11,023lb)
Max. gross weight	6,000kg (13,227lb)	7,790kg (17,174lb)	56,000kg (123,450lb)	22,679kg (50,000lb)	9,500kg (20,944lb)
Standard armaments load or payload	8 HOT 3 or TRIGAT[5] 4 Mistral or Stinger AAM	[6]	20,000kg (44,092lb)	11,793kg (26,000lb)[8]	3,500kg (7,716lb)
Passenger seats	–	–	85[7]	55[9]	20
Cruising speed	265km/hr (165mph)	315km/hr (196mph)	255km/hr (158mph)	276km/hr (171mph)	285km/hr (177mph)
First flight	27 April 1991	August 1995?	14 December 1977	11 May 1979	1994?

[5]The Gerfaut differs in having 4 Mistral, 44 × 70mm rockets and 450 × 30mm rounds. [6]The RAH-66 has six internal weapons stations and eight external stations on optional stub wings. Typical weapon combinations might be as follows:

Role:	Hellfire	Stinger	20mm Ammunition	Fuel for (hours)	Stub Wings
Reconnaissance	4	2	320	2.5	No
Attack	8	2	500	1.8	Yes
Air Combat	2	12	500	2.5	Yes
Deep Strike	10	-	500	925km (575 miles) range	Yes

[7]Combat-equipped troops. [8]Maximum underslung load. [9]Maximum combat-equipped troops; or 24 stretchers. [10]Specification. A joint venture between Agusta, Eurocopter and Fokker.

INDEX

69; HMM-365, 75; HMR-61, 20; HMX-1,
16, 18; VMO-6, 18
US Military Assistance Advisory Group, 64
US Navy, 20, 89, 107; Helicopter Attack
(Light) Squadron-3, 89
USSR, 114, 118, 120, 121, 126, 141, 150,
155
Ussuri River, 26
Ustinov, Defence Ministr, 115

Vanderpool, Col Jay D., 23, 24
Varennikov, Army Gen Valentin, 115, 144
Vertol H-21 Shawnee, 24, 46, 47, 50, 51,
53, 55, 59, 60, 68–70, 72, 74, 108
Vietnamese Air Force, 90
Viet Cong, 64–7, 69–73, 75–7, 83, 87, 95,
97–100, 104, 108, 110, 111, 116, 153; 9th
Division, 85
Viet Minh, 22, 49, 64, 109
Vietnamization, 65, 97–9, 101
Von Karman, Dr Theodore, 13

Von Senger und Etterlin, Gen, 186
Vung Tau, 76

Walker, Maj Gen Walter, 27
Warsaw Pact, 10, 11, 26, 62, 113, 176, 181,
185
War Zone C, 85
War Zone D, 93, 109
Wessex: *see* Westland helicopters
Westland helicopters: Lynx, 39, 177, 184;
Scout, 27, 28, 34, 35; Sea King, 35;
Wessex, 28, 34; Whirlwind, 17, 18, 24, 27,
50; WS-51 Dragonfly, 17, 22
Westmoreland, Gen William C., 65, 110
Whirlwind: *see* Westland helicopters
Wright brothers, 15

Yak-24 'Horse', 25
Yom Kippur War, 34, 163

Zhawar, 144
Zurovec, Ensign Wilhelm, 13